Holiness and the *Missio Dei*

Holiness and the *Missio Dei*

Andy Johnson

CASCADE Books • Eugene, Oregon

HOLINESS AND THE *MISSIO DEI*

Copyright © 2016 Andy Johnson. All rights reserved. Except for brief quotations in critical publications or reviews, no part of this book may be reproduced in any manner without prior written permission from the publisher. Write: Permissions, Wipf and Stock Publishers, 199 W. 8th Ave., Suite 3, Eugene, OR 97401.

Cascade Books
An Imprint of Wipf and Stock Publishers
199 W. 8th Ave., Suite 3
Eugene, OR 97401

www.wipfandstock.com

PAPERBACK ISBN: 978-1-4982-2161-0
HARDCOVER ISBN: 978-1-4982-2163-4
EBOOK ISBN: 978-1-4982-2162-7

Cataloguing-in-Publication data:

Names: Johnson, Andy.

Title: Holiness and the *Missio Dei* / Andy Johnson.

Description: Eugene, OR: Cascade Books, 2016 | Includes bibliographical references and index.

Identifiers: ISBN 978-1-4982-2161-0 (paperback) | ISBN 978-1-4982-2163-4 (hardcover) | ISBN 978-1-4982-2162-7 (ebook)

Subjects: LSCH: Holiness. | Mission of the church.

Classification: LCC BX8331.3 J65 2016 (print) | LCC BX8331.3 (ebook)

Manufactured in the U.S.A.   09/28/16

In memory of my father and mother, Clinton and Jeanette Johnson, who first introduced me not just to the *idea* of holiness, but also to what it looks like in the skin of not-yet-perfect human beings.

Contents

Acknowledgments | ix
Abbreviations | xii
Introduction and Orientation | xv

Section 1: Old Testament Soundings

1 Genesis 1–11: Holiness and God's Mission "in the Beginning" | 3
2 The Call/Election of Abraham and Israel: Living Out "the Way of the Lord" | 11
3 Except When They Don't: Holiness, Prophets, and Exile | 31

Section 2: Relocating Holiness in Jesus

4 Holiness and the Second Temple Context | 47
5 Relocating Holiness in a Jew from Nazareth: Soundings from the Synoptic Gospels | 53
6 Relocating Holiness in the En-fleshed *Logos* and His En-fleshed Community: Holiness and Life in the Gospel of John | 79

Section 3: Other New Testament Witnesses

7 The Community of the Holy and Righteous One: Bearers of the Name of the Lord of All | 107

8 Paul and New Creation "Colonies of Cruciformity" | 127

9 Revelation, Holiness, and Mission | 153

Conclusion: Holiness and the *Missio Dei* in Twenty-First Century North America | 181

Bibliography | 195
Author Index | 201
Subject Index | 203
Scripture Index | 207

Acknowledgments

THIS BOOK STARTED OUT as a vague suggestion I made to Chris Spinks early in the fall of 2008 when he came to Kansas City representing Wipf and Stock at a conference my seminary was hosting. When the Society of Biblical Literature meeting rolled around in Boston in November of that year, he took me to lunch, and I turned that vague suggestion into a vague promise that I would write something on the theme of holiness in Scripture. But over the next few years, I was so far behind on finishing another book that any writing time I could carve out had to be devoted primarily to it. During that time, though, my imagination was being shaped by the developing conversation regarding missional theology and interpreting Scripture through a missional lens. So when Hal Cauthron, Professor of New Testament at Southern Nazarene University in Bethany, Oklahoma, called and invited me to deliver the Rothwell Holiness Lectures in February 2012, he provided the spark that fanned my vague promise into a flame that resulted in this book. I entitled the series of lectures "Holiness and the *missio Dei*" and they became the basis for both the title and some of the substance of this book. I am very grateful to Hal, my other friends in the School of Theology and Ministry, and the university itself for the invitation to deliver these lectures, for the stimulating conversations, and for their warm hospitality.

I am also grateful to Chris for being so patient in waiting on a vague promise to develop into a book (and for all the dinners at SBL over the years!). Richard Middleton and Kent Brower generously offered their time in reading parts of the book, offering scholarly feedback with numerous suggestions that have improved the book. My colleague, Steve McCormick,

Acknowledgments

a historical and systematic theologian, has engaged with me in many helpful conversations about some of the ideas in this book. Dean Flemming not only read a portion of the book and gave helpful feedback, he also offered numerous suggestions in our weekly breakfasts that contributed to both the shape and substance of the book. I am especially thankful to Mike Gorman for making available to me a portion of his forthcoming book on John, reading the chapter on John at an earlier stage, and then reading the entire finished manuscript. His suggestions and comments have been invaluable in helping me to clarify various sections and improve the overall quality of the book.

I also want to thank the students I have had over the last four years for reading and interacting with portions of this book in a variety of classes. The discussions I have had with them have helped me to clarify my own thinking on some of the biblical passages and issues I write about in what follows. In particular, I wish to thank my faculty assistants during this time period, Jeb Flynn, Kaitlyn Haley, and Tim Hahn. Jeb and Tim handled various responsibilities in my classes that freed up precious time, allowing me to make progress on this book. Tim also chased down numerous references in the footnotes that helped me greatly as I was finishing the manuscript. Kaitlyn checked the Scripture references and helped with the indexes.

I wrote the bulk of this book on my sabbatical in the fall of 2015. I am extremely grateful to Nazarene Theological Seminary for their support of me and this project in granting me this sabbatical. In particular, I want to thank Roger Hahn, my academic dean and a New Testament scholar himself. During my fourteen years of teaching at NTS, he has worked tirelessly on the academic administration of the seminary, supporting all three of my requests for sabbaticals without taking one himself.

I wrote most of this book in my home office sitting in the same chair as I am sitting now. My office is not the quietest place in the house and almost every afternoon as I was writing, I was interrupted more than once by one or both of my teenage sons, Zac and Ben. Sometimes it would be to have a conversation with Zac before he went to work, or to shoot basketball with Ben. With Zac about to go off to college this fall, I am reminded of just how precious those "interruptions" were. I want to thank them for their "interruptions" that helped me unwind and get away from writing for a while. I also want to thank my wife Gina. Even though she has her own writing projects to worry about, she is always ready to listen with a sympathetic ear to my writing woes when the words just won't seem to get from my head to the screen. Without her support in so many facets of my life, this book would not have come to fruition.

Finally, I am dedicating this book to the memory of my dad and mom, Clinton and Jeanette Johnson. They both passed away unexpectedly within six months of each other in 1997 after almost forty years of marriage. They introduced me to the Lord and raised me in a church in the holiness tradition. While a good bit of the theology I learned very early in that local church—and even from my parents—badly needed an overhaul, the lives of many of those church members exemplified a faithfulness to God and a love for others that showed that they knew something about holiness and God's mission in the world. That was certainly true of my parents, whom I miss greatly and to whom I am eternally grateful for their example, encouragement and support.

Second Sunday of Easter, 2016

Abbreviations

AB	Anchor Bible
BNTC	Black's New Testament Commentary
BTCB	Brazos Theological Commentary on the Bible
CBQ	*Catholic Biblical Quarterly*
CEB	Common English Bible
DJG	*Dictionary of Jesus and the Gospels.* Edited by Joel Green et al. Downers Grove, IL: IVP Academic, 2013.
EvQ	*Evangelical Quarterly*
HBM	Hebrew Bible Monographs
HBT	*Horizons in Biblical Theology*
IBC	Interpretation: A Bible Commentary for Teaching and Preaching
IBT	Interpreting Biblical Texts
ICC	International Critical Commentary
Int	*Interpretation*
JSNTSup	Journal for the Study of the New Testament Supplement Series
JSOTSup	Journal for the Study of the Old Testament Supplement Series
JTI	*Journal of Theological Interpretation*
LXX	Septuagint

ABBREVIATIONS

NBBC	New Beacon Bible Commentary
NIB	New Interpreter's Bible
NIBC	New International Biblical Commentary
NIDB	*New Interpreter's Dictionary of the Bible.* Edited by Katherine Doob Sakenfield. 5 vols. Nashville: Abingdon, 2006-2009.
NIGTC	New International Greek Testament Commentary
NIV	New International Version
NRSV	New Revised Standard Version
NSBT	New Studies in Biblical Theology
NT	New Testament
NTL	The New Testament Library
NTS	*New Testament Studies*
OT	Old Testament
OTL	The Old Testament Library
PillarNTC	Pillar New Testament Commentary
RB	*Revue Biblique*
RSV	Revised Standard Version
SJT	*Scottish Journal of Theology*
SNTSMS	Society of New Testament Studies Monograph Series
SP	Sacra Pagina
THNTC	Two Horizons New Testament Commentary
VT	*Vetus Testamentum*

Introduction and Orientation

A Christian community in southern Bangladesh provides a clear picture of how a contemporary church might engage their culture in putting God's character of peace and justice on display. Most in the community come from a low-caste background and suffer oppression on a daily basis. That oppression only worsened when they became Christians. One of the poorest members, always seeking the good for his Christian brothers and sisters, donated a plot of land so that they would have a gathering place. As they met they discussed one of the biggest issues in their life together, i.e., their access to clean, safe water. There was a communal well in their village but because they were Christians, others in their village would no longer allow them to draw water from it and they had to walk three miles one way for water. They had seen numerous church members get sick and watched some of their children die when they had to resort to a closer, but unsafe, water source. With the support of a network of other churches, they were able to build a tube well on the donated plot to supply the church community with clean water. When it was finished, they had a ceremony of thanksgiving and dedicated the well to God's glory. Given that they were banned from a source of life itself, their being banned from using the central well was essentially an act of violence against them. As God's elect, they were, in effect, bearing the consequences within themselves of God's current wrath being poured out on their persecutors manifest in their rebellion and ignorance. But they refused to discriminate against any other villagers allowing all to come and share in the clean, life-giving water from their well. As a result, some of the very people who banned them from using the central well have now started attending their worship services. This is the result of one persecuted community always seeking the good not only for each other, but also for all, even for those who were their enemies. They were indeed a channel of God's love, a visible display of his character, through which the God of peace was at work to change violent enemies into God's own children, reconciling them to himself and to their former victims.[1]

This is a concrete example of the "theo-logic" we will see in numerous places throughout this book whereby God takes up the faithful human response of his elect people and incorporates it into his missional purposes and activity in order to display his holy character through them.

Thesis and Approach

There are numerous ways that one might choose to orient a book on holiness. This book will explore the topic by framing it with the question: What does holiness/sanctification have to do with the *missio Dei*, i.e., the mission of God in the world? The answer I intend to give to this question, the basic thesis of the book, is that for both Israel and the Church, to be sanctified is to be graciously taken up into, and set apart for witness to, and active participation in, the saving, reconciling, life-giving purposes of the missional God. For Christians this happens only as they become and remain part of an *ecclesia*, a people who are corporately and personally being shaped by the Holy Spirit into the image of the cruciform Son, and thereby being restored into the image of the holy, life-giving, Triune God—the *imago Dei*. Divine and human holiness, then, is associated with a particular (cruciform) pattern of activity effecting the saving, reconciling mission of the Triune God, whose ultimate desire is to draw all into the abundant, Spirit-saturated life of the new creation.[2] God's means of (re)shaping us into the *imago Dei*, of making us holy, is inseparable from—indeed, primarily constituted by—our participation in, and witness to, the *missio Dei* whose ultimate goal is to bring creation to its intended destiny.

At the very outset, however, I want to make it very clear that being engaged in God's mission whereby God is making us holy must itself be framed, shaped, and sustained by ecclesial practices internal to the life of the church (e.g., engaging in the daily and weekly rhythms of the church

---

1. All but the last sentence of this paragraph comes directly from my *1 & 2 Thessalonians* (240) and is a summary of Bumstead, "Pure Grace."

2. Some of the language in this paragraph is indebted to the initial paragraphs in my "Sanctification," 97 and my "Holy, Holiness, NT," 846.

in which the Word is proclaimed, Eucharist is celebrated, corporate and personal prayers are prayed, testimonies given, creeds recited, Scripture is read, taught, discussed, and performed, sick and elderly members of the congregation are cared for). Without these sorts of internal ecclesial practices undergirding attempts to participate in God's larger mission for the world, neither the goal of that mission nor the shape of any transformation associated with it will be clear.

As a biblical scholar, I will be arguing for my thesis by explicitly engaging Scripture *theologically*. This does not demarcate my approach along some sort of clear methodological boundaries. Interpreting the Bible theologically is characterized more by a particular orientation toward Scripture, in which interpreters self-consciously locate themselves and their interpretations within an ecclesial framework characterized by a commitment to the Christian canon(s), the historic creeds, and a variety of ecclesial practices. Moreover, my theological engagement with Scripture will be characterized by intentionally asking *missional* questions. In other words I will assume that God's mission to which Scripture bears witness is a primary orienting concern.

Structure of the Book

The book has three main sections bracketed by this introduction and a conclusion. In the first major section, we will be taking "soundings" from the OT with regard to the connection between holiness and the *missio Dei*. We will begin by focusing on Genesis 1–11 in terms of how it frames the biblical story as a whole and introduces the issue of holiness into that story (chapter 1). Our coverage of the rest of the OT will, of necessity, be very selective, limited primarily to portions of the Pentateuch (chapter 2) and some brief selections from the prophets Isaiah and Ezekiel (chapter 3). Hence the language of "taking soundings." The second major section will begin with a short introduction to the concept of holiness in Second Temple Judaism (chapter 4) and then focus on the gospel tradition, exploring what happens when holiness gets relocated in a Jew from Nazareth (chapters 5 and 6). The third section will deal with holiness and mission as it comes to expression in other parts of the NT. As in the OT we will be selective in our coverage of these parts of the NT, focusing primarily on portions of Acts (chapter 7), Paul's letters (chapter 8), and the book of Revelation (chapter

9). To conclude the book, I draw together its various strands and themes, and reflect theologically and missionally on their significance.

While it may already be evident from this description of the book's structure, the sheer number of biblical books left unexplored should make it clear that what follows is not intended to be a comprehensive treatment of the theme of holiness—or for that matter, the mission of God—in Scripture. No doubt, giving these other biblical books a voice in the conversation would enrich, complicate, nuance, and even challenge some of the generalizations made, and perhaps even the conclusions drawn in the overall study. In addition, an approach to the topic of holiness in Scripture other than that of an avowedly theological engagement intentionally asking missional questions would also nuance matters differently and emphasize other aspects of holiness than I do here. The following discussion, however, will show that some of the major biblical witnesses attest to the primary thesis of this book. That is, God's primary means of sanctifying or making his people holy is through their grace-enabled participation in his mission in the world.

SECTION 1

Old Testament Soundings

1

Genesis 1–11

Holiness and God's Mission "in the Beginning"

Framing the Biblical Story

WE BEGIN BY FOCUSING on the question of how Scripture frames the story it tells from Genesis to Revelation.[1] Some people read the Bible as though all the important stuff runs from Genesis 3 (where humans fall into sin) to Revelation 20 (John's vision of the last judgment where humans are judged). They tend to reduce the biblical story to God's attempt to deal with individuals' guilt so that when they die and face their own individual "last judgment," they can go to heaven.[2] But this ignores the way the Bible actually begins and ends. The Bible begins with God taking great care to create the physical world as his cosmic sanctuary or temple to become what we might call a "theater of his glory."[3] This is a world he calls "good" over and over at the

---

1. With the exception of some of the reflections on holiness, the material in this introductory chapter has a general affinity with similar introductory material in other missional readings of Scripture, e.g., Wright, *The Mission of God's People*. While its primary agenda is not to offer a missional reading of Scripture, Middleton's, *A New Heaven and a New Earth* does have a missional bent and has also influenced the shape and content of this initial chapter.

2. For a clarion call to abandon the idea that going to heaven when one dies is the primary point of the Bible, see especially, Middleton, *New Heaven*.

3. The theme of creation as the temple/sanctuary of God has become commonplace in contemporary biblical studies. For a very accessible introductory treatment, see Beale and Kim, *God Dwells Among Us*, 17–28. The theme is also important to Middleton's

Section 1—Old Testament Soundings

beginning of the Bible in Genesis 1. The Bible then ends with Revelation 21–22, with God "making all things new" (21:5). It ends with God's good creation made new, with creation reaching its intended destiny and flourishing with abundant life. Although creation is "very good" in this first chapter of Genesis (1:31), God does not make it "perfect,"[4] in the sense of some sort of static perfection. Rather, God gives humanity a "perfectly balanced and resourced starting point . . . a setting in which human beings, working with and enabled by God, could cause the created order to flourish."[5] In the first two chapters, then, God gives humanity a job to do, a role to play—a mission—from which he never releases us. Hence, from the outset, one important aspect of humanity's role vis-à-vis God can be summed up in the language and conceptuality of participation in the *missio Dei*.

This mission goes hand-in-hand with God's creation of human beings in God's own image.[6] Even though there are real differences between Genesis 1 and 2, when they are read against their ancient Near Eastern background, both essentially portray humanity as, in Middleton's words, "the authorized cult statue in the cosmic temple, the decisive locus of divine presence on earth, the living image of God in the cosmic sanctuary."[7] In Gen 2:7, the holy God graciously breathes his breath/Spirit/life into humanity—his own previously inert cult statue—thereby enabling humanity to re-present his gracious presence (like priests) in his cosmic temple and to rule over it (like kings) in a way that creation would flourish with well-ordered life (Gen 1:28; 2:15) and reach its intended destiny. Middleton's elaboration of this is worth quoting at some length:

> [W]hereas cult images of the gods are false images, and impotent to boot (Ps 115:4–8), humans are powerful, living images of the one true God, called to manifest God's presence by their active cultural development of the earth. By our obedient exercise of power, humanity as *imago Dei* functions like a prism, refracting the pure light of God into a rainbow of cultural activities that scintillate with the creator's glory throughout the earth. By our faithful

treatment of biblical eschatology (*New Heaven*, 46–49).

4. On this way of putting the matter, see Fretheim, *Creation Untamed*, 9–38.
5. Van Duzer, *Why Business Matters*, 36, 37.
6. From a Christian standpoint, it is the cruciform and risen Jesus who provides us with the definitive depiction of what it means to be the truly human image of God. Nevertheless, these first few chapters of Genesis already give us some clear direction for imagining what it means for humans to be created in God's image.
7. Middleton, *New Heaven*, 49.

Genesis 1–11

representation of God, who is enthroned in the heavens, we extend the presence of the divine king of creation even to the earth, to prepare the earth for God's full—eschatological—presence, the day when God will fill all things. Then (when God fully indwells the earthly realm) the cosmic temple of creation will have been brought to its intended destiny.[8]

The best place in the Bible to see a portrait of that intended destiny—creation reaching its full potential and flourishing with abundant life—is Revelation 21–22.[9] There God's garden creation with only two original inhabitants becomes a bustling city bursting with fruitful life with people living in complete harmony with God and each other (21:3). Not only is there no sin, suffering, or death, there is no capacity for these chaotic evil forces to ever re-emerge (21:1).[10] All this is because the entirety of the renewed creation will be soaked with God's unmediated holy, life-giving presence/glory (21:11, 22; 22:3–5; cf. 1 Cor 15:28) making all of it God's now completed holy temple/sanctuary. "The glory and honor of the nations" (21:24–26), that "rainbow of cultural activities that scintillate with the creator's glory,"[11] are gathered from all over the earth and brought into it. In it redeemed human beings fully represent God's gracious, life-giving presence/holiness like priests (Rev 22:3)[12] and share in his rule over God's renewed cosmic temple like kings (Rev 22:5). In short, this is *not* a restoration of the original creation to its original state but, in the words of Bauckham and Hart, "the unrealized promise of the first creation finally achieved."[13] However, even this "new creation" should not be imagined in terms of some sort of unchanging static perfection, but in terms of continuing and unhindered robust flourishing. To slightly modify the words of theologian, Robert Jenson, to fit this context: "[W]hatever blessing we may in a particular context invoke to speak of [creation's intended destiny], we must imagine a sort of spiral of the granting and pursuit of that blessing."[14]

---

8. Ibid.

9. In chapter 9, I discuss Revelation as a whole in more detail, including its last two chapters.

10. This is implied by the absence of the sea in the renewed earth. The sea, from which the first beast in Revelation emerges (13:1), symbolizes chaos in the ancient world.

11. Middleton, *New Heaven*, 49.

12. The language of this verse (*latreuō*) suggests that those dwelling in the new creation engage in priestly service.

13. Bauckham and Hart, *Hope Against Hope*, 149.

14. Jenson, *Ezekiel*, 336. The original context of Jenson's words is that of his

Section 1—Old Testament Soundings

To sum up, when all creation is fruitful and multiplying with abundant life and cultural development, when the holy God is dwelling directly with God's holy people in a holy place,[15] creation will have reached its intended, albeit non-static, destiny.

Taking the Bible's own framing seriously, then, helps us to see it as the story of God's mission to bring his creation to its full potential and to do so through the agency of humanity. Along the way, after Genesis 3, God will indeed deal with the sin and guilt of human beings along with its devastating consequences for the rest of the created order. But this "rescue operation" is a sub-plot in the main plot of God's mission to bring his creation to its intended destiny. Even so, it is a necessary sub-plot that occupies most of the Bible. So it is very important for us to pay some attention to how this sub-plot gets going, the way it develops in the early chapters of Genesis, and what holiness has to do with all of this.

Holiness and the Story's Sub-Plot

As we saw above, in Genesis 1–2, the holy God graciously creates humanity in God's own image to re-present his gracious presence in his cosmic temple and to rule over it in a way that would enable all creation to flourish with well-ordered life (Gen 1:28; 2:15) and reach its intended destiny. So that humanity could remain free to accomplish this task, God ordered this good creation with a boundary between every other tree and the tree of the knowledge of good and evil. Humanity was forbidden from eating the fruit from this tree (2:16–17). But you know the story. Even though they had been created in God's image, they crossed that boundary, refusing to fulfill the charge God had given them, succumbing to the temptation to "be like God" (Gen 3:5).

Before Genesis 3, although creation was not yet perfected so that God's presence fully saturated every nook and cranny of it, God had been immediately present to his good creation. All of creation, including humanity, had experienced God's direct holy presence *as blessing*, i.e., as generating

---

commenting on Ezek 47:1–12. His original quotation has the word "kingdom" where I have supplied "creation's intended destiny." There is little, if any, difference between what he means by "kingdom" in his original context and what I mean by "creation's intended destiny" here. As we will see in our chapter on Revelation, a main aspect of "creation's intended destiny" is precisely that the kingdom of God has come.

15. This last phrase is from Thomas, "Holy God," 53–69.

the capacity for fruitful life (1:22, 28; 2:7) and the means of sustaining it (1:29–30). In fact, Gen 2:3 is the very first time we hear the word "holy" or "sanctify" in the Bible: "God blessed the seventh day and made it holy, because on it God rested from all the work of creation."[16] Since God's blessing in 1:22 and 1:28 was for the express purpose of enabling well-ordered life to flourish and multiply, his *blessing* of the seventh day and *making it holy* can be assumed to have a similar purpose (i.e., to provide his creatures/creation the sustaining rest needed for the ultimate purpose of producing flourishing, well-ordered life).[17]

The first time we hear of God "sanctifying" or making something holy—setting it apart from other things (or days in this case) for his own use—the purpose of the action is so that well-ordered life can flourish. In other words, *holiness is explicitly connected with blessing and life*, the very things God's direct, unmediated presence had begun to generate for his creation prior to Genesis 3. Before Genesis 3, there was no need to demarcate secular from sacred space, no need to safeguard God's creation from his direct presence because that presence was universally experienced as bringing blessing and life.

The disobedience of the first pair, however, was disastrous. By refusing to live under God's rule respecting God's ordering of the cosmos, they became alienated from God (Gen 3:8), from each other (Gen 3:12, 16; 4:1–16), and from the rest of creation (Gen 3:15, 17–19). Their refusal to reflect God's gracious rule/image to the rest of creation in an attempt to "become like God" on their own terms was an exploitation of the status God had given them and a move toward (self) idolatry. This resulted in the very ground/earth being cursed (3:17) and made all of creation susceptible to the forces of sin and death resulting in injustice, violence, chaos, and disorder (6:5–6, 11–13). Before God graciously barred the entrance to the garden so that they would not be able to eat from the tree of life and live forever in the chaos and disorder they had unleashed (Gen 3:22–23), the first human pair instinctively did something that will become typical for the new situation their actions have set in motion; they hide themselves from the direct presence of God (Genesis 3:8–10).

---

16. Unless otherwise noted, throughout this book all OT quotations are from the Common English Bible and all NT translations are my own.

17. We will discuss the Sabbath later in more detail as part of the holy, life-giving patterns God provides to shape his people to embody his own holy, life-giving character.

Section 1—Old Testament Soundings

God never says hiding themselves was the wrong thing for them to do. Most of what follows in the biblical story, in fact, indicates that it was precisely the *right* thing to do. In the changed situation where rebellion has introduced injustice, violence, chaos, and disorder into God's creation, God's direct, unmediated presence in its fullness—God's holiness—is no longer *automatically* experienced as blessing and life, but *can* now be experienced as threat, or even curse (3:14–19). This is not to say that God gives up on his mission and leaves creation devoid of his graceful presence, as exemplified by his graciously clothing Adam and Eve and even by his driving them out of the garden, refusing to allow them to eat from the tree of life that would keep them alive forever to suffer the mess they have made (3:21–24). God's holy presence remains the necessary condition for there to be any beneficence and life on earth. But the circumstances have changed. Human beings are now inclined toward—or better, enslaved to—the death-dealing forces that threaten to plunge God's well-ordered creation into the chaos of injustice and violence (Gen 6:5; 8:21; 11:1–9). If God's unmediated presence, his holiness, is going to be experienced as beneficial and life-giving, it must be cordoned off, with humans protected from coming into casual contact with it.

Admittedly, some subsequent biblical stories narrate direct human contact with the holy God. God becomes really present to particular characters and to his people by appearing to them at times in ambiguous ways in which his identity as God only becomes apparent as each story progresses.[18] In other cases, particularly in Exodus, God's identity is never in question and he seems to come into direct contact with human beings who are said to "see God" (Exod 24:9–11). In fact, although he still seems to be in the pillar of cloud at the entrance to the tent of meeting, the Lord is said to speak to Moses "face to face, as one speaks to a friend" (Exod 33:11). But when Moses asks the Lord to show him *his glory* (Exod 33:18)—his visible holiness—things become more complicated. While God allows all his "goodness" to pass before Moses and proclaims his name and fundamental

---

18. E.g., Abraham and Sarah's visit from "three men" (Gen 18:2), one of whom somehow seems to turn out to be the Lord (18:16–17); Jacob's wrestling with "a man" in Gen 32:22–32 and his interpreting the wrestling match in terms of his seeing God "face to face" and yet having his life preserved (32:30). At other times, it is "the angel of the Lord" who appears who is very closely associated with the Lord himself, e.g., the call of Gideon where he sees "the angel of the Lord face to face" (Judg 6:22) and it is the Lord who is said to be speaking a few verses earlier (Judg 6:16); the circumstances surrounding Samson's birth where, after "the angel of the Lord" appears to his parents and ascends in a flame, Manoah says "We shall surely die, for we have seen God" (Judg 13:22).

character to him (33:19), the Lord tells him in no uncertain terms, "*you cannot see my face*; for no one shall see me and live" (33:20). God then shields Moses with his hand while his glory passes by so that Moses can see his back but not his face (Exod 33:21–23). Here, the implication is that "face" in this context is the fullness of God's very self.[19] While God's glory, his visible holiness, his very self, may be seen partially—from the back side as it were—humans still have to be protected from coming directly into "frontal" contact with God's holy presence in its fullness. Hence, when other passages use the language of seeing God "face to face," we might imagine that they are describing a very real—even intense—manifestation of God's holy presence, but this remains something less than direct, unmediated contact with God's holy presence in its fullness.[20] After driving the two humans from the garden, God will indeed remain truly present with his creatures and his creation. However, direct, unmediated contact with God's holy presence in its fullness will only come at the end of the biblical story when the servants of God and the Lamb "will see his face" (Rev 22:4) in a cosmos fully permeated with that holy presence.

In spite of the garden debacle, the Genesis narrator continues to remind us that God had created humanity in his own image (Gen 5:1–2). In fact, when God started things over with Noah and his family after the flood, even though the human heart remained inclined toward death-dealing forces (8:21), God himself reaffirms that he had made humankind in his own image (9:6). Even though Noah's family began to fulfill the creation mandate of being fruitful and multiplying, spreading out over the whole earth with a rich variety of languages and cultures (10:1–32), things apparently regressed in the Babel scene in Genesis 11 where humanity goes back to its old tricks in the garden.[21] Rather than exercising the mediating, royal role God has given them in creation in a way that brings honor to their creator—i.e., rather than fulfilling the creation mandate to move out and fill all the earth with the fruitful blessing of new life—all of humanity now hovers together in one place to try to "make a name for themselves" (11:4). They do so by building a tower that reaches the sky (another attempt

---

19. For a fuller discussion of this passage along similar lines, see Fretheim, *Exodus*, 299–301.

20. The passages under discussion in this paragraph are no doubt more complicated than what this summary sentence suggests. The whole issue deserves more attention than I have the space to give it.

21. On reading the Babel story as one of regression from diverse and fruitful human culture to that of imperial monolithic culture, see Middleton, *New Creation*, 54–55.

to reach God's level?) once again overstepping their bounds as creatures. Although the context has changed from a garden with two inhabitants to a valley where "all the people on earth" are gathered together *in one place*, humanity has not changed. Their actions amount to a defiant refusal to carry out their creational mandate of re-presenting God's gracious presence *throughout the whole* of his cosmic temple (as priests) and ruling over it in a way that all of creation would flourish with well-ordered life (Gen 1:28; 2:15) and reach its intended destiny. This time God has to forcefully divide and disperse their (imperial-like) project in order to restart the process of fulfilling his dream of bringing his whole creation to its potential through the agency of humanity. And it is out of this forced dispersion of humanity that God chooses one man and his barren wife to become the not-so-promising pair through whom God would begin to bring about that dream.

2

The Call/Election of Abraham and Israel

Living Out "the Way of the Lord"

Getting Things Started: Abraham

GENESIS 12 TO REVELATION 22 can be read as the story of God's mission to rectify what has happened in the biblical story to this point for the purpose of bringing about his goal for creation. In this story God never gives up on his dream of accomplishing his mission through the agency of humanity. After hearing all the genealogical details of Genesis 10 and 11:10–26 that, if nothing else, highlight the ability of humanity to be fruitful and multiply, we hear for the first time in the biblical story of one woman who was incapable of fulfilling God's creational mandate. "Sarai," we are told, "was unable to have children" (11:30). So it is somewhat surprising that the first step God takes to bring about his goal for creation is to single out—"set apart," "call" and/or "elect"—this barren woman's husband, Abram.[1] But that is what God does when three short verses after we are told of Sarai's condition, we hear:

---

1. Genesis does not use the root word for "elect/election" to speak of God choosing the Patriarchs. This does not mean, however, that the concept of election/calling is absent from the Patriarchs' stories, though it may indeed look somewhat different than what we see in places like Exodus and Deuteronomy regarding Israel's election. Admittedly then, stating matters as I have above and proceeding as I do in the rest of this section interprets Genesis in light of the language and conceptuality of other parts of the OT. On this issue, see esp. McDonald, "Did God Choose the Patriarchs?"

Section 1—Old Testament Soundings

> ¹ The LORD said to Abram, "Leave your land, your family, and your father's household for the land that I will show you. ² I will make of you a great nation and will bless you. I will make your name respected, and *you will be a blessing.* ³ I will bless those who bless you, those who curse you I will curse; *all the families of earth will be blessed because of you.*" (12:1–3)

God's presence with, and calling of, Abraham is clearly intended to generate blessing and life for him and his family. Christian readings of the OT should not ignore this intrinsic aspect of God's election of Abraham's family (Israel), i.e., in sovereign love, God elects Abraham's family *in the first place for their own benefit.*[2] But in addition, *because of* Abraham and his family, all the other families on earth (those in 10:1–32) will experience God's blessing and life.[3] Abraham and his family, then, are to become the primary channel of God's blessing to the nations. They are the particular human family through whom God chooses to work to accomplish his life-giving mission to defeat the death-dealing, chaotic forces of sin in order to bring humanity and the rest of creation to its goal.

God promises to start this great nation through Abraham's ninety-year-old wife, Sarah. Apparently, so that Sarah herself can hear the promise of God's life-giving *blessing* on her behalf (Gen 17:16), "three men," one of whom (somehow) turns out to be "the Lord," pay a personal visit to the old couple in Genesis 18.[4] With Sarah's laughter about the whole thing

---

2. On which, e.g., see Kaminsky, *Yet I Loved Jacob*; Moberly, *Theology of the Book of Genesis*, 143–61; Moberly, *Old Testament Theology*, 41–52.

3. The Hebrew of 12:3 could be translated "all the families of the earth will bless themselves [or bless one another] because of you." This would make the purpose of Abraham's initial calling less about his family becoming a channel of God's blessing to the other nations and more about God's election of Abraham for his own benefit. A good argument can be made for reading the text as an independent literary unit this way (see, e.g., Moberly, *Theology of the Book of Genesis*, 143–61). Even so, especially from a Christian perspective, larger canonical and hermeneutical considerations point toward the legitimacy of reading the text in a way that underscores the potential for seeing its missional aspect: (1) Its placement right after the dispersion of the larger human family at Babel; (2) the cosmic scope of the Exodus and the instrumental language of Israel's calling at Mt. Sinai in Exod 19:5–6 (cf. Isa 42:6; 49:6); (3) the Septuagint (a pre-Christian translation of the Hebrew scriptures into Greek) translates Gen 12:3 and its related texts in a way that reads Abraham's election as missional; (4) the only two direct quotes of 12:3 in the NT follow the Septuagintal interpretation of this text with the passive "will be blessed" (Acts 3:25; Gal 3:8) and both interpret this "blessing" as salvation. For these last four points, I am indebted to an unpublished paper by Richard Middleton.

4. On the face to face aspect of this meeting, see our earlier comments (pp. 8–9).

The Call/Election of Abraham and Israel

ringing in our ears, in the next few verses we hear what will turn out to be a paradigmatic theological pattern with regard to God's people and their participation in God's mission:[5]

> [16] When the men got up to leave, they looked down toward Sodom, and Abraham walked along with them to see them on their way. [17] Then the LORD said, "Shall I hide from Abraham what I am about to do? [18] Abraham will surely become a great and powerful nation, and all nations on earth will be blessed through him. [19] *For* I have chosen him, *so that* he will direct his children and his household after him to keep *the way of the LORD by doing* what is *right* and *just, so that* the LORD will bring about for Abraham what he has promised him." [20] Then the LORD said, "The outcry against Sodom and Gomorrah is so great and their sin so grievous [21] that I will go down and see if what they have done is as bad as the *outcry* that has reached me." (NIV)

Before focusing on the "theo-logic" of vv. 18–19, it is important to note that the context grounds these verses in a very concrete world, the world where the death-dealing, chaotic forces of sin have the cities of Sodom and Gomorrah in their grip so much so that their people's life together has become a channel of injustice and violence toward others (in a similar way that injustice and violence filled the whole earth in Gen 6:5, 11–13). The word the NIV translates as the "outcry" against these cities in v. 21, the CEB translates as "cries of injustice" (*tseaqah*). It is the sort of word that describes the cry of those who are vulnerable and helpless in the face of violence and injustice, like the cry of immigrant slaves who have helplessly watched the Egyptians throw their babies into the Nile (e.g., Exod 3:9; cf. Neh 9:9) or the cry of helpless widows and orphans (Exod 22:22–23). God prepares to deal with Sodom and Gomorrah because of the injustices they were perpetrating on those who were helpless to protect themselves from their violence (19:13). To be clear, Sodom and Gomorrah are not destroyed because their men attempt to engage in same sex relations per se. But there is no doubt that their attempt to gang rape those they take to be vulnerable visitors—essentially to show their dominance over them—illustrates the very kind of violent behavior and injustice that is pervasive among them. This kind of behavior not only dehumanizes victims, it also dehumanizes

---

5. What follows regarding this passage moves along similar lines as Wright's in *The Mission of God's People*, 88–94.

the perpetrators who become more like unruly beasts than truly human icons who mediate God's image to others.

What is important for our present purposes is that God decides not to hide from Abraham (v. 17) his compassionate concern for those enduring Sodom-like injustice. Granted, his compassion for them will ultimately be expressed in the destruction of the perpetrators and the conditions that make the violence and injustice possible. But what is on display is God's compassionate character manifest in his passionate resolve to make right that which is contrary to the flourishing life and well-being he intends for all his creatures—victims and perpetrators alike. God's judgment against the persistent opposition to his life-giving purposes is a manifestation of his loving sovereignty over his creation, his refusal to allow perpetrators to go on indefinitely treating their victims as less than the images of God they are and thereby become more and more beastly and dehumanized themselves. This is the concrete context for the Lord's decision not to hide from Abraham what he is about to do so that Abraham can learn his way.

In v. 18 it is as though God is reminding himself of his promise to Abraham and in v. 19 he gives the "theo-logic" of how this promise is to work out in Abraham and his family's life. Note the logical connectors in the following sentence:

> [18] Abraham will surely become a great and powerful nation, and all nations on earth will be blessed through him. "*For* I have chosen him *so that* he will direct his children and his household after him to keep the way of the LORD *by doing* what is right and just, *so that* the LORD will bring about for Abraham what he has promised him." (NIV)

Note that the first move in the whole sequence is God's. God makes a sovereign choice of Abraham before Abraham had done anything of consequence. But this sovereign choice of Abraham has a purpose. It is *so that* he will teach his family to keep the "way of the LORD," which is immediately defined in positive terms as doing "what is right and just." In both the Hebrew and Greek the language is that of *doing* "righteousness" (*tsedhaqah/dikaiosynē*) and "justice" (*mishpat/krisis*). Both terms are often used together with little difference in their meaning and have to do with acting rightly or justly in particular relationships and concrete situations.[6] But neither term refers to some sort of totally impartial "blind justice" of the sort that we are encouraged to imagine characterizes the American

---

6. See the discussion in Wright, *Mission of God's People*, esp. 90–92.

The Call/Election of Abraham and Israel

justice system.[7] Rather, enacting "social justice" is a more apt description of what these terms imply when used together.[8] "Doing righteousness and justice" is characteristic of the way the divine king acts (Ps 99:4; Jer 9:24) by actively opposing the forces of chaos and injustice and bringing deliverance from violence and oppression; it is a pattern of activity to be emulated by the human king (2 Sam 8:15; 1 Kgs 10:9; Jer 22:3; 23:5; cf. Isa 11:4–5).[9] The divine king's desire is to act in concrete situations *to restore the conditions of justice*, i.e., "the conditions that obtain when humans are right with God, with self, with others, and with the world."[10] In chapter 19 we find out that, in this particular situation, God does this by destroying the channels through which the forces of sin, chaos, and disorder are inhibiting his sustaining of rightly ordered life (i.e., *shalom*). However, as will become apparent when we trace the contours of Abraham's conversation with the Lord, God's move to destroy such channels—as in the earlier flood story—is *in response* to the *unchecked, rampant, and thoroughgoing* human violence in this particular place.

The whole episode of Abraham's attempt to involve God in a typical back and forth bartering contest in 18:22–33 underscores this point.[11] Abraham simply presupposes that God has already decided to destroy the cities, that "the way of the Lord" is always and only the way of retributive justice. But at this point in the narrative, God himself has only said that he is going to go down to investigate the charges against Sodom and Gomorrah (vv. 20–21). Abraham begins by assuming that he might need to educate (or at least remind) God about what constitutes justice when he asks "Will you indeed sweep away the righteous with the wicked?" (v. 23, NRSV) and then goes on to ask "Shall not the judge (*shophet*) of all the earth do justice (*mishpat*)?" (v. 25, NRSV). So he attempts to engage God in a bartering contest. Beginning with what in the logic of bartering would be a "low price," Abraham tries to persuade God not to destroy the city for the sake of fifty righteous (*tsadiqim*) people. Were God to engage in

---

7. See McKnight's reflections along these lines in *A Community Called Atonement*, 124–33.

8. Wright, *Mission of God's People*, 91; McDonald, "Listening to Abraham," 37.

9. Ibid.

10. McKnight, *A Community Called Atonement*, 125.

11. For an instructive reading of this passage that cautions against the common practice of listening more to Abraham than to God and imagining that God actually takes up the game of bargaining that Abraham initiates, see McDonald, "Listening to Abraham," 25–43. I am grateful to Richard Middleton for calling my attention to this article.

Section 1—Old Testament Soundings

this contest, there would be a counter offer that would be higher, but God never puts forward any counter offer, refusing to participate in Abraham's bartering contest. Rather, God simply allows Abraham to go as low as he appears to have the nerve to go, dropping the number down to only ten. As McDonald notes, "To every bid that Abraham lodges there is only a divine yes and never a no."[12]

God's refusal to engage in this bartering contest that is framed with Abraham's assumption that the "way of the Lord" is simply characterized by quantifiable retributive justice suggests that Abraham has misunderstood and that God is indeed educating him on the nature of divine justice. Abraham—here the paradigmatic representative of God's elect people—is given an opportunity to make intercession for these cities as a prophetic mediator.[13] However, as McDonald notes,

> Abraham does not appeal to the mercy of God and ask for full forgiveness; instead, presuming Yhwh to be a harsh judge, he prepares to barter with him. His strategy is undone by Yhwh's persistent acceptance of Abraham's offer; Yhwh turns out to be far more merciful than Abraham imagines. Drawing the line at ten indicates not only the depth of Sodom's sin but also that Abraham has not plumbed the depths of Yhwh's grace.[14]

The main point here is that, *as his initial move* to rectify situations of injustice, *God does not desire to destroy* those involved in that injustice, but rather to extend his mercy as far as is possible if there remains any real possibility for repentance and change in the situation.[15] In other words, *the Lord's way in doing justice is to lead with compassion and mercy* and in this text, God's elect people—represented by Abraham—are being taught that way and invited to become prophetic intercessors in situations characterized by injustice. Here "Yhwh seeks to instruct Abraham about 'his way,' and the dialogue is an interactive lesson in which Abraham learns

---

12. Ibid., 35.
13. For the details of this understanding of the text, see ibid., 35–41.
14. Ibid., 40.
15. Recall, for example, God's sparing of Ninevah even when Jonah functioned more as a prophet of doom than a prophetic intercessor. Also, note the extravagant mercy God is prepared to show to his own wayward people in Jerusalem if *only one* righteous person can be found in it (Jer 5:1).

The Call/Election of Abraham and Israel

the extent of Yhwh's mercy toward his creation, so that Abraham and his descendants may follow in that same way."[16]

In this particular case, the Lord, through the visit of the "two men/angels" in chapter 19, goes down and appears to finds out that the situation cannot be resolved with the offer of compassion and mercy.[17] In such a case, the way of the Lord—the way that the judge of the earth does justice in this sort of hopeless scenario where injustice and rampant violence is all pervasive—is to destroy the conditions (including its human channels) that make such unjust violence possible, thereby restoring *shalom* for those who are its victims. But again, this is not God's original intent for the way he would deal with his creatures and it is not the way God deals with any and every violation of his will for his creation, whether in the Old or the New Testament.

God's character is manifest in his compassionate concern for cries from people in distress who are experiencing injustice and in his actions to restore justice in the situation. Hence, we might describe "the way of the Lord" for God's elect people in this instance as: (1) exhibiting a compassionate concern for enacting conditions in their own community that God defines as right and just so that their own life together does not degenerate into Sodom-and-Gomorrah-like injustice toward others; (2) attuning their ears to the cries of injustice around them and speaking out against it, doing what they can to restore God's justice/*shalom* in the situation, *including imploring God as prophetic mediators to enact full forgiveness and mercy toward repentant perpetrators of injustice*. One word of caution about God's people doing what they can to restore God's justice is in order here. As we will note in a later chapter, after God's acting in a cruciform Lord to absorb violence into himself and purge the world of it, God's elect people acting violently toward others in the name of restoring God's justice should *in principle* be unthinkable.[18] In the NT, the holy people of God are never

---

16. McDonald, "Listening to Abraham," 41.

17. Perhaps Lot is to be considered "righteous" (in the sense of being innocent of the kind of behavior his fellow townspeople exhibit) since God saves him and his family, or perhaps God does this simply to exhibit his compassion for his covenant partner Abraham when he "remembered Abraham" (19:29).

18. The "in principle" represents my ongoing caveat to a total pacifism. For example, it would be difficult for me to argue from my very safe suburban home office that God's people should not support a governmental use of force to rescue kidnapped Nigerian girls from being tortured, killed, or used as sex slaves by violent means if there simply are no other means available. But even here the ambivalence I have toward this issue (if not the inconsistency in my position) comes to the fore when I have a difficult time

depicted as a channel through which God destroys others to bring about God's restoring mission.

Now to sum up our comments on Abraham. The "theo-logic" of this Genesis passage is that the middle term between God's sovereign choice to set Abraham and his family apart and God's fulfilling his promise to him is *obedience to the way of the Lord*, i.e., reflecting God's character/pattern of activity that manifests his desire to engender restorative justice in order to reinstate *shalom* in a chaotic and disordered world. It was through their doing so that God would mold their life together into a life-giving blessing for the rest of the nations. Since this theological pattern with regard to God's people and their participation in God's mission becomes paradigmatic for the biblical story, it is important to be as clear as possible about it. It is not as though God's purposes and promise of blessing for the nations will be completely frustrated and ultimately fail without the obedience of Abraham and his family. Rather, God always acts as a catalyst for his people's acting and will graciously incorporate their faithful human response into the fulfillment of his divine promise.[19] As we will see throughout the book, this theological logic of God's electing initiative followed by his call for, then taking up and incorporating faithful human response into his purposes and activity, is the underlying scaffolding of our language of God's people being elected in order to participate in God's mission.

Exodus and Mount Sinai: The Call/Election of Israel

It is not long before this divine mission hits a snag when Abraham's family finds themselves in slavery in Egypt. It appears that God's promise to generate blessing and life for them is in jeopardy. Before Joseph died, they were doing exactly what God had commanded humanity to do in the garden; they were being "fruitful and multiplying" (Exod 1:7//Gen 1:22). But then a new Pharaoh rose up, not just against this elect family—the stakes were higher than that—but against God's own intent for blessing and life to come to them and through them to the rest of the nations and ultimately to his whole creation.[20] You know the story, though, of how God made good on

---

imagining one committed to the cruciform Lord directly taking a perpetrator's life in carrying out such an operation.

19. Cf. Moberly's similar comments on the theological pattern of Gen 22:15–18 ("Earliest Commentary," 321).

20. For a more sustained reading of the Exodus narrative along these lines, see

The Call/Election of Abraham and Israel

his promises and rescued them through Moses in the Exodus and then led them to Mount Sinai.

In Exod 15:18, with the waters of deliverance still churning, Moses leads the Israelites in a praise song that ends with the first mention of the reign of God in Scripture: "The Lord will rule forever and always." When the Israelites later reached Mount Sinai, it should be clear that they were *already saved* and had *already confessed* the Lord not only as *their* royal sovereign but also as the king of the entire cosmos. Then, at the mountain, God, through Moses, reminds them of what he did to redeem them, declares them to be holy, and calls them to express that holiness in obedience to him, their royal sovereign who owns the whole world.[21]

> 4You saw what I did to the Egyptians, and how I lifted you up on eagles' wings and brought you to me. 5So now, if you faithfully obey me and stay true to my covenant, you will be my most precious possession out of all the peoples, since the whole earth belongs to me. 6You will be a kingdom of priests for me and a holy nation (Exod 19:4–6a).

There is a similar pattern of "theo-logic" at work here as in Gen 18:15, and God's covenant with Abraham's descendants here already assumes the earlier covenant he had made with Abraham (cf. Gen 17:7; Exod 3:6–7, 15–17). Prior to chapter 19, the Israelites have already been identified as Yahweh's "firstborn son" (Exod 4:22), emphasizing the fact that they were God's elect people before they ever arrived at Sinai. Hence, God's electing, delivering, and constituting Israel as a people is prior to anything God requires of them in response. By means of these actions, God has already set Israel apart or sanctified them, and therefore given them a holy status as he awaits their response. But God does require a response. *God's sanctifying action requires and makes it possible for Israel to engage in actions through which he continues their sanctification* (Lev 11:44–45).[22] In other words, God has acted but Israel must respond in faithful obedience and covenantal loyalty to the king of the whole world *if* they are going to be God's most prized tool with which to accomplish his mission, that is,[23] *if* they are going to fulfill their purpose

---

Fretheim, *Exodus*.

21. Wells's discussion of this "rather ambivalent state" of being declared holy, yet called to be holy, is helpful (*God's Holy People*, 52–57).

22. Indeed, the response that God enables and requires in the exodus event so that the life of God's people no longer conforms to their life in Egypt is itself a completion of their salvation begun in the exodus (on which see esp. Middleton, *New Heaven*, 87–88).

23. Following Wells's suggestion that the meaning of the phrase "precious possession"

Section 1—Old Testament Soundings

as the kingdom of priests and the holy nation God has called them to be. The "if" does *not* signal an offer to *become* God's people or a reward for obedience. Rather, the "if" essentially says to Israel: *If* you are to carry out your commission to be Yahweh's people on behalf of the other nations and on behalf of the whole earth, which belongs to him, your job description is to be a holy nation engaged in priestly service.[24]

The job description of priests in Israel included representing their fellow Israelites to God and God to their fellow Israelites in the ongoing offering of sacrifices and mediating God's gracious response to the people, teaching others God's Torah, and pronouncing blessings that mediated the beneficent, life-giving favor of God. At Sinai, then, God was calling the totality of Israel to take on this sort of job description on behalf of other nations.[25] They were to represent their particular God to the nations and the nations to their particular God.[26] It was *not* that they were called to go into the nations and be "evangelists" who preached repentance and tried to convert Gentiles over to the worship of Yahweh. Rather, *their faithful life together* was to function to teach the nations God's Torah, the "way of the Lord," thereby making them the mediator of God's life-giving blessings to the nations and indeed, even to the earth and its non-human inhabitants.[27]

At Sinai, then, it becomes clear that God has set Israel apart from other nations—has sanctified them—in order that they might be, and become, a publicly distinct people corresponding to his character through which he intends to carry forward his missional purpose. By living in faithfulness to the covenant, they were to be a light to the nations (Isa 42:6), a "showcase" or model for the way God had created humans to live. They were to be the instrument through which God would reestablish his reign over a world gone awry into chaos and disorder, thereby bringing healing and *shalom* to his creation.

---

is expanded and intensified in the following two phrases: "priestly kingdom" and "holy nation" (*God's Holy People*, 47–48).

24. See the similar, but not identical, claims of Wells, *God's Holy People*, 46; cf. Fretheim, *Exodus*, 212–13.

25. God addresses all of Israel in Exod 19:3 and the people all respond "with one voice" in 19:8. So the whole people together are depicted as exercising a singular priesthood.

26. A striking example of Israel's representative king engaging in this in a worship setting is Solomon's prayer for the foreigner in 1 Kgs 8:41–43 at the dedication of the first temple.

27. On which, see the discussion below of the effect of Israel's Sabbath laws for both domestic animals and the land itself.

However, even this redeemed, sanctified people who were living in a world where the forces of sin, chaos, and disorder had been released could not have a direct encounter with the holy God without "sanctifying" or "purifying" themselves to wash away any hint of impurity (Exod 19:10–25). Careless contact, just touching ground saturated with the presence of the holy God (v. 12), brings death not life. If God's holy presence, his holiness, is going to be experienced as beneficial, it must be adequately safeguarded. It must be cordoned off and protected from coming into casual contact with a rag-tag bunch of redeemed refugees who had earlier shown when they romanticized their former slavery (Exod 16:3) that they could still be inclined toward the death-dealing forces that threaten to undo God's well-ordered creation. In such a world and around such people—even God's redeemed missional people—God's holy presence had to be completely cordoned off from any hint of impurity if this people were to experience his holy presence as life-giving rather than as threatening (e.g., see the sad case of Aaron's sons in Lev 10:1–3).[28] This required that a sanctuary be built for God (Exod 25–26; 35–36) with altars that would allow the people to present offerings making it possible for them to live with the presence of the holy God among them (Exod 25:8). When the sanctuary was finished, the glory of the Lord filled it (Exod 40:34–35) as a foretaste of God's intent to fill the cosmic temple of creation with his full, eschatological presence/glory (cf. Rev 21:11). Its completion signaled to the people that the Lord's holy presence was indeed among them. But to continue experiencing that holy presence as life-giving rather than as threatening also required the people to take great care not to come into careless contact with it and, indeed, to engage in "sanctifying" actions of their own, actions through which God would continue molding them into a people reflecting his character as the channel of his holy mission.

God's Missional People Living Out God's Holy Calling

Israel's sanctification is both a fact—since God has set them apart from other nations (Lev 20:26)—and a job description to fulfill (Lev 18:2–4). While God's initial and sustaining sanctifying actions frame, enable, and provide their means, Israel must also engage in sanctifying actions both

---

28. This does not mean that purity and holiness are the same thing. As Dwight Swanson puts it, "Purity prepares the way for holiness; holiness leads to the presence of God" ("Leviticus and Purity," 47).

individually and corporately to live out their job description. God graciously gave his Torah to help Israel understand how their rather broad job description was to take shape in their daily lives. The covenantal demands of Torah gave "the way of the Lord" the specificity it needed in the particular social context and geographical location in which his people lived. In effect, it was their "employee manual" that would direct them how to fulfill their job description as God's vehicle of life-giving mission and the primary means through which God would continue molding them into that vehicle. Admittedly, I remain perplexed as to how certain ones of these instructions would help Israel fulfill its job description in its ancient social context. But taking into account their internal rationale as well as Israel's particular social context, it is not difficult to see how many might shape Israel's daily life in ways that would equip them to be the witness to, and vehicle of, God's life-giving mission to which God had called them.

Leviticus 19: Some Representative Instructions

To illustrate the missional nature of some of these covenantal demands, we will use Leviticus 19 as a launching pad. Christopher Wright calls this chapter "the finest commentary we have on Exodus 19:6,"[29] in which God says: "You will be a kingdom of priests for me and a holy nation." The chapter begins and ends with God's rationale for the specific pattern of activity in which he calls Israel to engage. The chapter opens with these words: "The Lord said to Moses, Say to the whole community of the Israelites: 'You must be holy, because I, the Lord your God, am holy'" (vv. 1–2). It closes with these words: "I am the Lord your God, who brought you out of the land of Egypt. You must keep all my rules and all my regulations, and do them; I am the Lord" (vv. 36b–37). Keeping the rules and regulations in this chapter stamps Israel's life together with a particular pattern that continues their sanctification, their being set apart from other nations to reflect the holy character of their particular God. This particular pattern exhibits "the way of YHWH" in the concrete daily life of this people in this specific social context.

Even a casual glance at the content of Leviticus 19 shows that holiness is not something limited to the "religious" sphere. This is a job manual for everyday life, giving instructions on things like respecting or taking care of your mother and father (v. 3), the way you farm your land (vv. 9–10,

29. Wright, *Mission of God's People*, 124.

The Call/Election of Abraham and Israel

19, 23–25), the way you treat your workers in a business and conducting your business with honesty (vv. 13, 35–36), how you treat the handicapped, senior citizens, and immigrants (vv. 14, 32, 33–34), not holding grudges (v. 18), what happens when you exploit someone sexually (vv. 20–23), and even your personal appearance (vv. 27–28). Being holy is about being engaged in a pattern of activity as a part of community in the messiness and particularity of that community's social context.

One could probably explain the rationale for *almost* every command in *this chapter* as to the way it functions to set Israel apart from other nations to reflect the holy character of their particular God and his commitment to righteousness, justice, and *shalom* (i.e., well-ordered, flourishing life). But we will only call attention to the way several representative types of covenantal demands function in this regard.

First, it should be self-evident by this point in the biblical story that for Israel to fulfill its job description, it would have to maintain exclusive loyalty to Yahweh. The first two of the Ten Commandments made this perfectly clear (Exod 20:3–4) and Lev 19:4 insists again that Israel is not to "turn to idols or make gods of cast metal." Obeying such a command would make Israel stick out like a sore thumb in the ancient world. Giving exclusive loyalty to one god in a world where worshipping a plurality of gods was the best insurance for your fortunes would have been striking. Perhaps even more striking, however, was the fact that Israel was absolutely forbidden to make any image of their god when everyone else in the ancient world could point to something very concrete to show what their god was like.[30] This was because God had already created God's own image in the world (i.e., living, breathing human beings), so all that Israel could point to as a concrete image of their god was . . . well . . . itself, its own life as a people!

Second, it is no wonder, then, that God gave other particular commands that would emphasize their distinctiveness among the nations. Commands like keeping Sabbaths (v. 3b), which makes one look odd, or

---

30. Hence, it is not surprising that even before the covenant could be fully enacted, the people made a golden calf, presumably as a representation of the god they believed had delivered them from Egypt (Exodus 32). While the ancients did indeed think that the image partook of the divine power/essence of their god, they were not so naïve as to think the image was the "real thing" so to speak—the ridicule of Israel's prophets and NT writers notwithstanding (on which see, Marcus, "Idolatry in the New Testament," 153; McBride, "Essence of Orthodoxy," 145).

even lazy when there are no weekends for anyone else.[31] Commands like not eating anything with its blood in it (v. 25) or, to bring in Leviticus 11 for a moment, commands to avoid particular foods that are sources of impurity (Lev 11, esp. vv. 44–45). As we briefly noted earlier, purity and holiness are not the same thing; the former prepares the way for the latter. Hence, keeping these sorts of commands distinguishes Israel from the surrounding nations and reflects the fact that the character of their God is as distinct from the character of other gods as is their diet distinct from what others eat.[32] Note the logic of a portion of Lev 20:24b–26:

> [24b] I am the Lord your God, *who has separated you* from all other peoples. [25] *So you must separate* between clean and unclean animals.... [26] You must be holy to me, because I the Lord am holy, and I have separated you from all other peoples to be my own.[33]

Third, some commands in Leviticus 19 and elsewhere (e.g., Exod 22:25–27) instruct Israel to mirror Yahweh's character, enacting Yahweh's justice by acting toward others inside and outside their community the way that God had already acted toward Israel.[34] Note especially 19:34:

> Any immigrant who lives with you must be treated as if they were one of your citizens. *You must love them as yourself, because you were immigrants in the land of Egypt*; I am the Lord your God.

The point here is that Israel was to treat immigrants in their own land differently than Egypt had treated them. They were not to mimic the ways of life considered "normal" in the idolatrous imperial culture from which God had delivered them. Rather, their actions were to reflect the graceful way the true God had treated them—even in something as messy as an

---

31. I will have more to say on keeping Sabbaths below.

32. The underlying rationale for the division of animals into clean and unclean remains debated, but the most common interpretation of the primary function of laws forbidding the eating of unclean animals is that they promote the idea of Israel as a holy, priestly nation and distinguish it from the surrounding nations (Ginsburskaya, "Purity and Impurity in the Hebrew Bible," 7–8).

33. It is common in studies that focus on dividing the Pentateuch into documentary sources to distinguish Lev 1–16 (P) from Lev 17–26 (H) by arguing that in the latter holiness has an ethical aspect whereas it does not in the former. That may or may not be true with regard to these putative sources when they are viewed as isolated documents. But when one views Leviticus as a whole and as part of the larger scriptural canon, examples like this one from Lev 20 show that in its final form, at least some of the material in 1–16 is already being given a particular rationale by the material in 17–26.

34. Cf. Middleton, *New Heaven*, 88.

immigration situation. It was simply a part of their job description of being a holy nation.

Obedience to "Ritual" Commands in Leviticus 19 (and other places)

Given Israel's social context, it is not difficult to see how the sorts of commands we have just been discussing would help Israel fulfill its job description of being the distinctive witness to, and vehicle of, God's life-giving mission. But how might some of the covenantal demands that are sometimes (unhelpfully) classified as "ritualistic" and juxtaposed over against "moral" demands shape Israel's life to reflect God's desire for creation to flourish with well-ordered life?

Sabbath, Sabbath Years, and the Year of Jubilee

We have seen that keeping Sabbaths underscores Israel's distinctiveness. But Israel's sanctifying action of ritually marking time in this way has clear *moral* consequences. As we have seen, God himself had originally "blessed" the seventh day and sanctified, or made it *holy* in order to provide his creatures the sustaining rest they need *for the ultimate purpose of producing flourishing well-ordered life* in the good creation (Gen 2:3; cf. Exod 20:11). God makes it clear in Exod 20:8–11 that in response to this graceful act, Israel is to imitate this action and "sanctify" the Sabbath as well:

> [8] Remember the Sabbath day and treat it as holy. [9] Six days you may work and do all your tasks, [10] but the seventh day is a Sabbath to the Lord your God. Do not do any work on it—not you, your sons or daughters, your male or female servants, your animals, or the immigrant who is living with you. [11] Because the Lord made the heavens and the earth, the sea, and everything that is in them in six days, but rested on the seventh day. That is why the Lord blessed the Sabbath day and made it holy.

In the surrounding nations all but the elite worked almost constantly in survival mode to the point of exhaustion. So Israel's keeping Sabbath not only made them quite conspicuous, it provided revitalizing, life-giving rest for every creature within its borders contributing to the well-being of all. Hence, in keeping or sanctifying Sabbath, Israel—whether aware of it or

Section 1—Old Testament Soundings

not—was bearing public witness to the character of their God as desiring blessing and flourishing life for all creation.

Every seventh year was to be set aside and observed as a Sabbath year in Israel. In addition, a special Sabbath year following the seventh Sabbath year (year forty-nine) in a series of seven sets of Sabbath years (i.e., the Jubilee year) was also to be set aside as holy.[35] Hence, not only every seventh year, but every fiftieth year, was to be set aside and observed as holy to the Lord. The practices involved in setting aside, or sanctifying, Sabbath years and/or the Jubilee year included[36] (1) allowing the land to lie fallow (Lev 25:1–7), enabling it to produce more abundantly in other years with life sustaining harvests, (2) allowing the poor to share in the produce of fields and vineyards with what is left going to the wild animals, (3) freeing all Israelites who had been forced by their poverty to sell themselves into slavery just to survive, and (4) return of all landed property to its original ancestral owner (in the Jubilee year).

We have no evidence that Israel ever actually practiced a Sabbath/Jubilee year in any full sense.[37] Perhaps this is not that surprising since—if we can borrow an analogy from a modern capitalist economy—doing so would have been a little like turning a Monopoly board over when a couple of people were winning big, giving each player an equal share of property deeds, and making everyone start again at "Go." Such a radical reordering of society would have kept the worst effects of economic misfortune and injustice from continuing into perpetuity in Israelite society. It would have distinguished Israel from the nations and simultaneously displayed the character of their God as committed to just socioeconomic practices that allow life to flourish for all, not just the few who happen to be winning the economic game. Israel's ritual marking of time in this way would embody Yahweh's own holiness by displaying "the way of the LORD," his righteousness/justice (Gen 18:19; Isa 5:16) to the nations.[38] The marking of time was intended to be one of the means by which God continued Israel's sanctification.

---

35. On the details of what follows in this paragraph, see Middleton, *New Heaven*, 254–58.

36. These practices are pieced together from Lev 25; Deut 15; Exod 21:1–11; 23:10–11.

37. There does appear to be a partial attempt to implement a Jubilee year of release for slaves in Jer 34:8–17, but only for a very short time after which their slave owners re-enslave them.

38. Cf. the similar comments of Middleton, *New Heaven*, 257.

Purity Laws

But what about all those commands that God gives to cordon off what is holy from what is impure? What about those instructions God gives for removing ritual impurities associated with common things like skin diseases, giving birth, having sex, or coming into contact with dead animals, human corpses, or blood? Before attempting an answer, we need to know a little more about the nature of impurity in the OT.

Every culture, including our own, has purity codes, whether or not they are explicitly acknowledged.[39] These codes are fundamentally connected with what is perceived to be *the proper ordering of the world* and govern the way we, often subconsciously, carry out our daily lives. We avoid some things because they seem to contaminate us with something out of bounds, something impure. Often we have a microbial explanation for our purity codes. For example, we will not wash our hands in the toilet before we eat—even though there is a bar of soap close by and plenty of water to do so—because of harmful bacteria. But it is not immediately obvious why many of us would find it difficult to spit into a new Dixie cup every couple of minutes and then drink it after a few minutes of spitting. The cup is clean and the spit just now came from our own mouths, so trying to give a microbial rationale will not work. It is just, well . . . nasty, and out of our world's proper bounds of order.[40]

Some of Israel's purity laws were probably a little like this too. Their rationale may not have been immediately obvious to them and they certainly are not to us. But Israel perceived that the world was ordered in a particular way. The cosmos had a fundamental order to it that was instituted by their particular God who had created it. But where we can discern the probable underlying rationale for this order, it is not a medical or microbial rationale. The whole issue is much more complex than we can do justice

---

39. For an accessible treatment with more extended reflections along these lines and along the lines of what follows in this section, see deSilva, *Honor, Patronage, Kinship, & Purity*, 241–49. His indebtedness to Mary Douglas and, to a lesser extent, Jacob Milgrom is obvious. I will also be drawing to some extent on his section regarding the purity maps of Torah and early Judaism and their meaning (256–74).

40. Without initially giving them an explanation for it, I have actually tried this experiment in some of my classes to try to help students understand how unstated purity codes are present in their own lives. I have had only one student who would follow through with actually drinking the contents of the cup (and I have no explanation for him!). I got the idea from Richard Beck, *Unclean*, 1. He, in turn, became acquainted with it from Paul Rozin's research.

Section 1—Old Testament Soundings

to here,[41] but at the risk of oversimplification, we could say that a good number of Israel's purity laws rely on a *theological* rationale, i.e., avoiding contact with anything that somehow displays characteristics that are out of line with the way God's own character was understood. After all, he had made the cosmos and given it its order in the first place.

As we saw earlier, especially after the first human pair unleashed the forces of chaos, death, and decay into the world, if God's holy presence is going to be experienced as beneficial, it must be adequately safeguarded. It must be cordoned off and protected from coming into casual contact with impurity, including impure human beings inclined toward the death-dealing forces that threaten to undo God's well-ordered creation and plunge it into chaos. In this respect, holiness is a little like electricity, a force generating all sorts of good things like light and heat, as long as it is properly cordoned off in a wiring system that prevents casual direct contact with it. But if you stroll up and stick a butter knife into the electrical socket, ignoring the way the system is wired or ordered, watch out!

I will focus on a couple of areas in particular to illustrate how the patterns discernible in some of the purity laws would symbolize Israel's commitment to avoiding that which it understood to be out of bounds with regard to God's ordering of the cosmos as well as his ultimate desire for the creation's flourishing with life. We begin with the avoidance of what is conceived to be incomplete, mixed, or blemished. God's character is assumed to be whole, complete, or perfect, and his desire is for well-ordered life in creation, not for disorder and chaos. Hence, Israel's public life was to reflect this assumption by, as much as possible, avoiding contact with that which seemed to reflect disorder or blemish. For example, Israel was not to crossbreed their livestock, mix two kinds of seeds together when they planted, or wear clothes made from mixed materials (Lev 19:19). Given their assumptions about God's nature and their social location within a very particular agrarian culture, mixing things together like this seemed to play fast and loose with the boundaries of creation's order. These sorts of things, then, symbolized disorder rather than the well-ordered life God intended for his creation. The same principle was at work with regard to the prohibition of blemished or deformed persons from entering the sanctuary in ancient

---

41. For an accessible discussion of some of the complexities regarding the rationale behind purity laws in the Hebrew Bible, see Ginsburskaya, "Purity and Impurity," esp. 19–24. Her general, cautiously stated rationale for understanding what makes something impure is similar (but not identical) to the way we describe things here. "Deviation of human nature from God's nature," she says, "is captured in terms of impurity" (19).

The Call/Election of Abraham and Israel

Israel, the locale of God's most focused holy presence (Lev 21:16–24).[42] On this logic, such people were walking displays of imperfection and lack of wholeness—of creation disordered—and would contaminate the holy presence of a whole and perfect God.

A second area of focus has to do with God's character, his holiness, being explicitly connected with blessing and life. Because "holiness at its source is life itself—the antonym of death,"[43] Israel's public life together was to reflect its commitment to life and avoidance of death by avoiding things that symbolized death or the loss of life. This is most evident in laws governing contracting impurity from contact with: (1) corpses, for obvious reasons; (2) those with skin/scale disease, usually called lepers, because with their skin "falling off" they were essentially seen as "walking corpses" (e.g., Num 12:12);[44] (3) blood or sexual fluids that, *as a part of the birth-death cycle,*[45] sustain or create life but when crossing the body's boundaries and flowing out symbolize the loss of life/death. Mary Douglas sums up the connection between death and impurity as well as the connection between death and idolatry this way: "The nature of the living God is in opposition to dead bodies. Total incompatibility holds between God's presence and bodily corruption. God is living, life is his. Other gods belong to death and the contagion of decay."[46]

Both impurity and holiness were understood as dynamic forces able to transfer their state from one person or thing to another person or thing by contact.[47] Contracting some form of ritual impurity was almost unavoidable in daily life even for priests when they were not actively carrying out

---

42. The Leviticus text only explicitly refers to members of Aaron's family (i.e., blemished/deformed priests) since they were the only ones who could enter the sanctuary and make sacrifices.

43. Harrington, *Holiness*, 179. Milgrom has summarized his exhaustive work along these lines in "Holy, Holiness, OT."

44. Milgrom, "Holy, Holiness, OT," 855–56.

45. The italicized qualification is an attempt to clarify why, for example, contact with menstrual blood is contaminating whereas blood from a wound or a bloody nose is not (see Ginsburskaya, "Purity and Impurity," 20).

46. Douglas, *In the Wilderness*, 24 (quoted from Harrington, *Holiness*, 179.)

47. This conceptuality of holiness and impurity representing opposed dynamic forces (whereas the related concepts of the pure and common represent static states) comes from Milgrom (see "Holy, Holiness, OT," 855–56). While it has been challenged by various scholars (e.g., see Ginsburskaya, "Purity and Impurity," 22n61; Trevaskis, *Holiness*, 68–69), it remains the most common way of understanding the way holiness and impurity are related.

their priestly duties. But it could usually easily be removed through various God-given means like cleansing (Exod 19:10–11), sacrificing (Exod 13:15; Lev 16:16–19), or anointing (Exod 30:26–30) so that the affected person or thing could be made pure or clean again. It was dangerous, though, to allow a person or thing that was impure to come into direct contact, even accidentally, with people, items, or places set apart within Israel itself for God's special use because they shared in God's holiness. Perhaps most dangerous of all was bringing impurity into direct contact with God's holiness in "concentrated form" in the sanctuary. Such actions were tantamount to ignoring the way God had structured the cosmos, contaminating the source of life itself with what might indeed be associated with death. As long as Israel was careful to cordon off God's holy presence from that which threatened to contaminate it, they would experience his holiness as life-giving and beneficial. But if they failed to do so, they would experience that same holiness as threatening.

Hence, many of Israel's purity laws appear to be based on a theological rationale. The pattern of activity they require Israel to embody symbolizes their commitment to God's intention for flourishing, well-ordered life in creation and their rejection of what is associated with death and disorder. Thus, Israel's very engagement in these purity practices was a sanctifying activity, one of the means by which God continued Israel's sanctification—his continued shaping of them into his instrument for carrying out his mission of bringing creation to its intended destiny of flourishing, well-ordered life that would scintillate with the glory of its creator.

3

Except When They Don't

Holiness, Prophets, and Exile

OUR OT SOUNDINGS TO this point have been almost entirely confined to the Pentateuch. In general, the prophets tend to shift the emphasis away from purity laws per se when dealing with the holiness (or lack thereof) of God's people. Although they do use the language of "pure" and "impure" occasionally, the prophets tend to give such language a different nuance than we saw in Leviticus.[1] Still, however, we will see a *similar pattern* regarding holiness and the *missio Dei* in the prophets as we have seen so far in the Pentateuch. While we will briefly reference a variety of prophetic texts in this section, we will focus on Isaiah and Ezekiel.

Isaiah and Holiness

The holiness of the Lord is a major focus of the book of Isaiah. Yet it opens with an indictment of God's people whose life together was expected to reflect that Lord's character, "the Holy One of Israel" (1:4).[2] Rather than fulfilling that expectation, their life together has begun to look like the way of Sodom and Gomorrah rather than the way of the Lord, so much so that the prophet says to the people of Judah: "Hear the Lord's word, you leaders of Sodom! Listen to our God's teaching, people of Gomorrah" (1:10). Although they seem to have paid close attention to getting their public worship just right (cf. Amos 5:20–23), they have lots of blood[3] on their

---

1. On which, see Shepherd, "Purity in the Prophets."
2. This is one of Isaiah's favorite ways of describing God (over twenty-five times).
3. The Hebrew word for blood is in the plural emphasizing the severity of the violence

Section 1—Old Testament Soundings

hands (1:11–15). Although Abraham's family has been taught "the way of the Lord" (Gen 18:19) quite extensively heretofore in the story, when the eighth century prophets (Isaiah, Amos, Hosea, Micah) come onto the scene, the family was failing to maintain the "justice" (*mishpat/krisis*) and do the "righteousness" (*tsedhaqah/dikaiosynē*) that characterizes that pattern of life. God's memorable plea to his wayward people in Amos 5:24 underscores this: "Let justice (*mishpat/krisis*) roll down like waters, and righteousness (*tsedhaqah/dikaiosynē*) like an ever-flowing stream." In Isaiah's early chapters, God's people had not only failed to attune their ears to the cries of injustice around them, their life together—like that of the cities of Sodom and Gomorrah—had itself become a channel for oppression and injustice. In fact, in some ways they have become even worse than these two infamous cities in that it is the weak in *their own* community who are experiencing this oppression and injustice at the hands of others in their community. Because of the greed and dishonesty of their leaders, widows and orphans—the most vulnerable among *their own* people—are being treated unjustly (1:17, 23). It is as though the powerful in their community are acting like those in Sodom and Gomorrah and like the imperial powerbrokers in Egypt did toward Jacob's family causing them to cry out in desperation.

Isaiah's well known parable of the vineyard drives this point home, especially the way the prophet concludes it in 5:7 with a play on words that by now has become familiar to us as characterizing "the way of the Lord":

> The vineyard of the Lord of heavenly forces is the house of Israel,
>
> and the people of Judah are the plantings in which God delighted.
>
> God expected justice (*mishpat*), but there was bloodshed (*mispaḥ*);
>
> Righteousness (*tsedhaqah*), but there was a cry of injustice (*tseaqah*)![4]

The cry of injustice (*tseaqah*) that arose from the people being oppressed by Sodom and Gomorrah (Gen 18:21), the same cry of distress that arose in Israel in response to Pharaoh's slaughter of their male babies (Exod 3:9), has now arisen in the very midst of God's chosen people (v. 7). God's expectation

---

and injustice they are perpetuating.

4. I have slightly modified the CEB's translation from "cry of distress" to "cry of injustice" in order to underline the fact that the word in the Hebrew text here in Isa 5:7 is the same word as in Gen 18:21 where the CEB renders it "cries of injustice."

Except When They Don't

that Abraham's family would walk in the "way of the Lord" by doing justice and righteousness has been frustrated. In the first few chapters of Isaiah, the prophet has several oracles indicting the sort of behavior that caused this cry to arise. Combining the language from several of these oracles, such behavior included the powerful greedily accumulating great wealth at the expense of the poor (3:14–15) and protecting the status quo with the typical military machinery of empires (2:7); unjustly taking over their land when the weak/poor could not pay their bills (5:8); allowing "money to talk" in public life and in the courts, thereby assuring that their injustice toward those who were weak would get stamped with the deceptive label of "justice" (1:23; 5:23); fraud and deception (5:18–21); self-indulgence and drunkenness (5:11–12, 22); the powerful and greedy idolatrously hedging their bets to protect their ill-gotten gains by paying homage to other gods besides Yahweh alone (2:8, 20; 1:29).

In this time and place, the prophet is not condemning the violation of Israel's purity laws. Rather, he is condemning behavior that exemplified the opposite of the justice and righteousness to which God had called his people, behavior that exemplified the opposite of the character of the Holy God that they were to embody. But living this way is essentially to live with blood-stained hands (1:15) and so it is not surprising that the prophet applies the language of purity/cleansing when referring to its remedy in 1:16–17:

> [16] Wash! Be clean! Remove your ugly deeds from my sight.
>
> Put an end to such evil; [17] learn to do good. Seek justice (*mishpat*):
>
> help the oppressed; defend the orphan; plead for the widow.

In this case, to be cleansed/purified of their "impurities" would not require a ritual washing, but a concrete turning away from their current pattern of life and instituting a different pattern through which God would continue their sanctification. In a word, their "cleansing" in this situation would require repentance; it would require *seeking/doing justice and righteousness* through which the Lord would continue making their life together holy, a life characterized by life-giving blessing and undivided loyalty to the Lord. To enlarge on what 1:17 makes explicit regarding treatment of the orphan and widow, being "cleansed" would be effected by ceasing the forms of behavior we described above in detail. But *ceasing* such behavior is simply a prerequisite to God's continuation of sanctifying their life together in a way that is analogous to Israel's being ritually pure is a prerequisite to God

Section 1—Old Testament Soundings

making the people holy. Here ceasing this behavior is not an end in itself. It must be accompanied by, and goes hand in hand with, *initiating* alternative practices through which God continues sanctifying their life together. This includes practices such as protecting the poor from the greed of the powerful; taking active measures to make sure that the poor/weak do not lose their land when they cannot pay their bills, thereby locking them in an endless cycle of poverty; taking active measures to stop the use of bribes in public life and in the courts so that justice for the weak is a reality rather than an illusion; dealing honestly in business deals and avoiding self-indulgence and drunkenness (5:11–12, 22); paying homage to Yahweh alone so that the powerful cannot hedge their bets with other gods to protect their ill-gotten gains. Such practices would embody not only singular loyalty to Yahweh but would engender a well-ordered communal life of *shalom* for all, including the weak in the community. It would constitute a context-specific pattern of life that testifies to, and moves toward, God's goal of bringing creation to its intended goal of brimming with fruitful life and *shalom*.

But isn't that asking an awful lot, especially from the powerful who are benefiting from the way things are? Can the people who call on Yahweh's name just fix things themselves? Or is there more to it? There is little doubt that for this situation to change, for his people to be "cleansed" and become holy, God has to do something. And that something will require painful judgment, but it will be directed toward restoring Zion, making Jerusalem again "the city of righteousness" (1:26). God promises that "Zion will be redeemed *by justice*, and those who change their lives [will be redeemed] *by righteousness*" (1:27). In 5:16 (a verse that appears shortly after the ending of the parable of the vineyard we quoted above) there is similar language when the prophet says: "But the Lord of hosts is exalted *by justice (mishpat/krisis)*, and the Holy God shows himself holy *by righteousness (tsedhaqah/dikaiosynē)*" (NRSV).[5]

Regarding 1:27, we might ask, by *whose* justice will Zion be redeemed and by *whose* righteousness will those who change their lives be redeemed? Is it God's justice or the justice of God's people? And about 5:16 we might ask, by *whose* justice is the Lord exalted and by *whose* righteousness does the Holy God show himself as holy? Again, is it God's justice or the justice of God's people? Many interpreters simply assume that it is God's own

---

5. The second part of this verse in the Septuagint is slightly different. It reads: "and the holy God *is glorified* by righteousness (*dikaiosynē*). However, given that "glory" is the visible form of God's holiness (as Isa 6:3 and other passages suggest), any difference in meaning is more apparent than real.

justice and righteousness that are in play here, and that this justice and righteousness refer to divine judgment. But Old Testament scholar Walter Moberly, bringing together a number of clues from the context, makes a compelling case for a different reading. He argues, in effect, that the answer to the question of whether the justice and righteousness in question is to be imagined as God's or God's people is "Yes."[6] In other words, the Lord is indeed exalted when the people of God's vineyard *enact God's own brand of justice* rather than shedding blood and the Holy God displays his own holiness when *his people enact God's own type of righteousness* instead of doing things to the weak that evoke distressed cries of injustice. In Moberly's words, "God's justice and righteousness remain 'his own' and still display Himself when they are seen in human lives that are faithful to him—for it is in nature transformed by grace that the divine is discerned."[7] In this case then, while the prophet clearly understands that divine judgment will surely come,[8] and even that divine judgment has a redemptive role to play for God's people, divine judgment itself need not be understood as the referent of justice and righteousness in passages in the early part of Isaiah like Isa 1:27 and 5:16. Zion will indeed be redeemed when God works his justice *through his people's enactment of it* and the lives of those in a Sodom-like Zion will be redeemed when their lives are changed *and they embody God's own righteousness*. It is only then—when God acts as the catalyst of his people's acting—that Jerusalem will be called the "city of righteousness" (1:26).

But judgment does come, and as we move through the first thirty-nine chapters of Isaiah, Jerusalem does not become this "city of righteousness." Many among God's people continue to have blood-stained hands and "unclean lips" (6:5), falling well short of embodying the character of their thrice holy God whose glory fills the whole earth (6:3). The result is indeed the judgment that God says is coming when he calls Isaiah (6:9–13). Thus, we encounter a different setting for the second part of Isaiah (chapters 40–55), where God's people are assumed to have experienced God's judgment in the form of being in the bondage of exile.[9] In this second part, the language

6. This is an oversimplified expression of Moberly's reading of the verse in "Whose Justice? Which Righteousness?" 55–68. See esp. the summary comments on page 63.

7. Moberly, *Old Testament Theology*, 171n59.

8. And come it will as passages like 6:9–13 assert and as the setting of chapters 40–55 clearly assume that it has.

9. Historically, it seems likely that the prophet largely responsible for the content of Isaiah 1–39 was not responsible for 40–55 ("Deutero Isaiah") and that yet another

of righteousness (*tsedhaqah/dikaiosynē*) is used with what most recognize is a different nuance than the way it was used in the first part of the book. In this second part, at important points the word is used in parallel to the language of salvation that God promises to bring to his now judged and exiled people. The NRSV recognizes that, in these places and others in Isaiah 40–55 (e.g., 51:5–6), the word *tsedhaqah* is a way of speaking about God's covenantal faithfulness manifest in his Exodus-like acts of saving/delivering; it therefore translates the word as "deliverance." For example, in 46:12–13 in the NRSV the prophet says:

> [12] Listen to me, you stubborn of heart, you who are far from deliverance (*tsedhaqah/dikaiosynē*):
>
> [13] I bring near my deliverance (*tsedhaqah/dikaiosynē*), it is not far off, and my salvation will not tarry;
>
> I will put salvation in Zion, for Israel my glory.

It is not surprising that in the verse that introduces the third section of Isaiah (chapters 56–66), we see a similar usage of this language, particularly in the last line:

> Thus says the Lord:
>
> Maintain justice (*mishpat/krisis*), and do what is right (*tsedhaqah/dikaiosynē*),
>
> for soon my salvation will come,
>
> and my deliverance (*tsedhaqah*) be revealed (Isa 56:1, NRSV).

Whatever the exact historical situation in this passage, as in the second part of Isaiah, the prophetic speaker still awaits deliverance and a new age that he assumes is near.[10] Here the Lord's saving/delivering covenantal faithfulness (*tsedhaqah*) is associated with the Lord's command to his people to maintain justice and do their own *tsedhaqah/dikaiosynē*. Because God's own saving/delivering action that manifests his covenant faithfulness is on its way, God's people are to maintain the way of the Lord by doing justice and righteousness—by engaging in corresponding actions that manifest their own faithfulness to God's covenant. In the immediate

---

prophet was largely responsible for 56–66 ("Trito Isaiah"). Be that as it may, given our decision to engage in a theological reading of Scripture, our focus here is on the final canonical form of the book of Isaiah.

10. Cf. Childs, *Isaiah*, 456.

context of this passage, Isa 56:2–8 describes the righteousness/covenant faithfulness of God's people and foreigners whom God will gather in general terms of a life lived under Torah, albeit with an emphasis on keeping Sabbath. While the focus is somewhat different, this is not at odds with the exemplary specific practices the prophet calls God's people to enact in the first part of Isaiah that we described earlier. "Keeping the way of the Lord by doing justice and righteousness" (Gen 18:19) was what this particular people of God had always been called to do.

As a reminder, the changes the prophet calls the people to make in their communal life in the first part of Isaiah would not only embody singular loyalty to Yahweh but would also engender a well-ordered communal life of *shalom* for all, especially for the weak in the community. Together with the observance of Sabbath emphasized in 56:2–8,[11] this specific pattern of life would testify to, and move toward, God's goal of bringing creation to its goal of brimming with the blessing of fruitful life and *shalom*. Engaging in this pattern of life where justice and regular revitalizing rest are given to the weak and helpless would be a clear contrast to the imperial pattern of life in Sodom and Gomorrah, Egypt, and Babylon. The latter was a pattern of life under which God's people had suffered in Egypt, had mimicked in their own communal life (as we saw above), now were suffering under again in Babylon, and from which the prophet is expecting God to deliver his people. It is precisely *because* God's act of deliverance—his righteousness/*tsedhaqah*—is directed toward rescuing them from that oppressive, death-dealing form of life that their corresponding righteousness/ *tsedhaqah* takes the form of a pattern of life that contrasts with the injustice and oppression from which they are delivered. When this happens—when God acts as the catalyst of his people's acting—Jerusalem will indeed be called the "city of righteousness" (1:26) and nations will be drawn to the glory of the Lord which his people's life together reflects (60:1–3).

Noting this correspondence between God's own *tsedhaqah* and that of his people takes us back to the prophet's assertion in 5:16: "But the Lord of hosts is exalted *by justice (mishpat/krisis)*, and the Holy God shows himself holy *by righteousness (tsedhaqah)*" (NRSV). While the whole earth might indeed be "full of his glory (i.e., his visible holiness)," *the primary way that this sovereign Lord displays himself to be holy is through his own redemptive*

---

11. Recall how keeping Sabbath not only displayed a conspicuous loyalty to Israel's God but also, because of the revitalizing rest it provided, bore public witness to the character of this God as desiring blessing and flourishing life for all creation.

pattern of activity that his people then reflect in the way they pattern their public life. This language recalls the logic of the "way of the Lord" we initially encountered in Genesis 18. Here again, both divine and human holiness is associated with a particular pattern of activity that furthers the life-giving, missional purposes of Israel's holy God.

Such a way of life could have had the effect of confronting the nations' idolatrous way of life with a clear alternative society flourishing with justice and life. With no typical images of its god allowed, this was a way of life that would have provided the only visible image of Israel's God to the nations around them. If Israel's particular version of the divine was going to be discerned by the nations, its life together would have to reflect Yahweh's own character. For better or worse, Yahweh's name was inextricably and publicly linked to the way that Israel patterned its life together. Perhaps better than anyone else, Ezekiel makes this clear, and his book will be the last place in the OT from which we take a representative sounding.

Ezekiel and Holiness

As the first part of Isaiah affirms, Israel often failed to confront the surrounding nations' idolatrous way of life and, instead, was absorbed into it (sounds a lot like the Church!). The result, as the second part of Isaiah makes clear, was exile. The prophet Ezekiel says that the reason for Israel's exile was that they had profaned God's holy name (36:20–21), "had dragged it through the mud," so to speak, before the watching nations. As is the case with the book of Isaiah, Ezekiel's prophecy does not emphasize Israel's violations of ritual impurity per se. However, Ezekiel often uses language originally from the sphere of ritual purity/impurity (e.g., impurities, uncleanness, make unclean/defile, profane) in reference to various covenant violations. For example:

> [16] The word of the Lord came to me: [17] Mortal, when the house of Israel lived on their own soil, they *defiled* it with their ways and their deeds; their conduct in my sight was like the *uncleanness* of a woman in her menstrual period. [18] So I poured out my wrath upon them for the blood that they had shed upon the land, and for the idols with which they had *defiled* it. [19] I scattered them among the nations, and they were dispersed through the countries; in accordance with their conduct and their deeds I judged them. [20] But when they came to the nations, wherever they came, they *profaned* my holy name, in that it was said of them, "These are the people

of the Lord, and yet they had to go out of his land." ²¹ But I had concern for my holy name, which the house of Israel had *profaned* among the nations to which they came (Ezek 36:16–21, NRSV).

Verse 21 reflects what is arguably the primary question addressed in Ezek 33–39: what will God do to vindicate his holy name/reputation after it has been profaned by his people's sinful actions in the sight of the nations? In Ezek 33:10–11, God first has Ezekiel remind Israel of their own self-diagnosis for their dire situation and then has the prophet voice God's initial response to that self-diagnosis:

> ¹⁰ You, human one, say to the house of Israel: This is what all of you are saying: "How our transgressions and our sins weigh on us! We waste away because of them. How can we live?" ¹¹ Say to them, This is what the Lord God says: As surely as I live, do I take pleasure in the death of the wicked? If the wicked turn from their ways, they will live. Turn, completely turn from your wicked ways! Why should you die, house of Israel?

This self-diagnosed covenantal infidelity is precisely the reason for—even the substance of—God's holy name having been profaned among the nations. It was indeed their sins (39:23; cf. 37:23), lawless deeds (36:33; 37:23; 39:24), injustice (39:26), unclean acts (36:17, 25; 39:24), and idolatry (36:18, 25) that constituted their "dealing treacherously" with God (39:23) so that his holy name was desecrated among the nations. In addition, this self-diagnosis essentially gives the reason why the House of Israel is "chanting their own death dirge"¹² in the lifeless valley of death in chapter 37: "Our bones are dried up, and our hope has perished. We are completely finished." (37:11)." Their question here in 33:10, "How can we live?" anticipates the Lord's question to Ezekiel in 37:3 as he stands gazing out at the valley: "Can these bones live again?"

In the hopeless situation brought on by their covenantal infidelity, they describe their situation metaphorically as *existing in a state of death*. But not only do they describe themselves with language borrowing from the realm of (the extreme in) ritual impurity, the prophet depicts unfaithful Israel in the most "unclean" way possible, as a valley of dry bones with no life at all. They need a divine act that is transformative, an act that unquestionably includes a covenantal pardon, but that also enables a (cleansing) transformation of their whole pattern of life whereby they turn away from

---

12. Jenson's language (*Ezekiel*, 282).

Section 1—Old Testament Soundings

these lawless deeds, sin, and acts of injustice to a pattern of "doing justice (*mishpat/krima*) and righteousness/covenant faithfulness (*tsedhaqah/dikaiosynē*)."[13] Such a transformative turn is indeed a turn from living in a state of death to life itself, a (re)turn to the *living* God (cf. 33:10) and faithful covenant relationship with him. Whether or not 33:11–20 assumes that individual Israelites might somehow change their pattern of life themselves, the rest of this larger section in Ezekiel makes it clear that the God who is himself the source of life will have to act on behalf of the House of Israel if they as a people are to be transformed into a faithful covenant partner. Such a transformative divine act is precisely what Israel is depicted as receiving in chapters 36–37.

That transformative act involves God's Spirit and is depicted as a lifegiving "heart transplant" in chapter 36 and as a resurrection to new life (a "new creation") in chapter 37. The "heart transplant" passage is a familiar one:

> [24] I will take you from the nations, I will gather you from all the countries, and I will bring you to your own fertile land. [25] I will sprinkle clean water on you, and you will be cleansed of all your pollution. I will cleanse you of all your idols. [26] I will give you a new heart and put a new spirit in you. I will remove your stony heart from your body and replace it with a living one, [27] and I will give you my spirit so that you may walk according to my regulations and carefully observe my case laws. [28] Then you will live in the land that I gave to your ancestors, you will be my people, and I will be your God. [29] I will save you from all your uncleanness, and I will summon the grain and make it grow abundantly so that you won't endure famine. (Ezek 36:24–29)

Given that the sprinkling of purifying water was the means by which one could be cleansed from corpse pollution (Num 19:13–20), the metaphor of sprinkling clean water upon Israel as the means by which Yahweh cleanses them from their idols and polluting acts (36:25) underscores the graphic imagery of God's people living in a state of death brought on by their covenantal infidelity. This cleansing divine action has as its very content the giving of the Spirit that follows in vv. 26–27. That is, Yahweh's "cleansing" those living in a state of death brought on by their covenantal infidelity is accomplished by the giving of his own life-giving personal presence by

---

13. This way of putting the matter is a summary of the content of 33:11–20 where the familiar language of "doing justice (*mishpat/krima*) and righteousness/covenant faithfulness (*tsedhaqah/dikaiosynē*)" is used three times (vv. 14, 16, 19).

which their death-bound pattern of life—their malformed stony heart—is transformed into a life of fidelity to their covenant partner. This gracious giving of his own Spirit to Israel is a transformative act of cleansing deliverance that conforms God's people's minds, bodies, and communal life to his own life-giving patterns; it is the means by which Yahweh restores the covenantal relationship (v. 28) and thus *saves* [Israel] from all [their] *unclean* acts (v. 29).

Since the state from which Israel must be "saved" is that of an unclean state of death, Ezekiel goes on in 37:1–14 to describe this transformative cleansing act as God's life-giving Spirit raising them from death to life. Because Israel's actions had *desecrated* God's holy name among the nations, they are appropriately depicted in an *impure* state, as human bones in a valley of death, in a grave where holiness/life is most absent because it is devoid of God's personal life-giving presence. In what is essentially a life-giving embrace, God's cleansing, pardoning action comes with the rush of the Spirit/Breath of life into the valley of death. With echoes of Gen 2:7 (where God breathes his breath/Spirit into the lifeless human to bring him to life), Ezekiel speaks about this Spirit entering into the whole community of exiled Israel as well as into each set of bones, bringing them all to life together. No fewer than four times does Ezekiel emphasize that the Spirit enters *into* these dry bones (37:5, 6, 10, 14). Two of these times he uses the language of God's "giving" his Spirit "into you all" (37:6, 14). This is God's own personal presence that brings his people up out of their graves (37:12–13) and decisively answers their earlier question from 33:10: "How can we live?" They will only live by means of God's own presence/Spirit dwelling with, among, and indeed, in them (i.e., in their newly received transplanted hearts). As guilty covenant violators lying dead in exilic bondage, they will only live when Yahweh's personal presence delivers them by transforming them into faithful covenant partners whose restored covenantal life together is *the means by which* God sanctifies and vindicates his holy name.

The very name of Yahweh, the Holy One of Israel, was simply too inextricably and publicly linked to the way that Israel patterned its life together for God's action on behalf of either Israel or his own name not to impact the other. Hence, immediately prior to the promise of the "heart transplant," Yahweh says:

> [22] Therefore say to the house of Israel, Thus says the Lord God: It is not for your sake, O house of Israel, that I am about to act, but for the sake of my holy name, which you have profaned among

> the nations to which you came. ²³ I will sanctify my great name, which has been profaned among the nations, and which you have profaned among them; and the nations shall know that I am the Lord, says the Lord God, *when through you I display my holiness before their eyes* (Ezek 36:22–23, NRSV).

God's mission may be delayed, but it has not changed in its overall goal or in the means by which God will accomplish it. Its goal is still that the nations will come to know Israel's particular God, Yahweh, that blessing will come to them as a result, and the means by which this is to happen is that of God's displaying his holiness before the eyes of the nations through Israel's life together (v. 23). But for an Israel who is as good as dead and singing their own funeral dirge in exile to be able to pattern their life after "the way of the Lord" by doing justice and righteousness, God will have to bring about a life-giving act of deliverance that includes a "heart transplant," a resurrection to new life. One might say that Israel will have to be made into a new creation by the life-giving breath/Spirit in order to reflect the image of the Holy God to the nations who do not currently acknowledge him. In essence, the Holy God would have to continue his sanctifying activity by sending the life-giving Spirit of holiness into the death valley of their existence, raising them to new life, and conforming their minds/imaginations, bodies, and communal life to his own life-giving patterns.

Section 1 Summary

We now need to draw this excursion into the OT to a close. We have seen that God's dream was to bring his good creation to its goal through humanity but that the first pair failed in their role of imaging God to the rest of creation. So God chose Abraham and his family as a means of rectifying the situation. Following the "way of the Lord" would have this family reflecting God's character/pattern of activity in a chaotic and disordered world, thereby becoming the channel of God's life-giving blessing to the rest of the nations. We saw this same theological pattern when God sanctified this family, setting Israel apart by electing, delivering, and constituting them as a people. Choosing to enter covenant with this God came with a job description: to mediate his blessings to the nations by becoming a "showcase" or model for the way God had created humans to live, thereby bringing healing and *shalom* to his creation. His initial sanctifying action required and made it possible for them to engage in practices guided by their "employee manual" (i.e., Torah) through which the Holy God would continue their sanctification, conforming their minds/imaginations, bodies, and communal life to his own life-giving patterns.

Hence, God's initial and continuing sanctification of Israel is ultimately aimed at restoring Israel as a people into the *imago Dei*, the image of God. This restoration is constituted by the corporate formation of a distinct and public people whose obedient actions are one means God uses to conform them to his holy life-giving patterns, thereby shaping them into his set-apart instrument for the *missio Dei*. Therefore, God's means of (re)shaping Israel into the *imago Dei*, of making them holy, is inseparable from—indeed, primarily constituted by—their participation in, and witness to, the *missio Dei*, which is God's mission to engender life in all its fullness for Israel, and through Israel, for the nations and creation as a whole. So then, both divine and human holiness in the OT is associated with a particular pattern of activity effecting the life-giving, missional purposes of Israel's holy God.

But as we saw in the last section, the tragic fact is that Israel often failed to confront the surrounding nations' idolatrous way of life and, instead, was absorbed into it. Prophets like Isaiah and Ezekiel were acutely conscious that something had to change and articulated the shape and particulars of that change in ways that did not come to immediate and/or literal fruition when the people of God came home from exile and built a Second Temple for Yahweh. This reflects a basic orientation of prophetic speech in Scripture regarding prophecies of restoration from the exile. In general, there was an excess of promise(s) over the fulfillment that actually took place. For example, although there was indeed a remnant of God's people who experienced a return from Babylon, which they interpreted as God's act of deliverance manifesting his covenantal faithfulness, their post-exilic life fell far short of the vivid "new creation" imagery of Isa 65:17–25. And while the return of Israel from Babylonian exile giving them a new start in their own land may have initially restored honor to their particular God's name, their new life together fell short of the hoped for "heart transplant" way of life described in Ezek 36:24–29 that would reveal Yahweh's holiness to the watching nations. Even more obviously, the quite modest Second Temple simply could not come close to Ezekiel's glorious description of the new temple to be built to house Yahweh's glory when God's people were delivered from exile and living in this God's holy presence in their own land again (chapters 40–48). Rather than being rejected as false, however, these excess promises were taken up into Jewish and Christian patterns of hope for the future in varying situations. In any case, the prophets, Isaiah and Ezekiel in particular, knew that something had to change for Israel to be able to embody Yahweh's own holiness so that they could become the display people God intended them to be. They knew that something had to happen, and something totally unexpected did. Yahweh's own holiness became relocated in a Jew from Nazareth who wound up as a corpse on a Roman cross.

SECTION 2

Relocating Holiness in Jesus

4

Holiness and the Second Temple Context

Introduction

IN THE PRECEDING SECTION we took some soundings from the OT focusing on holiness and the *missio Dei*. We described God's mission as being to engender life in all its fullness for Israel and, through Israel, for the nations and creation as a whole. God's initial sanctification of Israel required and made it possible for them to engage in practices guided by their "employee manual" (i.e., Torah) through which God would continue their sanctification, conforming their minds, bodies, and communal life to his own life-giving patterns. God's ultimate sanctifying aim was to restore Israel as a people into the *imago Dei*. As we noted at the end of the last chapter, this restoration is constituted by the corporate formation of a distinct and public people whose obedient actions are one means God uses to conform them to his holy life-giving patterns, thereby shaping them into his set-apart missional instrument. Thus, God's means of (re)shaping Israel into the *imago Dei*, of making them holy, is inseparable from—and largely constituted by—their participation in, and witness to, the *missio Dei*. Both divine and human holiness in the OT is associated with a particular pattern of activity effecting the life-giving, missional purposes of Israel's holy God.

In this section, we ask what happens when holiness—God's very essence, God's dangerous yet beneficent, presence—is relocated in a Jew from Nazareth. Declaring the risen Jesus as "my Lord and my God" (John 20:28)

Section 2—Relocating Holiness in Jesus

was, as Stephen Barton notes, "a development of momentous proportions."[1] To confess that the one who was the visible *imago Dei*, the image of the unseen Holy God (Col 1:15), hung naked in public shame on a Roman cross, became a corpse and was buried, was problem enough. But the further clarifying claim that "the fullness of *this particular* deity"—all of God with no parts left over—"dwelled bodily in" his crucified and buried flesh (Col 2:9) heightens the scandal and signals a dislocation and relocation of holiness itself. Something has happened to the "electrical system" that channels God's holy presence in life-giving, rather than threatening ways. In Second Temple Judaism the heart of that metaphorical "electrical system" was understood as the Jerusalem Temple, and concerns about Israel's purity and holiness were intensified.

Holiness in Second Temple Judaism

As we saw earlier, the Bible begins with God creating the physical world as his cosmic sanctuary or temple where he could dwell in an unmediated way with his creatures. But after the garden rebellion, if God's holy presence, his holiness, was to be experienced as beneficial and life-giving, it had to be adequately safeguarded, cordoned off and protected from coming into casual contact with impure things and people. Both the moveable tabernacle in the wilderness and Israel's first Temple had symbolism indicating that they represented creation as a whole, creation rightly ordered with God on the throne in the Holy of Holies dwelling with his people in a way that mediated his beneficent presence safely.[2]

Not surprisingly then, in the first century, the primary locus of God's holy presence was widely understood to be the Second Temple in Jerusalem. From its Holy of Holies the dynamic force of holiness was thought to radiate outward through the rest of the Temple and on into Israel's land and to its people. As long as the daily sacrifices were maintained, God's beneficial, salvific, forgiving presence was understood to be safely available to the land and its people. While the giant cherubim throne and the ark of the covenant that were fixtures of the Holy of Holies in Solomon's Temple were absent from this Second Temple, its iconography still reflected the "imperial theology of Yahweh's kingship, his rule over the powers of chaos,

---

1. Barton, *Dislocating and Relocating Holiness*, 197.
2. Beale and Kim, *God Dwells Among Us*, 51–64; Roberts, "Temple, Jerusalem," 501–2.

and his glorification as the source of life, abundance, and world order."[3] By the time of the Second Temple, this assumed connection between the Temple as God's dwelling place and "world order" was widespread. As was the case with some Greco-Roman temples,[4] it was understood as directly connected to the cosmos itself.[5] It was "the point from which creation proceeded," the "meeting place of heaven and earth."[6] It was a microcosm of the cosmos, and one of its functions included maintaining the order of the cosmos as set up by the creator God,[7] the order necessary if God's powerful holy presence was to continue to be experienced as life-giving rather than as threatening, as generating well-ordered life rather than chaos. Some Second Temple Jews could even ask the question: If the Temple is destroyed, will the structures of the cosmos be undone and the world return to chaos?[8]

As in the OT, in the Second Temple period there were dangerous consequences for bringing the holy into contact with impurity since impurity was a dynamic, contagious force and might contaminate God's holy presence. Having to share the land with impure Roman occupiers—who even had military barracks connected to the Temple—heightened concerns about the dangerous effects of impurity. Hence, especially in and around the Temple, diminishing the effects of impurity by enlarging the realm of the pure was of paramount concern and required careful observance of Torah.

However, this concern for purity went well beyond a concern for keeping the Temple itself pure. While observant Jews throughout Israel were not unconcerned about what we might call "inner purity," the archeological evidence suggests that they had heightened concerns about sources of impurity (e.g., unclean foods, corpses, skin diseases, discharges from sexual

3. Roberts, "Temple, Jerusalem," 501–2, 507. The quote comes from 501.

4. In Rome the rounded form of the Pantheon appears to have been built to resemble the heavens (at least in the opinion of Dio Cassius, *Roman History*, 53.27.2) suggesting that it may have been intended to function as an embodiment of the universe. Pausanias describes Apollo's sanctuary at Delphi as the "navel of the world" (10.16.3).

5. Levenson, *Sinai and Zion*, esp. 89–184. On the axiomatic character of a temple-centered cosmic ideology in Second-Temple Judaism, see Fletcher-Louis, "Destruction of the Temple," 156–62 and the extensive literature he cites. See also Beale, *Temple and the Church's Mission*, 29–80.

6. Levenson, *Sinai and Zion*, 118, 123.

7. Ibid., 133, 139, 141.

8. "Or will the universe return to its nature and the world go back to its former silence?" (2 Bar 3:7–8).

Section 2—Relocating Holiness in Jesus

organs, improper sexual relationships) and engaged in practices to limit their effects.[9] Some groups like the Qumran community and the Pharisees intensified purity concerns even further and were what we might call first-century "holiness movements."[10] As a member of the Pharisees, Saul of Tarsus, then, belonged to a "holiness movement."

Earlier we saw that the purpose of avoiding some forms of impurity was to sanctify the people's mind/imagination (i.e., their whole self-understanding) by conforming it to the life-giving patterns of the holy God. Hence, in the political and social situation in which Jews in Israel in the first century found themselves, there is something *profoundly right* about this heightened concern to avoid impurity.[11] After all, God had not changed, nor had the structures of the cosmos. God's cosmic ordering designed to fend off chaos and safely cordon off his holy presence so that it could be experienced as beneficial rather than as threatening remained solidly in place.

With the land politically controlled by impure foreigners who embodied the imperial power of Rome, these heightened concerns for purity tended to fuel Jewish political resistance more so than a desire to fulfill their priestly role of embodying the character of God for the sake of the nations/Gentiles. It was understandably difficult for Jews to imagine being a channel of God's life-giving blessing toward those occupying their land and polluting it to boot. One legitimate aspect of holiness, that of *distinction and separation*, began to dominate the way it was conceived—for example, clear distinctions between more or less holy classes of Jews, separation of Jew from Gentile, (sources of) life from (sources of) death, pure from impure. This led to a purity-based social system whose primary purpose was to maintain boundaries between pure and impure.

---

9. Note, for example, the plethora of stone vessels throughout the land of Israel which were impervious to impurity. This and other evidence indicates that even ordinary Jews handled not just sacred food (Lev 7:19–21) but even their daily ordinary food in accordance with a stringent form of purity (Milgrom, "Holiness, OT," 857). In addition, the presence of ritual baths in the remains of pre-70 Palestinian synagogues suggests that ordinary Jews did not even enter synagogue without attending to their purity status (Brower, *Holiness in the Gospels*, 2).

10. Unlike most Jews, such groups would even be concerned with "secondary pollution," i.e., pollution that results when one comes into contact with something that a person or thing in an unclean state had touched (deSilva, "Clean and Unclean," 145).

11. As Brower puts it: "If the people of Israel were a kingdom of priests and a holy nation, and if the holy God were ever to make his dwelling again in their midst, then it followed that purity must be maintained at a higher level than had heretofore been the case" (*Holiness in the Gospels*, 2).

Holiness and the Second Temple Context

Within this larger social system, there could indeed be competing "purity maps," different ways of classifying persons, places, times, and things as pure or impure, in bounds or out of bounds.[12] For example, the Pharisees might have one purity map, the Qumran community another, and Jews—not belonging to either group—might operate by a different purity map altogether. But that the social system itself should in some sense be purity based was not questioned. In fact, it was built right into the structure of the Temple. In the Temple's "holiness electrical system" the force of holiness was understood to radiate outward in concentric circles beginning from the Holy of Holies. From there it radiated into gradually less holy spheres represented by the various Temple courts: the court of the priests, the court of the (male) Israelites, the court of the (Israelite) women, and the court of the Gentiles. (It was something like the way a Wi-Fi signal becomes gradually weaker the further one moves away from its primary modem.) Hence, the purity-based social system built into the Temple's structure was understood to reflect *God's own cosmic ordering designed to fend off chaos* and safely cordon off his holy presence so that it could be experienced as beneficial.

Such was the cultural world of the early Jewish Christ followers of the NT, people like Jesus' first disciples and the Pharisee, Saul of Tarsus. As a Pharisee, Saul would have found this purity-based social system to be second nature, since he was concerned, no doubt, not only with his own personal holiness but also with Israel's corporate holiness. What happened to convert ordinary Jews and people like Saul from one view of holiness to another?[13] The obvious answer is that they became convinced that God had raised a man crucified as messiah from the dead.[14] But I want to push beyond this question and broaden it a bit. What happened to change the very nature of holiness itself? Granted, the NT nowhere gives a specific answer to that question. But connecting its theological dots gives a relatively clear answer: Through the Christ event, God himself entered into creation, setting into motion the end of the old creation and the birth of a new creation (2 Cor 5:17; Gal 6:15). In other words, God has ontologically, or really, changed the cosmos and therefore the way it is ordered. The whole Christ-

---

12. See the helpful discussion in Neyrey, "Idea of Purity."

13. Hooker and Young speak of his conversion as "a change from one understanding of 'holiness' to another" (*Holiness and Mission*, 17).

14. Gorman moves in this direction (*Inhabiting*, 131–37). Agreeing with his arguments regarding Saul's "will to purity," here I attempt to trace some of the train of thought that might have deconstructed this "will to purity."

Section 2—Relocating Holiness in Jesus

event—incarnation, birth, life, death, resurrection, ascension, exaltation, and the pouring out of the Spirit—has somehow changed the order and structure of the cosmos. Therefore, the way holiness itself was conceived would also have to change. In short, holiness would have to be relocated in a Jewish man from Nazareth.

5

Relocating Holiness in a Jew from Nazareth

Soundings from the Synoptic Gospels

Introduction

IN THIS CHAPTER, WE will take some soundings regarding the nature of holiness from the Synoptic Gospels: Matthew, Mark, and Luke. We will be using Mark as our primary base but will also draw on material from the other two.[1] No doubt, if we were to focus instead on either Matthew or Luke—especially their particular way of narrating Jesus' relationship to the Temple, his death, and his resurrection appearances—the following chapter would have different nuances. But there are enough similarities among all three of these gospels that the different nuances of Matthew and Luke would tend to complement, rather than undermine, the basic gist of what follows.

Before focusing on Mark, we begin with some very brief, general remarks on Jesus' birth, an event only recorded in Matthew and Luke.

The Birth of Jesus

In the gospels, Jesus is called *the* Holy One of God[2] (Mark 1:24; John 6:68–69) and Matthew and Luke tell us that he came into his creation through

---

1. For more thorough treatments of holiness in each individual gospel (including John), see esp. Brower, *Holiness in the Gospels*.

2. This does not seem to have been a recognized title for a specific figure in Jewish

a young girl (Matt 1:18–25; Luke 2:1–7). Richard Beck's words capture something of the scandal of this:

> Shockingly, and contrary to human expectation, God was born as a human being, covered in sweat, blood, and amniotic fluid . . . God is squeezed out into the world through a woman's birth canal, attached to her by an umbilical cord. In the Incarnation God crashes through the quarantine of holiness and purity erected around Him.[3]

According to Lev 12:1–8, the mother of a newborn son was impure for seven days and had to stay home for thirty-three more days, not coming into contact with anything considered holy. It is not completely clear whether a newborn was conceived as sharing in the mother's impurity or was perhaps contaminated by her impurity through contact with her in these thirty-three days.[4] But one thing is clear. The holy one of God, through whom creation was made according to John 1:3, came into that creation right *in the midst of impurity*, not being cordoned off from it. Not surprisingly, that is also the way he lived.

Jesus' Appearance and Baptism

At the beginning of Mark, we encounter "all the people from the Judean countryside and all the people in Jerusalem" who were coming out into the wilderness to be baptized by John, confessing both their own sins and the sins of Israel as a whole (1:5).[5] The primary mode of "forgiveness of sins" was through the sacrificial system of the Temple. Hence, the early movement of these people *away from* Jerusalem in connection with the "forgiveness of sins" would suggest that the primary locus of God's forgiving, salvific, beneficent, and holy presence had begun to shift away from

---

literature (France, *Gospel of Mark*, 104). In Mark, at the very least, it seems to be one way of underscoring the unique, elect sonship of Jesus (cf. the words from unclean spirits in 3:11, 5:7). In any case, it marks him out as "the embodiment of the holy in the midst of the people in confrontation with the unclean" (Brower, *Mark*, 73).

3. Beck, *Unclean*, 153.

4. Luke 2:22 can be read as implying that Jesus had somehow contracted impurity as well: "When the time came for *their* purification according to the Law of Moses, they brought him up to Jerusalem to present him to the Lord."

5. In various sections of this chapter, I have adapted and borrowed heavily from my "The 'New Creation.'"

the Jerusalem Temple at the very "beginning of the good news about Jesus Christ" (1:1). This will be confirmed in 2:1–12 when Jesus himself forgives the paralytic's sins in a (his own?) house in Capernaum with a simple pronouncement, completely circumventing the Temple and embodying what God was understood to be doing through the system of daily sacrifices on behalf of the people and their sins. The implication of this is that throughout Mark, the Jerusalem Temple is no longer to be imagined as the *primary* locus of God's holiness. It is no longer the heart of that metaphorical "holiness electrical system."[6] Jesus is.[7]

God's holiness is relocated in the man from Nazareth, who stands in line awaiting baptism, totally identifying himself with his people, who have gathered with the expectation of God doing something and wanting to become the cleansed, set apart, holy people who participate in it. They were, in essence, saying: "Do something that will make things right, that will set a new age in motion and make Israel the people you have called us to be."[8] Or, in Isaiah's words: "If only you would tear open the heavens and come down" (Isa 64:1)!

And that is what God does. God's Spirit rips open the heavens and comes down right *into* Jesus[9] (1:10)—not "upon" him as in Matthew and Luke—which is followed by an announcement of Jesus' sonship. When Jesus is coming up out of the water, he sees the heavens in the process of *being* ripped apart (1:10), an action not given final closure at this point in the story.[10] So we are alerted up front that Mark will be narrating the rip-

---

6. In Matthew and Luke/Acts, the Temple is presented in somewhat more positive terms as a continuing locale of God's holy, beneficent presence (e.g., Matt 23:21; Luke 1:8–20; 2:21–38; 24:52; cf. Acts 2:46; 3:1–26). Still, in both Jesus is depicted as the most important locale of God's holy presence (e.g., Matt 12:6). In addition, by the end of Matthew, there has been a decisive shift away from the Temple to the risen Jesus and those who will follow him as the ongoing locale/new temple of God's holy presence (Matt 21:42; 18:20; 28:18–20; on which, see Beale and Kim, *God Dwells Among Us*, 86–98). One also sees this shift gradually happening in Luke and continuing into the story of Acts (on which see Green, "Demise of the Temple").

7. For a detailed historical argument that Jesus and his followers understood themselves as a counter-temple movement with Jesus as the decisive embodiment of Yahweh's eschatological temple, see Perrin, *Jesus The Temple*.

8. See the similar comments of Hooker, *Gospel*, 44.

9. The language reminds us of Ezek 37:6, 14 where God promises to give his Spirit "*into* you all" thereby restoring a "dead" people so that they can become the display people that God intends in Ezekiel 36.

10. The verb form translated "being ripped apart" (*schizomenous*) is present tense depicting the action as being in progress and somehow incomplete or ongoing (as noted

Section 2—Relocating Holiness in Jesus

ping apart of "the great cosmic curtain that separates creation from God's presence ... [so] that the protecting barriers are gone and that God, unwilling to be confined to sacred spaces, is on the loose in our own realm."[11] In the absence of a birth story, this seems to be Mark's way of depicting the beginning of God's action to change the "holiness electrical system," and thereby the old structures of the cosmos itself. But it is just that, the *beginning* of a single, extended divine action *in the life of a human person* that comes to a climax in Mark's story when "the great cosmic curtain" of the Temple is "ripped open" at Jesus' death (15:38).[12] As we will see, in the crucifixion scene, we have essentially the mirror image of what happens here, so that the baptism scene and the crucifixion scene function as "book ends" to Mark's story of Jesus.

In this initial scene, then, God the Father, through the Spirit, initiates a "gracious gash in the universe,"[13] and inhabits the body of the Son who becomes the primary locus of God's holy presence. As we hear in 1:24, he is "the Holy One of God," and as John the Baptist had already said when speaking to the crowds: "He will baptize you all with the Holy Spirit" (1:8). While this baptism may also reference an event after the end of Mark's story (i.e., Pentecost), this cleansing metaphor should be taken seriously in terms of its meaning for the characters *in Mark's story*. As we will see, as the primary locale of God's holiness, Jesus is not contaminated by impurity but rather brings the Spirit's cleansing, holy presence to bear on the lives of those he encounters by cleansing their impurity, giving them life, and making them whole.

The very first words we hear Jesus speak in Mark are words of God's good news: "The time has been [and is] fulfilled and the kingdom of God has come [and is now] near. Repent and believe in the good news" (Mark 1:15). The way the (perfect tense) verbs work in the immediately preceding sentence implies that the coming near of God's kingdom has happened right in the story Mark is telling. The coming near of God's kingdom in Jesus is a major emphasis in the Synoptic Gospels, and in Mark the most obvious moment for it to have "come near" is the moment of the "gracious

---

by Juel, *Master*, 34).

11. Juel, *Master*, 34–35. I have modified the order of Juel's words here in a way that still does justice to his primary point.

12. The verb translated as "ripped apart" (*eschisthē*) in 15:38 comes from the same basic verb as the form in 1:10. These are the only two places in Mark where this verb is used.

13. Marcus, *Mark 1–8*, 165.

gash"[14] when the Spirit descended into the Son. As the primary locus of God's holy, beneficial presence in Mark's gospel, Jesus goes beyond symbolizing Yahweh's kingship over the cosmos as did the Temple. He channels that holiness in a missional direction as he both announces and executes God's reign by reclaiming many for his lordship who are victims of the chaotic forces of evil, impurity, sickness, sin and death. Before going further in Mark's story, we pause for a few remarks about those chaotic forces that will be helpful.

Excursus: Forces of Chaos in the Synoptic Gospels

Moving from the OT to the stories of Jesus in the Synoptic Gospels can be a bit unsettling, particularly with regard to the assumed presence of the demonic on almost every page. The gospels assume the existence of the Devil/Satan, a commander-in-chief of demons/malevolent spirits who are in opposition to God's reign and purposes. In the Synoptic Gospels, there is one healing encounter that assumes a relationship between sickness/physical maladies and human sin (Mark 2:1–12; Matt 9:1–8; Luke 5:17–26).[15] Just what that relationship is in the paralyzed man's case remains unstated. However, there are far more passages in these gospels that assume some sort of connection between sickness/physical maladies and the demonic.[16] Although all three Synoptic Gospels can distinguish between physical disorders healed and demons being cast out (e.g., Mark 1:34; 6:13; Matt 8:16–17; Luke 4:40–41), there are passages in each of them where Jesus heals a person or persons of a physical illness with an exorcism (e.g., Mark 9:14–29; Matt 12:22–23; 4:24; Luke 6:18–19).[17] Generally speaking, the boundary between healing and expelling the demonic becomes more blurred as one moves from Mark to Matthew and then to Luke where "almost every account of healing . . . is portrayed as an encounter with diabolic forces."[18]

---

14. Ibid.

15. For an insightful treatment of this passage and passages in the OT that regularly assume some sort of relationship between disease and human sin, see Gaiser, *Healing*, 191–206.

16. For the summary comments about this issue that follow in this paragraph, see R. H. Bell, "Demon, Devil, Satan," *DJG*, 2d ed., 193–202, esp. 195–97.

17. For an exegetically nuanced and theologically rich discussion of this connection between the demonic and physical illness focused on the healing of the epileptic boy in Mark 9:14–29, see Gaiser, *Healing*, 132–50.

18. Green, *Theology*, 95.

Section 2—Relocating Holiness in Jesus

There is also some sort of nexus between demonic activity and impurity in the Synoptic Gospels, although it is somewhat fluid and imprecise.[19] Even so, it is not hard to see a connection between impurity as a dynamic, polluting force associated with death/loss of life and demonic activity opposing the reign of the living God whose holiness—when properly cordoned off—was thought to generate blessing and life. Indeed, about the time of the first century, certain "Jewish biblical passages about death in general and corpse defilement in particular were coming to be read in ways that exemplify a demonization of death and of things associated with it."[20]

We might even move a little further along these lines and note that the gospels at least give hints of a connection between the demonic and the occupying imperial power of Rome. For example, in Jesus' encounter with the Gerasene demoniac in the most unclean of settings in the gospels (Mark 5:1–13, discussed below), some have drawn attention to the possible connection between the demonic name, Legion, and anti-Roman sentiments, since legion is a Latin loan word that often referred to a group of Roman soldiers.[21] Linking the kingdom of Satan and that of the (unclean) occupying kingdom of Rome with such a reference would certainly be subtle, but not farfetched in first-century Jewish circles. After all, Revelation makes the link overtly, as we will see later. This is not to suggest that the story of this enslaved man is only a cipher for a political point Mark is making or that he is casting Jesus as another Jewish revolutionary to overthrow Rome's power in Palestine. But if, as seems likely to me, we are to make some such link in the story of the Gerasene demoniac between the violent military power by which Rome ruled its empire and the demonic power standing behind it, Mark is subtly depicting such occupying imperial power as another force of chaos, an "unclean" death-dealing force that disorders human life. In this story, then, we see a connection not only between impurity, death, and the

---

19. The sheer prevalence of the language of "*unclean* spirit(s)" in all three Synoptic Gospels demonstrates that some sort of connection between impurity and demonic activity is assumed (e.g., Mark 1:23; 3:11; 6:7; Matt 10:1; 12:43; Luke 4:36; 6:18; 8:29; cf. 4QDamascus Documenta 6 i 6–13). On this connection, see T. Klutz, *Exorcism Stories*, 125–37. For the contours of the continuing debate over whether demonic power is associated with impurity in the OT itself, particularly in the priestly material of Leviticus, see Swanson, "Leviticus and Purity," 31–32.

20. Klutz, *Exorcism Stories*, 134.

21. See the discussion in Brower, *Mark*, 145–46; Marcus, *Mark 1–8*, 351–52. As we will see below, the language of the unclean pigs rushing headlong into the sea is similar to that of Pharaoh's soldiers rushing into the sea and drowning.

demonic, but also a link between these three and death-dealing political power.

In the Synoptic Gospels then, Jesus, the Holy One of God, the vehicle of God's reign, engages a nexus of debilitating forces somewhat fluidly and imprecisely connected to each other, namely, Satan/the demonic, physical disorders/sickness, impurity, death-dealing political power, and human sin itself. Taken together, these are forces opposing God's reign by oppressing, enslaving, contaminating, and generally distorting God's creatures and his creation, keeping his beneficent, life-giving holy presence at bay. Although they are never called "forces of chaos" anywhere in the Bible, the phrase seems to be a good short-hand description for forces that disorder God's good creation in an attempt to keep it from reaching its intended destiny.

Jesus versus the Forces of Chaos

As the primary locus of God's holy, beneficial presence in Mark's gospel, Jesus channels that holiness in a missional direction as he announces and executes God's reign by reclaiming many for his lordship who are victims of the sorts of forces we just described. Only a few verses after Jesus' announcement of God's kingdom, Jesus enters a synagogue and encounters a man with an unclean spirit who identifies Jesus as *"the Holy One of God"* (1:24). "Rebuking" him and commanding him to "be silent," this *Holy One* delivers the man from the control of the *unclean* spirit (1:25–26). Shortly after that, he restores Peter's mother-in-law to health by "raising" her so that her fever leaves her, a life-giving action that might also imply a deliverance from demonic activity.[22]

Some time later, in a story that appears in all three Synoptic Gospels, Jesus is encountered by a leper, one of those "walking corpses" (Mark 1:39–44; Matt 8:2–4; Luke 5:12–16). Jesus enacts compassion by intentionally touching him so that his leprosy goes away and he is cleansed (1:41–42). But before he can be fully reintegrated into the community, he has to be declared clean by the priest at the Temple and so Jesus sends him there for that purpose. Jesus does not contract impurity when he, the Holy One of God, touches the leper. Rather, he brings the holy presence of God to bear on him by cleansing his impurity/pollution, which also restores him

---

22. Note that in Luke's parallel account, he has Jesus "rebuking" the fever (4:39), using the same word he had just used in the previous story when he had Jesus "rebuke" the demon (4:35).

Section 2—Relocating Holiness in Jesus

to physical health and wholeness, making it possible for him to participate in the community of God's people. This story is paradigmatic for the way Jesus, with mercy and compassion, intentionally crosses the purity boundary associated with lepers and brings God's holy, cleansing presence to bear on their bodies (cf. Luke 17:11–19) or, "baptizes them with the [cleansing] Spirit." Jesus even appears to up the ante regarding these purity boundaries by staying at the house of Simon the leper (Mark 14:3; Matt 26:6) in flagrant violation of these purity codes, "because whoever stays under a roof with a leper, as with a corpse, contracts defilement."[23]

Speaking of exposure to corpse impurity, touching a corpse, being in the same room with it, or even allowing your shadow to pass over it in a funeral procession was considered polluting in the Jewish world of Jesus' day.[24] Nevertheless, in Mark 5:1–13 Jesus goes strolling right into a Gentile cemetery (par. Matt 8:28—9:1; Luke 8:26–39). Before he gets there, however, he and his disciples encounter a storm with demonic characteristics so that the sea itself—a symbolic manifestation of chaos in the ancient world[25]—rises up against them in 4:35–41 to keep them out of a place under demonic control, full of impurity and death, a place about as void of holiness as a place could be. But the Holy One of God—using the same two words as when he addressed the unclean spirit in 1:25–26—"rebukes" the wind and commands the sea to "be silent" (4:39), effectively thwarting the attempt by the forces of chaos to keep him out of their stronghold. Starting with this battle with the chaotic wind and sea through the end of chapter 5, we do not see Jesus in a defensive stance to protect the holiness he bears from the worst of impurity's pollution. Rather, we see a vivid portrayal of the life-giving power of holiness intentionally pitted against, and conquering, the death-dealing forces of chaos.

When Jesus and his disciples get to the other side of the "sea," we are told that they arrive in the country of the Gerasenes (5:1).[26] From what we go on to learn about this place, we can be sure that Jews were scarce in those

---

23. deSilva, "Clean and Unclean," 146.

24. deSilva, *Honor, Patronage, Kinship, & Purity*, 263.

25. Mark's gospel is the first historical record to call the Lake of Galilee a "sea," allowing him to invoke the image of Jesus as a "divine warrior" who brings liberation by conquering the sea/sea monsters (Ps 74:12–15; 77:16–20; 89:9–10; Isa 51:9–11) which represent(s) the forces of chaos in numerous cultures in the ancient world.

26. Whether Mark's gospel originally contained the word Gerasenes, Gergesenes, or Gadarenes (as in Matthew) is difficult to say but is not particularly important for our purposes.

Relocating Holiness in a Jew from Nazareth

parts and that it was not a popular first-century Jewish vacation spot! A typical Jew concerned even a little with issues of purity and holiness would have considered it out of bounds because impurity was rampant. Pigs, for example, are most unclean, and their presence clearly indicates that this is *Gentile* territory. Since most Jews understood Gentiles to live in a perpetual state of impurity, there are already two strikes against the purity status of the place (pigs and Gentiles). There is also a graveyard close by, a source of extremely contagious corpse impurity. Even worse, from out of those tombs comes a man, almost certainly a Gentile, with death's contagion all over him. To top it all off, Mark says the man has an *unclean* spirit and then says: "he lived in/among the tombs and no one was able to bind him any longer, not even with a chain; for he had often been bound with shackles and chains and the chains had been torn apart by him and the shackles had been smashed. And throughout the night and day he was screeching and cutting himself with stones in/among the tombs and on the hills" (5:3–5). Whether this man actually resides inside the tombs or lives among them, he is perpetually contaminated by a corpse pollution that he can pass on to others. Not surprisingly, this man has an unclean spirit, which somehow becomes a whole army (a legion[27]) of unclean spirits as the story progresses (5:2, 8–9). This is a human being out of control, exponentially unclean, and enslaved to chaotic forces that are slowly forcing him to destroy himself. He is a walking exhibition of chaos itself, of creation disordered by impurity, death, and the demonic. As David Garland puts it, "His howling night and day (5:5) reveals him to be a microcosm of the whole of creation inarticulately groaning for redemption (Rom 8:22)."[28] And if the word Legion subtly suggests a link between Rome's violent military power by which it ruled and a demonic power standing behind it, his situation is a microcosm of those suffering from the chaotic force of occupying imperial power, another "unclean" death-dealing force that disorders human life.

When the holy one of God arrives, God's holiness goes on the offensive. Inhabited by the Holy Spirit, making him the vehicle of God's reign, Jesus goes into battle to reclaim this helpless human being for God's lordship.[29] But the battle is over almost before it starts. The unclean spirits

---

27. Legion is a Latin word commonly referring to a Roman division of five to six thousand foot soldiers and 120 cavalrymen.

28. Garland, *Theology of Mark's Gospel*, 273.

29. For the numerous military allusions coloring this as a battle scene, an invasion by Jesus into enemy territory, see Dowd, *Reading Mark*, 54.

Section 2—Relocating Holiness in Jesus

are reduced to begging in an encounter with one stronger than they are as he "plunders their house" (cf. 3:27) and acquiesces to their pleas to be sent into the herd of pigs (5:11–13). "In a delightful tour de force, the spirits themselves choose the means of their own destruction"[30] when the pigs rush headlong (*hormaō*) down a steep slope and drown in the sea. Interestingly, some first-century Jewish accounts of the exodus use similar language of Pharaoh's forces "rushing headlong" into the sea where they were drowned.[31] In that case, Yahweh used the very thing that represented chaos in the ancient world to deliver Israel from slavery and demonstrate his reign.[32] In this passage, we see another exodus and another demonstration of God's reign where the sea comes into play. Here the unclean spirits opposing God's reign by enslaving one of God's creatures fittingly meet their demise in unclean animals as they are drowned in a recently conquered, formerly chaotic, sea. This Holy One of God, who is the primary locale of God's holy presence, is not threatened with the polluting impurity all around him. Instead, in this healing battle, Jesus brings the beneficent presence of God to bear on the man's situation by liberating him from his living death in perpetually polluted surroundings and restoring him to *shalom* (5:15).

Jesus hardly has time to catch his breath before new battles with the chaotic forces of impurity and death are underway, but this time after he crosses the "sea"—now absent any sign of chaos despite the pigs' plunge into it—again into Jewish territory (5:21). Although now in Jewish territory, he is once again confronted with the sort of impurity that Jews concerned with holiness would attempt to avoid. In 5:21–43 Mark brackets a story of a woman suffering from a twelve-year-long menstrual hemorrhage between the opening and closing of a story of a twelve-year-old girl in critical condition and about to die. In these stories, Jesus has his work cut out for him, with two females who have the chaotic powers of death and impurity at work in their bodies.

With regard to the woman with the hemorrhage, we should recall that blood or sexual fluids, as a part of the birth-death cycle, may indeed sustain

---

30. Juel, *Gospel of Mark*, 112. Cf. *T. Sol.* 5:11 where a demon who is going to be exorcised begs not to be condemned to the water, presumably for destruction.

31. Josephus uses the same verb (*hormaō*) as in Mark (*Antiquities* 2.340, 342), whereas Philo uses a related word (*Moses* 2.254).

32. Recall that the first time we hear about God's reign in the canon is beside the sea in Exod 15:18 as the conclusion of the song of deliverance sung by Moses and the Israelites.

or create life. However, when crossing the body's boundaries and flowing out, they symbolize the loss of life/death. This woman who had a continuous menstrual hemorrhage would have been seen as perpetually unclean, with the ability to pollute whatever and whoever she touched (Lev 15:25–30). She was essentially another walking exhibition of chaos itself, of creation disordered by death, since she was in a perpetual state of "losing her life." The physical toll this would have taken on her is obvious, but it would have been compounded and furthered by the economic and social implications of her predicament. Not only had she spent everything she had to try to get better (5:26), for twelve long years her life would have been void of regular human embrace and (most probably) an inability to engage in synagogue activities or Temple worship. Her perpetual pollution excluded her from participating in the people of God. In every way then, one might say that she "has been dying as long as the child has been living—twelve years."[33]

But this nameless, pollution-bearing woman engages in a bold and dangerous action when she comes up behind Jesus in a crowd and intentionally touches his clothes, no doubt making contact with others in the crowd as well (5:27–28). Instead of her polluting Jesus with impurity, the power of holiness flows from him to her, immediately neutralizing the power of impurity and death in her body (5:29–30). With her physical malady cured, Jesus summons her and addresses her as "daughter," as a loved member of a family, effectively announcing an end to her social isolation with the words "your faith has saved you."[34] In addition to physical healing then, "[w]hat Jesus does for the bleeding woman here and for the leper in 1:40–45 is to restore the right relationships symbolized by the purity codes; he restores people to the presence of God and to the human community."[35] He then commands the woman to go forth in the overall *shalom* that now characterizes her situation (5:34).

Stopping to deal with this woman delayed Jesus long enough that the little girl dies, with professional mourners already on the scene commencing her funeral (5:35, 38–39). From the standpoint of those who report this news to her father, there is no more reason to bother a Jewish teacher who would be rendered unclean by laying his hands on the corpse of a little

33. Dowd, *Reading Mark*, 56.

34. The Greek word translated as "saved" above (*sesōken*) is usually translated as "healed," but it comes from the same word family as "salvation," indicating that salvation includes physical, social, and economic aspects and therefore is not simply about one's "spiritual" condition as it relates to life after death.

35. Dowd, *Reading Mark*, 57.

Section 2—Relocating Holiness in Jesus

girl who was now beyond help in any case (5:41). But once again, when Jesus takes her by the hand, she is, in effect, "baptized with the life-giving Holy Spirit" and thereby restored to life and made clean from any residual impurity (5:41–42). Jesus, the Holy One of God, is not contaminated by corpse impurity but restores the dead child to a state of purity, health, and life. Whereas death was at work in both the bleeding woman and the dead child, they encountered the one who was giving his life as a means of their liberation from the forces of chaos at work in their bodies (Mark 10:45), the one in whom life was at work, and they received a share of that life (cf. Paul's language in 2 Cor 4:12).

These stories in Mark 5 are representative of numerous episodes in the Synoptic Gospels in which Jesus intentionally crosses purity boundaries with mercy and compassion, bringing God's holy cleansing presence to bear on contaminated, debilitated, weak, and isolated bodies, healing and rescuing them from the forces of chaos and reincorporating them into human community. Such stories vividly portray the life-giving power of holiness overcoming the death-dealing forces of chaos, rather than being threatened by them.

Table Fellowship and Sabbath Actions

Two other aspects of Jesus' action in the Synoptic Gospels that bear on the issue of holiness are Jesus' meal practices and his actions on the Sabbath.

Table Fellowship

Jesus also crossed purity boundaries when it came to engaging in table fellowship with those considered outsiders and "sinners" by the Pharisees (e.g., Mark 2:15–17; Matt 9:9–13; Luke 15:1–2; 19:1–10). In these contexts the term "sinner" is sometimes introduced by Jesus' antagonists (e.g., Luke 5:27–32). It refers to someone whose behavior, including his or her relative lack of attention to avoiding impurity, is considered outside the bounds of the group that regards them as a "sinner." The Pharisees, who had high status in Palestinian society primarily because of their careful attention to purity issues, attempted to apply a standard of purity appropriate for priests on duty in the Temple to their daily lives, not least at mealtime.[36] In the

---

36. E.g., as Mark 7:1–3 confirms, in accordance with the traditions of the elders,

Pharisees' view, someone like Jesus, whom they assumed was concerned with matters of holiness, should have been much more careful to draw tight boundaries around those with whom he created bonds by sharing a table with them. It was bad enough that Jesus would eat elbow-to-elbow with over five thousand people, fully aware that he was likely to contract various sorts of impurity from such people. But to share meals intentionally with people with low status in the Jewish world, like tax collectors (whose work for, and close contact with, the Roman occupiers made their loyalty to God's people and their purity status suspect), the desperately needy, and those with a variety of physical disabilities (damaged/blemished bodies lacking wholeness), was virtually a guarantee that one would be defiled. The daily lives of such people simply made it very difficult for them not to be contaminated with various forms of impurity, and eating with them would be out of bounds for "holiness-minded" Jews like the Pharisees. But Jesus was in the process of reforming all existing Jewish purity maps, including that of the Pharisees. In this regard, "Jesus reversed the purity regulations and boundary markers of the community that kept the 'lost' lost, the sinner sinful, and the outsider outside."[37]

However, a brief word in defense of the Pharisees is in order. First, Jesus did not hesitate to engage in table fellowship with those very Pharisees with whom he had sharp religious disagreements about purity boundaries and the nature of holiness (e.g., Luke 7:36–37; 11:37; 14:1). They too were invited to become part of the extended family of Israel that Jesus was forging around himself, represented by his twelve closest disciples. Second, the Pharisees' careful attention to purity issues was an attempt to help the community become the priestly people God had called Israel to be. It was also an attempt to maintain the order they understood that God had built into the cosmos by keeping persons and things in their proper places. At least theoretically, those who were outsiders to their group might be able to share table fellowship with them if they were first to repent and also pay careful attention to purity issues. But this sort of stance ignored the social and economic obstacles such outsiders would have faced. While the Pharisees required repentance and attention to issues of purity *before* engaging

---

Pharisees will not eat *ordinary* meals without first washing their hands to remove ritual impurity. There is no command to do this in the OT. There is, however, a command to *priests* to wash their hands *at the time they are engaged in tabernacle service* (Exod 30:19–21, cf. 40:12–13) prior to partaking of holy food from the altar (their portions of sacrifices).

37. Thompson, "Gathered at the Table," 84.

Section 2—Relocating Holiness in Jesus

in table fellowship with outsiders, Jesus ate with such low status outsiders—essentially implying that they were *already* a part of his extended family *in order to* bring them to repentance and life.[38] The implication was that where Jesus was, there was the locale of the holy, cleansing presence of God where "baptism with the Holy Spirit" neutralized impurity and reincorporated low-status "sinners" and outsiders into God's own family.

Sabbath Actions

We saw earlier that Israel's sanctifying/keeping holy the Sabbath (Exod 20:8) responds to, and imitates, God's own initial sanctifying activity (Gen 2:3; Exod 20:11). In doing so, it provides revitalizing rest for all within its borders and, since no one else in the ancient world had one day of the week off, keeping Sabbath marks out Israel as distinct. At the same time, it publicly displays the character of God as desiring blessing and flourishing life for all creation and assures Israel that God continues to sanctify them (Exod 31:13). The problem is that Scripture, while clear on God's intent that his people keep Sabbath, is a bit short on exactly what constitutes "work" in their changing circumstances. Complex Sabbath regulations began to develop that were meant to help Jews draw clear boundaries between actions that kept Sabbath, and those that went too far and might be considered "work." Just what keeping Sabbath truly meant was a very live, and crucially important, issue in first-century Judaism. In the situation where Jews were enveloped by their pagan occupiers, proper regulations were crucial so as to mark off clear boundaries between God's people and others, to clearly distinguish Israel from those around them. In such a situation, one can understand how, with no malicious intent, one proper function of Sabbath (the boundary-keeping function of marking off God's people as distinct) began to be the primary emphasis.

Jesus' Sabbath activities, particularly his healing acts (Mark 3:1–6; Matt 12:9–14; Luke 6:6–11; 13:10–17; 14:1–6), challenge the idea that the primary function of keeping Sabbath is boundary maintenance. Such actions thus provoke controversy in his context because they might appear to threaten the identity and existence of Israel. In the case of the healing of the man with a withered hand, which appears in all three Synoptic Gospels (Mark 3:1–6; Matt 12:9–14; Luke 6:6–11), the man's disabled/blemished body marks him out as less than whole, locating him far from the center of

38. On this issue, see especially Thompson, "Gathered at the Table."

the purity maps of those in attendance at the synagogue. In such a blemished state, some have suggested, he would appear to be unclean in some way and thus be unable to participate in Temple worship (Lev 21:16–24).[39] If so, one might say that in Mark's telling at least, the "Temple" housing the beneficent presence of God's holy, cleansing power comes to him. In any case, as with others Jesus encounters, this man experiences a "baptism with the Holy Spirit" as Jesus simply gives a command and utters a word that heals the man's hand, restoring him to health and wholeness of life, and perhaps to full (Temple) participation in the community of God's people.

Nothing that Jesus does in these stories constitutes a violation of any specific Sabbath command in Scripture. But as later rabbinic literature attests, healing on the Sabbath when a human life is clearly not in imminent danger was indeed understood by some to violate Sabbath.[40] Jesus' actions of "doing good" and "saving life" on the Sabbath, however, essentially confirm his (authoritative) pronouncement that "the Sabbath was made for the sake of humanity and not humanity for the sake of the Sabbath" (Mark 2:27). He never undercuts Sabbath-keeping per se, but privileges its life-giving, salvific purpose over its boundary-keeping function. This does not mean that keeping Sabbath holy now no longer includes a pattern of participating in life-giving rest for one's self and one's community. But Jesus reconfigures that pattern so that it also includes engaging in healing, life-giving activity for the sake of debilitated others one encounters on the Sabbath so that they too may experience true Sabbath *shalom*.

Jesus' "Purity Map": Teachings on Clean and Unclean

In the Synoptic Gospels, it is not that Jesus is unconcerned with issues of purity; nor does he reject the whole notion of mapping the world in terms of purity and impurity. While he does reject many of the specifics of existing purity maps, these gospels suggest that he operates by a different sort of purity map, redrawing the lines in different places.[41] By drawing lines in

---

39. E.g., Hurtado, *Mark*, 50. The Leviticus text in its original context only appears to apply to those who would be priests. Even so, if groups like the Pharisees who were in attendance tended to argue that purity regulations that in the OT only applied to priests while engaging in priestly service should be applied to all in the nation, such logic might exclude this man from entering the Temple. Whether this sort of purity map was actually operative in keeping such people out of the Temple is not clear.

40. See France, *Gospel of Mark*, 149–50.

41. Neyrey, "Idea of Purity," 113, 115–23. On this issue, see also Brower's excellent

Section 2—Relocating Holiness in Jesus

particular places that order life in a particular way, a purity map attempts to guard its community against the impurity/chaos that would engulf it otherwise. In Mark 7, in a surprising and unprecedented pronouncement, Jesus declares that nothing that goes into a person from the outside is able to make him or her unclean: "There is nothing outside a person that, by going into them is able to defile her/him. Rather, the things which come out of a person are the things which defile her/him" (7:15).

For any religious movement in Jesus' day—Jewish or otherwise—this pronouncement would be startling. In fact, the disciples themselves find it so radical and perplexing that they take it as some sort of parable (7:17). And who can blame them because, with respect to Leviticus 11 concerning clean and unclean foods, it appears to "make void the word of God," the very thing Jesus accuses the Pharisees of doing earlier in this context (7:13). In Jesus' explanation to the disciples, he redraws the boundary of existing purity maps by redefining what makes a person unclean:

> "Don't you see that everything outside the person, by going into the person is not able to defile them because it doesn't go into their heart but into their stomach and it goes out into the sewer?" (Thus he declared all foods clean.[42]) And he said "That which comes out of a person defiles the person. For from inside, out of the heart of people, come evil patterns of thinking: sexual immorality, stealing, murder, adultery, greed, wickedness, deceit, lack of self-constraint, envy, slander, arrogance, lack of moral sense. All these evil things originating inside the person come out and defile the person" (7:18b–23).

There is no separation here between the "internal" and the "external," as though Jesus is redrawing purity lines that are in some sense "internal" in nature as opposed to other Jewish groups' "external" purity maps. Patterns of thinking that are naturally performed inside a person's heart/mind are tied closely to the patterns of behavior in which they engage. According to Jesus, it is when the dispositions toward destructive behaviors reach fruition

---

treatment of Mark 7 (*Mark*, 191–201).

42. The syntax of this phrase marks it out as an interpretive insertion by Mark, albeit one that draws out the clear implications of the discussion heretofore. Jesus' statement in this section and this interpretive insertion raise complex historical questions. If the historical Jesus was this direct about clean and unclean foods, it is odd that people like Peter, who was apparently present, would continue to draw such distinctions later (Acts 10:14), even if it was in a vision. Our focus here, however, is on the sense and significance of Mark's telling of the story.

and are *externally enacted* that the person is defiled (7:20, 23). Most of these destructive behaviors are manifestations of violations of the portion of the Ten Commandments that deal with injustices against one's neighbor.[43] If left unchecked, such behaviors would pollute the relational networks of any human community and plunge it into the chaos and destruction against which purity regulations attempt to guard.[44]

While Mark's emphasis in this passage is on what *makes* one unclean, a similar passage in Luke hints in a complementary way at the way one *avoids* being "unclean." In Luke 11:37-42, Jesus is critiquing a particular group of Pharisees and experts in the interpretation of Torah, juxtaposing his own interpretation of Torah's larger concerns with their Torah inspired practices. The catalyst for the confrontation is Jesus not washing his hands to be sure he had removed ritual impurity before mealtime (v. 37). When his Pharisee host expresses amazement at this, Jesus retorts: "Now you Pharisees cleanse/purify the inside of the cup and the dish, but your inside is filled with exploitative greediness[45] and wickedness. Fools! Didn't the one who made the outside make the inside also?" (vv. 39b-40). In v. 41, Jesus essentially gives the cleansing cure for this inner defilement: "With regard to these things inside [namely, your exploitative greediness and wickedness], give alms, and voila, all things will be clean for you [i.e., both your inside and your outside]."[46] Jesus certainly focuses on inner integrity here, but his prescription for a "cleansing cure" assumes that outward compassionate and merciful actions that participate in restoring justice and *shalom* in people's lives begin to change the dispositions of one's heart, thereby making one completely "clean." Jesus goes on in the next verse to affirm these particular Pharisees' close attention to small matters of Torah, but says that

---

43. Neyrey, "Idea of Purity," 120.

44. All Jews in the first century would have proscribed such behaviors. Many Jews viewed these behaviors as morally defiling in a way that was *distinct from, but analogous to,* the way ritual defilement worked (Klawans, *Impurity*, 158 and *passim*). Perhaps this is how Jesus viewed things.

45. The Greek word for what I have translated "exploitative greed" is *harpagē*, from the same word family as *harpagmos*. The latter is the word used by Paul in Phil 2:6 when he says that Jesus refused to regard his equality with God as "something to be exploited," but rather willingly lowered his status and became a slave who, out of fidelity to God went to his death for the sake of others. In other words, the exploitative greed characterizing these particular Pharisees issuing in self-exalting behavior (11:43)—like that of Jesus' disciples themselves (e.g., Luke 9:46-48)!—is the very opposite of the character manifested in the Holy One of God.

46. For a similar interpretation of this verse, see Carroll, *Luke*, 259-60.

Section 2—Relocating Holiness in Jesus

their overall pattern of life is to "neglect the justice and the love of God" (v. 42).[47] Not neglecting "the justice and the love of God" is another way of stating what Jesus—in a sort of summary statement of Torah—explicitly calls for in the lives of his followers. That is, they are to love God with all their heart, soul, mind and strength and love their neighbor as themselves (Luke 10:27; Mark 12:28–31; Matt 22:35–40). The implication here is that engaging in an overall life pattern of participating in just, *shalom*-restoring, actions towards others and whole-hearted love/fidelity toward God makes one "pure" inside and out on Jesus' purity map. This is the life-pattern of Jesus himself, the Holy One of God, in the Synoptic Gospels. His just, liberative, and *shalom*-restoring actions characterized by compassion and mercy display not just purity, but the very character of God, and thus explicate the nature of holiness in these gospels.[48]

Here we might anticipate a connection between what we are describing and what we will see when we turn to Paul's letters. That is, the Synoptic Gospels portray this Nazarene in whom holiness was relocated as demonstrating fidelity (love) to God even to the point of death (Mark 14:36) and self-giving love for others throughout these narratives as he was—to use Mark's specific language as a sort of summary statement—giving his whole life as a means of their release/liberation (10:45). Jesus' life-pattern, therefore, not only reforms existing purity maps in a way that begins to dismantle the structures of the old cosmos; it also gives positive content to the nature of holiness in the new cosmos. It is a pattern of missional activity characterized by fidelity to God (*pistis*) and self-giving love (*agapē*) for others through which the Triune God carries out his saving, reconciling purposes and points toward his goal of *shalom* for his creatures and creation as a whole.

Jesus and the Temple

In his activities prior to coming to Jerusalem in the Synoptic Gospels, we might describe Jesus as a moveable tabernacle housing God's holy

---

47. The Greek verb translated "neglect" is in the present tense underscoring its habitual nature (i.e., an overall pattern of life).

48. Note how the Father in Luke is depicted as compassionate (15:20, cf. 1:76–78; mimicked by the Samaritan in 10:33) and merciful (6:36), both primary characteristics of holiness. It is no accident that Luke 6:36 (Jesus' command to his followers to "be merciful just as your Father is merciful") appears to be loosely modeled on Lev 19:2 ("Be holy because I myself, the Lord your God, am holy").

presence.[49] As the holy one of God, he lived right in the midst of impurity without being contaminated by it. Like the divine fire of the Temple's altar, he was not defiled by impurity but cleansed and sanctified those whom he encountered.[50] He repeatedly crossed purity boundaries of the old creation bringing God's holy, cleansing presence to bear on the (often polluted) bodies and relationships of those who were debilitated and enslaved by the forces of chaos, excluded from a full relationship with God and God's holy people. In doing so, Jesus goes beyond symbolizing Yahweh's kingship over the cosmos as did the Temple in Jerusalem. Instead, he becomes the vehicle through which God's Holy Spirit *enacts God's reign* in the lives of those he encounters so that they become signs of a new creation/cosmos characterized by forgiveness and justice, health and wholeness—in a word, *shalom*.

As the primary locale of God's holiness, the bearer of his gracious beneficial presence, Jesus' actions in Mark in particular suggest that God's people could get along without the Temple. In the first-century Jewish world, such a suggestion was dangerous. And, although the controversies Jesus generates prior to coming to Jerusalem in Mark are heated, after he enters the Temple, matters reach a boiling point. Perhaps more than anything else, what Jesus does in the Temple in Mark gets him into serious trouble because his actions symbolize its coming destruction (Mark 11:15–18). No matter how many Bibles have the title "Jesus' Cleansing of the Temple" over Mark 11:15–18, the narrative clues add up to a "cursing" rather than a "cleansing."[51] Implicitly "cursing" the Temple and predicting its demise sealed the deathly deal for the Holy One of God.

The Death of Jesus

"Anyone who touches the body of a human who has died and doesn't cleanse himself defiles the Lord's dwelling (*skēnē* in Greek). Such persons must be cut off from Israel" (Num 19:13). As we noted already, touching a corpse, being in the same room with it, or even allowing your shadow to pass over

---

49. Again, on Jesus as the decisive embodiment of Yahweh's eschatological temple, see Perrin, *Jesus The Temple*.

50. "If an inappropriate or unclean offering was accidentally placed on the altar, the fire was so powerful that it incinerated the impurity and sanctified the item.... The process of holiness is dynamic, almost chemical in that the very nature of the offering is transformed by contact with holy power" (Harrington, *Holiness*, 53).

51. Among others, Brower sets forth these narrative clues in a compelling way ("'Let the Reader Understand'").

Section 2—Relocating Holiness in Jesus

it in a funeral procession was considered polluting in the Jewish world of Jesus' day.[52] Holy things, holy places, and holy people needed to be kept as far as possible from such contamination. John 1:14 tells us that Jesus, as the Word become flesh, "tabernacled (*eskēnōsen*)" among us; he became "the Lord's dwelling/tabernacle (*skēnē*)," the Temple on the move. But Mark tells us explicitly that this moveable tabernacle—Jesus himself—wound up where the chaotic forces of impurity, death and decay finally take all the rest of the old creation. He *became*, in Mark's sober and explicit language, *a corpse* (15:45). Unlike Matthew and Luke who speak of Jesus' dead *body* (*sōma*), Mark emphasizes that all that remains of Jesus is a *corpse* (*ptōma*), the end result of the apparent victory of the forces of chaos. This flesh-and-blood human being who was somehow *homousios* (of same substance) with the Father, very God of very God, went one step further than refusing to be cordoned off from death's impurity. Humiliated on a Roman cross, he entered into the bowels of death itself and became a corpse whose impurity would have made those who buried it unclean.[53]

This is to up the ante on bringing the holy into contact with impurity. When death somehow enters into the very life/dwelling of God—the source of all holiness and life—the way the cosmos itself is structured and ordered cannot but be affected. The ultimate boundary has been crossed. The crucifixion scene in Mark's gospel can be read along these very lines.

> [37] And Jesus let out a loud cry and breathed out the Spirit (*exepneusen*) [38] with the result that the curtain (*katapetasma*) of the Temple was ripped in two from top to bottom. [39] And when the centurion who was standing facing him saw that he breathed out [the Spirit] this way, he said: "Truly this person was the Son of God" (15:37–39).

We will first focus on the splitting of the Temple curtain in 15:38. There were two Temple curtains to which Mark could have been referring. The inner curtain separated the Holy of Holies from the remainder of the Temple. The outer curtain hung in front of the doors that separated the sanctuary from the forecourt. We have little information about either apart from Josephus' description of them, and he refers to both with the same word that Mark

---

52. deSilva, *Honor, Patronage, Kinship, & Purity*, 263.

53. As we will see below, the corpse of Jesus becomes, at least for a time, devoid of the cleansing, life-giving Holy Spirit so that it would have been defiling for those who came into contact with it.

uses in v. 38 (*katapetasma*).⁵⁴ Which curtain we are to imagine as having being torn cannot be settled simply on the basis of historical information.⁵⁵ No matter what, we all have to be supplied with information about one or both these curtains prior to, or during, our reading of Mark for the tearing to generate anything but a question mark.⁵⁶

At this point it is helpful to remember the theology of creation's order that was commonly connected to the Jerusalem Temple in the first century. That is, the Jerusalem Temple was widely understood to be the place where heaven and earth met, a microcosm of the cosmos that functioned to maintain the order of the cosmos as the creator God had set it up. Key for our purposes is that this theology of creation's order was graphically depicted by means of the craftsmanship of the *outer* Temple curtain. Josephus implies such with his description of it:

> Before these hung a veil (*katapetasma*) of equal length, of Babylonian tapestry.... Nor was this mixture of materials without its mystic meaning: it typified the universe (*hōsper eikona tōn holōn*) ... On this tapestry was portrayed a panorama of the heavens.⁵⁷

Hence, the craftsmanship of the outer curtain graphically depicted the widespread assumption that the Temple was an image/icon (*eikōn*) or microcosm of the universe as a whole.⁵⁸

With this in the background, we return to Mark, recalling that throughout the narrative the primary locus of the Spirit, God's holy presence, has not been the Holy of Holies but the body of God's Son, the Holy One of God. Jesus' entrance into the story was marked by the movement

---

54. *Jewish Wars*, 5.5.5 § 212 and 219.

55. Generally one's decision on the issue is wrapped up with the meaning one assigns to the event itself. Geddert lists thirty-five different suggested meanings in *Watchwords*, 140-45.

56. Anyone reading this gospel publicly in the first or second century would likely have studied it in advance, marked it for reading purposes, and read it aloud expressively. They might also have explained aspects of the meaning of the text and would have probably expected to receive and answer to questions from their audience during their reading (Beavis, *Mark's Audience*, 124, 13-67; cf. also the comments of Shiner, *Proclaiming the Gospel*, 26-28).

57. *Jewish Wars*, 5.5.5 § 212-14; cf. the cosmic symbolism related to the Temple and its cultus also in *Antiquities* 3, 180-87; 123.

58. While even the inner curtain contained cosmic symbolism in that, like all the curtains/veils in the Temple, its color resembled the color of the heavens (Beale, *Temple*, 46, 190), only the outer curtain graphically portrayed the cosmic symbolism with its panoramic heavens.

Section 2—Relocating Holiness in Jesus

of the Spirit who ripped open the heavens and descended into (*eis*) him (1:10). His exit from the story is marked by the mirror image of the activity of this same Spirit. At Jesus' death in 15:37, Mark uses a word (*exepneusen*) that was not commonly used as a euphemism for dying in everyday Greek, suggesting that he wants us to hear something more than just that Jesus died. Especially since we were told that the Spirit went *into* Jesus in his first appearance in the story, this word suggests that in Jesus' final appearance the Spirit exits his body. That is, his last breath is a breathing *out* of the Spirit who came *into* him at the beginning.[59] As a result of the Spirit's movement, the heavens are ripped apart (*eschisthē*) as they were when the Spirit descended in 1:10, but this time in the form of the outer Temple curtain with the heavens painted on it (v. 38). God's Spirit, his personal dynamic force of holiness, is thus portrayed as moving *out of* Jesus *into* the Temple, *not as moving out of the Holy of Holies*. The ripping apart of "the great cosmic curtain that separates creation from God's presence,"[60] which began at Jesus' baptism, is now completed at his death.[61] The idea of the Temple as a microcosm of the cosmos was implicitly but graphically portrayed by means of the outer curtain; therefore, its ripping signifies the end of the old order of things, *including the purity-based social system built into the Temple structure* itself that was understandably thought to reflect God's own cosmic ordering.

The Resurrection, Exaltation, and Ascension of Jesus

Of course, the story doesn't end here, and Mark assures us that Jesus has been raised. His account, however—assuming it ends at 16:8[62]—is quite sparse, with no resurrection appearances. But Mark's overall story encourages us to connect some dots that are legitimate theological inferences based on the narrative's movement heretofore, even if they are not on the surface of the narrative. There is good reason for us to imagine that the splitting of

---

59. The word *exepneusen* is a compound word made up of *ex* (whose basic meaning is "out of," the opposite of "into") and *pneuō* (whose basic meaning is "to breathe"). The latter is the verbal form of the noun *pneuma* that is translated as "Spirit/spirit/breath."

60. Juel, *Master*, 35.

61. The type of Greek verb used here (*eschisthē*) suggests a completed action.

62. The earliest manuscripts do not have verses 9–20. The issue is more complicated than this might indicate, but for our purposes it is sufficient to say that almost all scholars admit that vv. 9–20 were not originally a part of Mark's gospel.

the Temple curtain was not the Spirit's last act in Mark's story. In remaining with and enabling the Son to bring to completion his giving of his life as a means of release for the many (10:45), the Holy Spirit is now marked with the same cruciform character as is the Son.[63] Mark's narrative movement implies that it is this now cruciform Spirit who is the agent through whom God the Father raises his obedient Son from the tomb (16:6).[64] By entering into the tomb and bringing life where there was no potential for it, where there was only a corpse, this life-giving Spirit forges a new creation from the ruins of the old.

Note the way the young man in the tomb describes the *risen* Jesus in v. 6. Using a particular Greek verbal form, he describes Jesus the Nazarene as (to paraphrase it) "the one forever stamped with the legacy of crucifixion."[65] In other words, the effects of crucifixion—the wounds Jesus received in his liberating battle against the forces of chaos—are not erased in the Lord's risen body. Hence, the character or essence of this Jew from Nazareth in whom holiness is relocated, remains *cruciform*. Luke and John make a similar theological point by explicitly noting that his risen body remains marked by the scars of crucifixion (Luke 24:39; John 20:25–27), marks Jesus continues to carry into his exaltation and ascension in both gospels.

There is one more theological connection to make between the dots generated by Mark's story. But first, let us recall for a moment that as Jesus was pouring out his life for others in life-giving beneficent ways prior to his crucifixion, we could say similar things about him as we could say about the Temple. As was assumed of the Temple, he was the primary locale of

63. That the Holy Spirit is cruciform in character is also at home in Paul's letters (Gorman, *Cruciformity*, 17–18, 50–74).

64. There is ambiguity here in that elsewhere in the NT, only God (the Father) is regarded as the agent of Jesus' resurrection (e.g., Acts 2:23–24; 3:15). But since the Spirit who comes from God the Father in 1:9–11 empowers Jesus' ministry throughout, everything Jesus does, he does through the agency of the Spirit, *including raising a little girl from the dead* (5:35–43). So, while we would certainly say the Son raises the little girl from the dead, he does so through the agency of the life-giving Spirit. Therefore, it is not inconsistent to imagine that God the Father does indeed raise the Son, but he also does so through the agency of the life-giving, Holy Spirit in 16:6. For further reflections along these lines in a wider biblical context, see my *1 & 2 Thessalonians*, 308–12.

65. Mark describes the risen Jesus with exactly the same word (*estaurōmenon*) as does Paul in 1 Cor 1:23 and 2:2 to make a similar theological point. Revelation also uses the same sort of Greek verb form (a perfect tense participle) of a different word to describe the Lamb as—again to paraphrase it—"stamped forever with the legacy of slaughter" (e.g., 5:6).

Section 2—Relocating Holiness in Jesus

God's holiness from which God's beneficent presence radiated in cleansing, healing, forgiving, and life-giving ways. While the structure and furniture of the Temple *symbolized* God's reign, Jesus *became* the very vehicle of that reign. The purity-based social system built into the Temple's structure was understood to reflect *God's own cosmic ordering designed to fend off chaos* and safely cordon off his holy presence so that it could be experienced as beneficial. But God's holy presence in Jesus was not cordoned off from impurity, and Jesus was not defiled by it. Instead, like the divine fire on the Temple's altar, Jesus, as the bearer of the divine Spirit, incinerated impurity and brought overall *shalom* to those who were previously excluded from the benefits of the "holiness electrical system" by the existing purity maps. In his activities and teaching, then, Jesus redrew the purity map into a social system that allowed those who were previously unclean outsiders to experience God's holy presence as beneficial. In Jesus' battle against the forces of chaos and especially in his death and resurrection, God reordered the cosmos itself. He overhauled the "holiness electrical system," giving positive content to the nature of both divine and human holiness in the new cosmos. It is now cruciform in shape and manifest in Jesus' boundary-crossing faithfulness to the Father's life-giving, saving mission (*pistis*) expressed in costly, self-giving actions for others (*agapē*) in order to restore his creatures and creation to *shalom*.

With these connections between Jesus and the Temple in mind, we can see more clearly how to connect some more of the dots in Mark's story. If the Jerusalem Temple was a microcosm of the old creation, we might expect there to be a similar relationship between the cruciform body of the risen Son and the new creation God set in motion by his resurrection. That is, in raising the body of the faithful, self-giving Holy One of God from the dead, the Spirit replaces the image/icon (*eikōn*) or microcosm of the old order (i.e., the Jerusalem Temple) with the image/microcosm of the new order (i.e., the risen body of Jesus). Hence, while Jesus' risen body remains absent from Mark's story, connecting the story's dots suggests that his cruciform body becomes a new temple that functions as an image/microcosm of the new creation with a redrawn (yet still purity-based) social system built into its structure.

Summary

At the end of the next chapter on the Gospel of John, we will offer a more synthetic summary that draws together the themes of that chapter as well as this one, centering on the question of what happens when holiness gets relocated in Jesus. However, it will be helpful at this point to remind ourselves briefly of the major themes relating to Jesus, holiness and God's mission that we have highlighted in this chapter.

Jesus, *the* holy one of God, entered into creation right *in the midst of impurity* and lived in such a way that he did not cordon himself off from it. As the primary locus of God's holy, beneficial presence in Mark's gospel, Jesus goes beyond symbolizing Yahweh's kingship over the cosmos as did the Temple. As the Spirit-bearing Son, with mercy and compassion, he intentionally crosses purity boundaries to channel God's holiness in a missional direction as he both announces and executes God's reign by reclaiming many for his lordship who are victims of the chaotic forces that disorder God's good creation in an attempt to keep it from reaching its intended destiny. Jesus' boundary-crossing activity also reconfigures missionally what it means to be holy at mealtime. Without regard for their purity status, Jesus ate with low status outsiders like they were *already* a part of his extended family *in order to* bring them to repentance and life. In addition, Jesus' words and actions indicate that keeping Sabbath holy includes not just participating in life-giving rest for one's self and one's community, but also engaging in healing, life-giving activity for the sake of debilitated others one might encounter on the Sabbath, so that they too may experience true Sabbath *shalom*. None of this, however, means that Jesus is unconcerned with issues of purity. Rejecting many of the specifics of existing purity maps, he redraws the lines of what counts as purity and impurity. Jesus' words and actions suggest that on his purity map, participating in just, *shalom*-restoring actions towards others and whole-hearted love/fidelity toward God makes one "pure" inside and out. This is the life pattern of Jesus himself, whose just, liberative, and *shalom*-restoring actions characterized by compassion and mercy display not just purity, but the very character of God, thereby explicating the nature of holiness in the Synoptic Gospels.

In his battle against the forces of chaos and especially in his death and resurrection, God overhauls the "holiness electrical system," reordering the cosmos itself. In raising from the dead his body that had been the moveable tabernacle housing God's holy presence, the Spirit replaces the image/

Section 2—Relocating Holiness in Jesus

microcosm of the old order (i.e., the Jerusalem Temple) with the image/microcosm of the new order (i.e., the risen body of Jesus). Hence, Christ's wound-marked, cruciform body becomes a new temple which functions as an image/microcosm of the new creation. The theme of Christ's body as a new temple with Christ's resurrection as the catalyst for a new creation is also present in other NT documents,[66] not least of which is the Gospel of John to which we now turn.

---

66. In the chapter on Paul's letters, we will also see similar conceptuality regarding the body of Christ, the new creation, and its redrawn purity map.

6

Relocating Holiness in the En-fleshed *Logos* and His En-fleshed Community

Holiness and Life in the Gospel of John

> *I have come that they may have life, and have it in profuse abundance (John 10:10).*
>
> *Sanctify them in the truth. Your Word* (logos) *is truth. (John 17:17)*

Introduction

IN THE SYNOPTIC GOSPELS, we saw that the pattern of activity that now constitutes *both* divine and human holiness is cruciform in shape and manifest in Jesus' faithfulness to the Father's life-giving, saving mission (*pistis*) expressed in costly, self-giving actions for others (*agapē*) even to the point of death. It is this missional life pattern that reconfigures holiness in such a way that Jesus turns out to be—to use Paul's language—the visible *imago Dei*, the image/*eikōn* of the unseen Holy God (Col 1:15), embodying what humanity was created to be. John's gospel differs in many ways from the other three gospels (e.g., chronological order, language and tone, a lack of parables and exorcisms, inclusion of long teaching units where it is sometimes difficult to distinguish Jesus' words from those of the narrator). John offers a rich and unique narrative Christology by weaving together a complex tapestry of images and concepts, each of which—sometimes in dizzying ways—overlaps with and helps interpret the others. Yet, there remains a conceptual pattern in the fourth gospel that is similar to what we saw in the last chapter regarding Jesus' reconfiguration of holiness in terms of a missional life pattern.[1] As we will see, that missional life pattern takes on a slightly different hue in light of John's more overt identification of Jesus with Israel's God and with life itself, depicting Jesus as the fleshly, very human embodiment of the living—and life-giving—God who tabernacles with his people.

Jesus as Divine Logos and Life Itself

Unlike the Synoptic Gospels, John's gospel does not begin in Galilee or Judea but at the very beginning of creation itself. In fact, its beginning words are the same as those in the first verse of Genesis, an early signal that in John we have to do with the beginning of a new creation.[2] Referring to Jesus as the (preexistent) Word (*logos*),[3] the first four verses explicitly locate him within the unique divine identity of Israel's God and claim that he is the very source of life itself:

> [1] In the beginning was the Word (*logos*), and the Word was with God, and the Word was God. [2] This one was with God in the beginning. [3] All things came into existence through him, and apart from him not even one thing came into existence. What has come into existence [4] in him was life, and that life was the light of all humanity (John 1:1–4).

Just as God brought all things into existence by creating life through a spoken word in Gen 1:3, John declares that all life came into being through the Word (*logos*). God's life-creating word in Genesis can be distinguished, but not separated, from God himself. When one hears the voice/word of a

---

[1]. For insightful missional readings of John that are broader in scope than the current chapter, see Flemming, *Recovering*, 113–31 and *Why Mission?* 53–71. This chapter has much in common with Michael Gorman's forthcoming *Abide and Go*, a detailed, sustained interpretation of John that focuses on participation in the missional life of the Triune God. I am grateful to him for making an early version of this work available to me.

[2]. This becomes clearer in John 20.

[3]. For a succinct discussion of the possible background(s) to this concept and the way *Logos* Christology pervades John's gospel, see Reynolds, "Logos," 523–26.

person, one hears the person herself.⁴ Similarly, God's life-creating Word in John can be distinguished from God since he was "with God" but not separated from God since he "was God."

This kind of language sounds a bit abstract and can be difficult to come to terms with, but God's audible Word—God's life-creating act of communication with God's world—is not an abstract concept. John lays any such possibility to rest in 1:14 when he says: "And the Word (*Logos*) became flesh and tabernacled (*eskēnōsen*) among us, and we beheld his glory, the glory as of the only Son from the Father, full of grace and truth." God's audible word becomes visible in the flesh of a particular Jew from Nazareth, and "[t]o become flesh is to become human, completely."⁵ Just as the glory of the Lord filled the wilderness tabernacle (*skēnē*) in Exod 40:34–35, this human being becomes the moveable, fleshly tabernacle manifesting the Father's glory. "Glory" in this sense has to do with the Father's visible splendor, "the radiance of his character, of his goodness, of who he truly is."⁶ Now, rather than being veiled by a cloud (e.g., Exod 16:10; 24:15–18; 33:18–23; 34:5–7), that visible splendor—God's holiness made visible—is located in, and *unveiled* by, human flesh. In a completely surprising and unexpected way, God takes the first step in making good on the promise in Ezekiel 37:27–28: "My dwelling place (*kataskēnōsis*) shall be with them; and I will be their God, and they shall be my people. Then the nations shall know that I the Lord sanctify Israel, when my sanctuary is among them forevermore" (NRSV). John's language and imagery suggesting that Jesus takes over the functions of the Jerusalem Temple and becomes the eschatological temple is even more pronounced than that in the Synoptic Gospels.⁷ In John, Jesus

---

4. Cf. Craig Koester, *Word of Life*, 28–29.
5. Ibid., 84.
6. Bauckham, *Gospel of Glory*, 50.
7. Jesus' claim to the Samaritan woman to be the source of a "spring of water surging up to the life of the new age" (4:14) and then connecting himself to "rivers of living water" (7:37–39) in the Temple during the feast of tabernacles also connects him with Temple imagery. For example, note the river making life possible in the sanctuary of Eden (Gen 2:10–14), the life-giving river flowing from the expected eschatological temple in the OT (Ezek 47:1–12; Joel 3:18; cf. Zech 14:8), and "the river of the water of life" flowing from the throne of God and the Lamb in Revelation's new creation, the whole of which is God's sanctuary/temple (Rev 22:1). Cf. Beale and Kim, *God Dwells Among Us*, 86. For a more detailed treatment of the way Jesus takes over the functions of the Temple in John, see Kerr, *Temple of Jesus' Body*; Perrin, *Jesus the Temple*, 53–55. On the way that water imagery in John also identifies Jesus with Israel's God himself, see Crutcher, *That He Might Be Revealed*.

Section 2—Relocating Holiness in Jesus

is clearly depicted as the moveable tabernacle of the Father's glory whose very body is the temple/sanctuary (*naos*), the Holy of Holies housing the presence of the holy God (2:19–21).

Taking up Israel's mandate as the obedient Son, Jesus is in intimate relationship with the Father (10:30, 38). He is sanctified/set apart by the Father and sent into the world (10:36). As the Son who is "close to the Father's heart," he reveals the Father's character (1:18); and therefore, as "the Holy One of God" (6:69), he reveals the nature of holiness itself. John's gospel tells the story of the Father sanctifying/setting apart the Son and sending him into the world to engage in a pattern of saving, life-giving activity ("the works of my Father") that expresses the essence of the Father's life-giving, holy character (10:36–38).

In this gospel, that pattern of saving activity is so focused on giving life to the world that Jesus can summarize his mission as: "I have come that they may have life, and have it in profuse abundance" (John 10:10). Or, to quote a very familiar passage from John:

> And just as Moses lifted up the snake in the wilderness, so also must this Human One[8] be lifted up so that everyone who believes in him may have *the life of the new age*. For God so loved the world that he gave his one and only Son so that everyone who believes into him may not perish but have *the life of the new age*. (3:14–16).

Most will have expected to hear the words "eternal life" rather than "the life of the new age" as I have translated the underlying Greek phrase above. The life of the new age is indeed life that never ends, but just referring to it as "eternal life" sometimes generates visions of an everlasting, disembodied, wispy type of never ending life "up in heaven."[9] The type of life Jesus is referring to here, however, is a new quality of life in the present that requires a "(new) birth from above" (3:3, 5) because it transforms our fundamental allegiances to begin aligning us with the sort of never-ending life that will characterize creation when it reaches its goal.[10] That life is far from an individualized version of a disembodied soul knocking on the pearly

---

8. Like the CEB, I have translated the more familiar phrase, "Son of Man," with the phrase "Human One" because I am convinced that the intent of the underlying Greek phrase (*ho hyios tou Theou*) is to emphasize the true humanity of Jesus (on which see below).

9. John, in fact, never explicitly says that heaven is the place people go when they die, or for that matter, when Jesus raises them on the last day.

10. Cf. the similar comments of Middleton, *New Heaven*, 246.

gates. It is the full-bodied, abundant and flourishing, Spirit-saturated life of *shalom* that pervades the new creation where diverse people are reconciled to, and in intimate relationship with, God and one another.[11] In John, those who are joined to the life-giving vine as fruit-bearing branches (15:1–2) already have this life of the new age, and even death cannot cut them off from it because they have "passed from death to life" (5:24). Their intimate knowledge of "the only true God, and Jesus Christ" whom the Father sent (17:3) transforms their allegiances and priorities and aligns them with the life of *shalom of* the coming new creation. However, they must still await Jesus to "raise them up on the last day" (6:54, 44) to finally share the life of *shalom in* that Spirit-saturated new creation where their knowledge of God reaches an even higher level of intimacy when they see God's face in the full sense that Moses could not (Rev 22:4).[12] In short, "abundant life," "life," or "eternal life/life of the new age" in John is "the renewal of the whole of life through participation in the divine life."[13]

Jesus' mission matches his person because he is the embodiment of life itself. He is "the bread of life" (6:35, 48), "the resurrection and the life" (11:25), "the way, the truth and the life" (14:6). Since the Father has granted him to have life in himself (5:26; cf. 1:4), he is the one who will raise the dead (5:25–29; 6:39–40, 44, 54) and is thus able to grant the life of the new age (6:27, 33; 17:2). His mission of bringing life to the world is graphically illustrated in the "signs" of the healing of the royal official's son in 4:46–54 ("Your son *will live*."), healing a paralyzed man (5:2–9), giving bread to a crowd of hungry people (6:1–15), restoring the sight of a blind man (9:1–12), and raising Lazarus from the dead (11:1–44).[14] Since Jesus

---

11. We more fully discuss this way of characterizing the new creation in the chapter on the Book of Revelation.

12. In alluding to Revelation here, I am not suggesting that it and the Fourth Gospel have a common author nor even that the gospel's author would necessarily have described things the way I am doing here (although I doubt he would have objected). I am simply reading John's gospel as part of a canon of Scripture with the way that canon ends in mind.

13. Bauckham, *Gospel of Glory*, 71. Cf. Thompson's description of the multiple connotations of "abundant life" in John: "It looks back toward creation; it anticipates the blessings of the new life of the resurrection, especially the blessing of being in the divine presence; and it lies at the intersection of past and future, while in the present it offers communion with the living God" (*John*, 91).

14. Since death is at work not only at the final moment of one's last breath, but in ways that impair life being experienced to the full, one can see how the feeding of the five thousand signaling Jesus as the "bread of life" (6:1–15) and these healings are signs of the

Section 2—Relocating Holiness in Jesus

is "the Holy One of God" (6:68–69), and death and the impurity associated with it is the antonym of holiness, it is fitting that he embodies life itself. Indeed, it is because Jesus speaks words of the life of the new age that his disciples know him to be "the Holy One of God" (6:68–69).

Divine Glory, Love, and the Death of Jesus

We saw earlier that in the OT Yahweh's glory is itself a visible manifestation of his holiness (e.g., Lev. 10:3), and just above we noted that the glory on display in the *Logos* is the visible splendor of God, "the radiance of his character, of his goodness, of who he truly is."[15] Hence, to behold the glory of the *Logos* (1:14) who was "with God" and "was God" was to catch a glimpse of the holiness of God, the "radiance of his character, of his goodness, of who he truly is."[16] It was to see the life-giving power and presence of the Holy God revealed in human flesh. One important way in which the disciples behold this divine glory revealed in Jesus is as he is engaged in "the works of [the] Father" (10:37). These "works" are broader than, but do include, Jesus' miraculous "signs," beginning with his turning water into wine which "revealed his glory" (2:11). In the raising of Lazarus, in particular, one can see the "glory of God" (11:40), the powerful life-giving presence and action of the Holy God in the human flesh of the Son (11:40). Because of their miraculous character and because they were signs of the abundant life of the new age that Jesus had come to give,[17] all of Jesus' signs "revealed his glory"—and thus, the glory of God—to those who saw him in the flesh. Seeing Jesus' glory, then, was to catch a glimpse of divine holiness made visible as a pattern of life-giving, redemptive activity as he went about doing "the works of the Father." It is, however, a risky pattern of activity that inexorably leads to his death, as becomes evident in the aftermath of the penultimate sign of his raising Lazarus from the dead (11:46–53).

---

abundant life of the new age (cf. Bauckham, *Gospel of Glory*, 71–72).

15. Bauckham, *Gospel of Glory*, 50.

16. Ibid.

17. The connection of the sign at the wedding in Cana with the life of the new age may need clarification. By providing fine wine in abundance, Jesus saves a family from social humiliation and enhances fellowship, thereby enhancing life at the celebration. In addition, the wedding feast itself points toward the abundant life of the new age in that it anticipates Isaiah's eschatological banquet (25:6–8) which includes "a feast of well-aged wines" and takes place on the same mountain where God "will swallow up death forever" (Bauckham, *Gospel of Glory*, 71–72).

"Glory" in John's gospel also has another important meaning quite at home in his first-century context. It can mean "honor" or "praise" that one gives out to others or receives from them. In engaging in this missional life-giving pattern of activity, Jesus does not seek his own glory (honor or praise) but seeks the glory (honor or praise) of the One who sent him (7:18). That is, by engaging in the mission which the Father has given him to do, Jesus seeks to glorify the Father in the sense of bringing honor to him. Hence, at one and the same time these very God-centered actions not only embody God's glory (visible splendor/holiness) in human flesh, they also bring glory (honor) to God and result in Jesus, the one who models what true humanity is, receiving glory (honor) from God.[18]

These ways of understanding "glory" in John's gospel come together and overlap when Jesus is "glorified" by being "lifted up"/"exalted" on the cross,[19] raised from the dead, and then ascends to the Father. This single trajectory composed of three distinguishable events (suffering/crucifixion, resurrection, and ascension) is the pathway on which Jesus "goes to the Father" in John's gospel, the pathway of his being "glorified." While Jesus is glorified in each of these events, John places most emphasis on the first, the moment of suffering, shame and humiliation on the cross as— paradoxically—a moment of glory. As such, Jesus' crucifixion stamps the whole trajectory with the shape of the cross, imprinting divine glory with a cruciform character. Hence, a key moment in which the audience sees Jesus' glory—God's holiness made visible—is as he, the truly Human One, is physically elevated or "lifted up" on the cross:

> And just as Moses lifted up the snake in the wilderness, so also must this *Human One* be *lifted up* so that everyone who believes into him may have the life of the new age (3:14–15).
>
> Jesus answered them, "The hour has come for the *Human One* to be *glorified*. Truly I tell you, unless a grain of wheat falls into the earth and dies, it remains a single grain. But if it dies, it bears much fruit.... And I, when I am *lifted up* from the earth, will draw all to myself." He was saying this to signify what sort of death he was going to die (12:23–24, 32–33).

---

18. Cf. Bauckham, *Gospel of Glory*, 57–61.

19. There is debate as to whether "lifted up"/"exalted" refers only to the crucifixion (e.g., Koester, *Word of Life*, 122) or to both the crucifixion and Jesus' exaltation/ascension to the Father (e.g., Bauckham, *Gospel of Glory*, 73). For our purposes, we need not take a position on the issue.

Section 2—Relocating Holiness in Jesus

As I said earlier, I have translated the more familiar phrase, "Son of Man," with the phrase "Human One" because I am convinced that the intent of the underlying Greek phrase (*ho hyios tou Theou*) is to emphasize the true humanity of Jesus; it is not a way of emphasizing his deity. The phrase communicates that Jesus is the prototypical human being, the "last Adam," to use Paul's language (1 Cor 15:45), the one who fulfills "God's design for humanity as God's coworker, vice regent."[20] By being "lifted up" on the cross as the visible result of unbelief and sin, the "sort of death" that this truly Human One dies takes away the sin of the world—the enslaving antipathy toward God leading to death (8:24)—transforming it into faith by drawing all to God and thus to the life of the new age itself (3:16; 6:44), the final goal of creation.[21] Craig Koester's elaboration of the connection between the story in Numbers 21 and John 3:14–15 illuminates this point:

> [B]oth episodes show God transforming the visible result of sin into a means of giving life. In the Old Testament story, Moses puts a bronze serpent on a pole so that people can see it. When they turn to the serpent on the pole, they are confronted with what is killing them. Yet in so doing they receive life by being restored to health (Num 21:9). In John's gospel it is Jesus who hangs on the pole or cross. When people turn to him they are confronted with the results of the sin that is killing them. Yet as they turn to the crucified Jesus, they receive eternal life.[22]

This one who somehow is the presence of the holy God is at the same time the one true human in whom God is realizing his dream of bringing creation to its final goal of flourishing with life. This selfless, life-giving death he dies is the pinnacle of his seeking God's glory (honor) rather than his own, the means by which the Father is "glorified" (17:1, 4–5; 13:31–32). At the same time, it is the apex of his revelation of God's glory (visible splendor/holiness) in human flesh. This is because Jesus' profound act of selfless human love both honors God and reveals the depths of divine love at the very heart of who God is. In the words of Koester, "If glory defines

---

20. Hastings, *Missional God, Missional Church*, 310.
21. For a clear and concise description of the nature of sin in John's gospel, see Koester, *Word of Life*, 65–74.
22. Ibid., 45.

what the crucifixion is, the crucifixion defines what glory is. The crucifixion manifests the scope of divine power by disclosing the depth of divine love."[23]

We have already seen that the catalyst for the Father's sending of the Son to bring life was the love of God for the world (3:16). Not surprisingly, Jesus' voluntary act of laying down his life for his friends (15:13) not only delivers his flock from death (10:11–18) and displays his glory/visible holiness as a pattern of redemptive, life-giving activity; it is also the consummate demonstration of love. We see this encapsulated first in the Lazarus story and then fleshed out in more detail in the rest of the gospel. While Jesus knows that his going back to Jerusalem to raise Lazarus will both honor God and display God's glory (11:4), he is also fully aware that it will lead to his death (11:7–16). But out of love for Lazarus and his sisters, Jesus goes anyway, forcing the hand of the high priest and his council (11:45–53) and in effect, laying down his own life for his friend. As Jesus stands weeping at the tomb, "the Jews" rightly say, "See how he loved him" (11:36).[24] After Jesus raises Lazarus, delivering him (at least temporarily) from death as a manifestation of God's glory (11:40), in what follows in the rest of the gospel, John portrays Jesus' death as the consummate demonstration of *complete/perfect* love.

In chapters 13–17 Jesus shares a final meal with his disciples and prepares them for his departure. John introduces that section in 13:1 in this way:

> Now before the festival of Passover, Jesus knew that his hour had arrived for him to depart from this world and go to the Father. Having loved his own in the world, he loved them completely/to the end (*eis telos*).

The Greek phrase in parentheses can have two meanings at once, something that happens often in John's gospel. It can mean that Jesus loved his disciples perfectly/completely and that he loved them to the very end of his life. That Jesus does both becomes evident first in the story of the washing of his disciples' feet and then in the narration of his death. To describe the foot washing (13:2–20) with appropriate Pauline language from Phil 2:6–8, this one who was "in the form of God" essentially "poured himself out by taking the form of a slave . . . and humbled himself" by doing something

---

23. Ibid., 122.
24. On this aspect of the Lazarus story, see Bauckham, *Gospel of Glory*, 66–67.

Section 2—Relocating Holiness in Jesus

that one would only do for oneself or have a slave do; he washed his disciples' dirty, smelly feet (graciously including those feet he knew would soon run off to betray him [13:27]!). The implication is that this self-lowering, extremely scandalous action parabolically displays what loving completely/perfectly (*eis telos*) looks like in practice and thus offers the disciples an example (13:15) that they are to replicate in their life together (more on the imitation of Christ a bit later). This demonstration of perfect love continues in his "obedience to the point of death" and foreshadows his ultimate act of self-giving on a scandalous cross:

> After this, when Jesus knew that all was now finished/completed (*tetelestai*), in order that the Scripture might be completed, he said, "I am thirsty." . . . Then when Jesus received the wine he said, "It is finished/completed (*tetelestai*)." And after bowing his head, he handed over the Spirit (19:28, 30).

Jesus' voluntary status-lowering, self-giving actions of obediently pouring himself out for the sake of the particular historical persons who were close to him (and for the sake of the whole world, as 3:16 makes very clear) is finished/completed at his death.[25] Hence, his death is the culminating demonstration of perfect/complete love (cf. 15:12–13) that gives a particular shape to divine glory, the visible manifestation of holiness.

In John's gospel, then, divine glory has a cruciform shape that explicates divine holiness in terms of the depths of divine love. It may surprise us to find out that the disciples themselves—in all their humanity—are granted a share in this very divine glory (17:22). Participating in this glory means that their corporate life together as well as their individual lives must take a similar cruciform shape that will explicate divine holiness in term of the depths of the divine love that they themselves have experienced. This divine love is to be mirrored in relationships in human communities (13:34–35; 15:12–17) and replicated in missional patterns of redemptive activity for the world God loves.[26]

---

25. "In Jesus' love for his friends God's love took human, historical form in order to embrace the world" (Bauckham, *Gospel of Glory*, 69).

26. For further development of the claim in this sentence, see Gorman, *Abide and Go*.

The Sanctified Community in Union with God and One Another Engaged in Mission

In Jesus' "high priestly prayer" in John 17, Jesus prays for the sanctification of his disciples who have been gathered together since he washed their feet in chapter 13. In John's gospel the verbal form of "sanctify" is only used in 10:36 and in this high priestly prayer in 17:17–19. The context of 10:36 is that of a dispute with "the Jews"[27] over what they perceive as Jesus' blasphemy for claiming a unity with the Father:

> Are you all saying that the one whom the Father *sanctified* and sent into the world is blaspheming because I said, "I am God's Son?" If I'm not doing the works of my Father, then don't believe me. But if I am doing them, even if you don't believe me, believe the works so that you might come to know and recognize that the Father is in me and I am in the Father (10:36–38).

In this context the Father's sanctification of the Son refers to the latter's being set apart as the personal agent of God's life-giving mission to the world. As the "the Holy One of God" whom the Father has set apart and granted to have life in himself (5:26; cf. 1:4), his mission flows directly from his person.

In his prayer for the disciples, Jesus echoes this language in 17:15–19:

> I'm not asking that you take them out of the world, but that you guard them from the evil one. They don't belong to the world just as I don't belong to the world. *Sanctify* them in the truth. Your Word/word (*logos*) is truth. Just as you sent me into the world, I also have sent them into the world. And on their behalf *I am going to sanctify myself*,[28] so that they also might *become and remain sanctified*[29] in truth.

---

27. Both Jesus—not to mention all his disciples—and his opponents in this passage are Jews who share the same religious heritage. To use passages like this, then, to demonize Jewish people in general in the name of Christ is actually to share the spirit of the antichrist (cf. Koester, *Word of Life*, 76).

28. I have translated the Greek verb *hagiazō* as a futuristic present to underscore that it is Jesus' *ensuing actions* in John's story that explicate what Jesus means with regard to sanctifying himself.

29. John uses a particular Greek construction (a perfect periphrastic) to underscore not just an initial action of being set apart but its ongoing reality. Hence, the translation of "become and remain."

Section 2—Relocating Holiness in Jesus

In John, "the world" has two significant dimensions. On the one hand, the world is under the control of sin, death, and the "evil one," and therefore is in rebellion against God. Used in this sense, neither Jesus nor the disciples "belong to the world." Those gathered around Jesus do not belong to the world in its rebellion against God because they already have begun to share the life of the new age with transformed priorities and allegiances; they have already passed from death to life (5:24). Like Jesus, they are "hated" and opposed by "the world" (17:14). At the same time, "the world" remains the object of God's love (3:16), the object of the Father and Son's life-giving mission—even as it is in rebellion against God (cf. Rom 5:8–10).[30]

Here Jesus prays that just as the Father had sanctified him and sent him into that world, he would also sanctify his disciples, setting them apart *from* the world as instruments for God's life-giving mission *in* that same world. In the logic of the passage, the means through which the Father sanctifies them is Jesus' imminent self-sanctification/consecration (17:19) which begins when he allows himself to be arrested, effectively setting himself apart as a sacrifice, i.e., the Lamb of God who "takes away the Sin of the world" (1:29).[31] As we noted above, in taking away the enslaving antipathy toward God leading to death (8:24) and transforming it into faith by drawing all to God, on the cross he draws all to the life characteristic of the new age (3:16; 6:44). Like the death of the Passover lamb (see below), this culminating act of costly love issues in life in Johannine terms (3:14–17; 6:47–51; 10:17–18, 27–28). And in this context, it also provides the grounds and ultimate means of the disciples becoming and remaining sanctified (i.e., set apart as instruments for God's life-giving mission). In a section below, we will return to the imagery of the Passover lamb and explain more fully how Jesus' self-sanctification provides such grounds and means for his disciples' sanctification. But before that, we will focus on another portion of Jesus' prayer that clarifies certain aspects of what Jesus means by asking the Father to sanctify his disciples.

In 17:20–23 other aspects of the disciples becoming and remaining sanctified come to the fore, without which engaging in God's life-giving mission could not get underway. Here Jesus continues his prayer in this way:

> I'm not asking for the sake of these [disciples] only, but also for the sake of the ones who are going to believe *into (eis) me* through

---

30. On "the world" in John's gospel, see Koester, *Word of Life*, 80–81.
31. Cf. the similar line of interpretation in Bauckham, "Holiness of Jesus," 108–12.

their word. [I'm asking] that they all may be *one*. Just as you, Father, are in me and I in you, may they also be *in (en) us* so that the world may believe that you have sent me. The *glory* which you have given to me, I have given to them so that *they may be one just as we are one, I in (en) them* and you in me so that they may be *completely one* in order that the world might know that you have sent me and *loved them just as you have loved me.*

This is rather remarkable language. It suggests that "believing" as it relates to Jesus is more than simply believing a proposition, or for that matter, more than simply trusting Jesus for everlasting life, although it certainly includes both. Rather, here "believing" transfers people "into" Jesus himself (cf. believe into [*eis*] in Gal 2:16) in a way that they now share in, and are a part of, his very person (cf. 15:4–5). But at the same time, he also inhabits them ("I in them," cf. 15:4–5), both individually and as a unified corporate body ("completely one"). In addition, since Jesus is in the Father and the Father in him, being in Jesus and having Jesus in them can only mean that the disciples are also "in" both the Father and the Son ("in us").

Theologians draw from such language to speak about *theosis* or deification, becoming like God.[32] Broadly speaking, *theosis* is that process in which humans become like God by participating in God's own life, thereby taking on certain attributes of God. Humans do not cease being creatures in this process nor somehow lose their personal identity by being absorbed into God's being. But, *at God's initiative* (e.g., 15:16), they really come to share in at least some of God's attributes, including at the very least, God's *holiness and immortality*.[33] As this language suggests, the disciples' goal to become and remain sanctified includes participating in the life of the Father and the Son as they also share intimate life with one another in a unified corporate body. Here sanctification *assumes a corporate framework*; it is not something that happens to isolated individuals. In Johannine logic, participating in the life of the Father and Son entails experiencing their mutual love for each other that spills over into their love for those who believe

---

32. We are only offering a minimal, quite general, definition of the *theme* of *theosis* in this section. The *doctrine* of deification/theosis developed especially by Eastern Orthodoxy is more complex (cf. Barbarick, "'You Shall Be Holy,'" 289–90). For a development of the theme in this context of Jesus' high priestly prayer, see Brower, *Holiness in the Gospels*, 74–76. On *theosis* more broadly in John, see Gorman, *Abide and Go*. For more general introductions to the theme, see Finlan and Kharlamov, *Theōsis*; Christensen and Wittung, *Partakers*.

33. Cf. the comments of Gorman, "Romans," 16–18.

Section 2—Relocating Holiness in Jesus

"into" Jesus. And that love spills over into, and characterizes, the relationships between those who are "in Jesus" (13:34–35; 15:12–17). As we saw earlier, such intimate knowledge of, and participation in the Father and the Son *in the present* is a real anticipation of the everlasting life of the new age that is characterized by the intimacy of seeing God face to face and sharing in reconciled, intimate relationships with others. Hence, it is already an anticipatory—and very real—taste of God's own immortality that those who believe "into Jesus" will finally and fully share *in* the new creation.

But becoming and remaining sanctified means that the love that characterizes this community must also spill over into the world itself since it was God's own love for the world that was the catalyst for the sending of the Son (3:16) and these sanctified disciples are being sent into the world just as he was. Indeed, according to Jesus' prayer, the very purpose of his disciples sharing in the life of the Father and the Son is "so that the world may believe that you have sent me." And Jesus goes on immediately to say, "The glory which you have given to me, I have given to them." This divine glory—the visible manifestation of the holiness of God—that characterizes the Son must also characterize the community of those who are in the Father and the Son. And that glory is most fully seen in Jesus' costly status-lowering, self-giving actions of obediently pouring himself out for the world in life-giving mission, most especially as he is "lifted up" on the cross as a demonstration of perfect/complete love. Hence, the disciples' sanctification means sharing in divine glory that has a cruciform shape and explicates divine holiness in terms of the depths of a divine love enacted in life-giving mission for the whole world. Ultimately, in becoming and remaining sanctified, the disciples are set apart *from* the world to become instruments for God's life-giving mission *in* and *for* that same world. By visibly practicing cruciform love for each other that illustrates their unity with God and each other, their communal life exhibits the power of divine love to a self-absorbed, ethnically divided—often violently so—world, whether that of the first century or today.[34] As Flemming aptly states, "Here the church's union with the triune God and with one another leans outward."[35] Such communal life, especially when accompanied by loving acts toward those outside the community, tends to have the effect of drawing others to experience the love God exhibited for the world in the sending of the Son.

---

34. On the missional effect of practicing love and oneness, see esp. Flemming, *Recovering*, 122–23; Flemming, *Why Mission*, 67–68.

35. Ibid., 67.

We may now be better able to see what Jesus means when he asks the Father to sanctify the disciples "in the truth" and then immediately declares "your Word/word (*logos*) is truth" (17:17). Jesus, the Word (*logos*), is not only the embodiment of life in John's gospel but also the embodiment of truth (14:6). He is indeed "the way, the truth, and the life," claiming that "no one comes (*erchetai*) to the Father except through me" (14:6). Hence, his whole cruciform way of life is what constitutes truth. Dare we say, it is the ultimate truth about what both true divinity and true humanity looks like, as opposed to the lie that the Devil has been telling since the beginning (8:44)? In any case, it is that way of life that he is about to model in a paradigmatic, act of self-sanctification that culminates on the cross. That cruciform way is the way through which Jesus himself must pass in going (*erchomai*) to the Father (17:11, 13) when he ascends after the resurrection (20:17). Hence, when Jesus asks the Father to sanctify the disciples "in the truth," he is asking the Father to set them apart and immerse them in the way of the cross that engenders life for others, the way of life that explicates both the true character of God and God's truly human image.[36] Clearly, immersion in such a way of life will require a transformation of the disciples' hearts and lives, including a cleansing from sin. Hence, the language of sanctification here presumes not just a "setting apart" but an inner and outer transformation—something like a new birth/birth from above.[37] Such transformation may be a necessary prerequisite of engaging in this cruciform missional way of life (as perhaps implied in 13:10). However, the Father's immersion of the disciples into this cruciform missional way of life may itself be the means of the disciples' *ongoing* transformation.

It is important to recognize that Jesus uses the active voice to speak about "sanctifying himself" whereas the disciples are not the active agents of their sanctification. The Father sets them apart and immerses them in this cruciform, missional way of life. This is indeed *imitatio Christi* (imitation of Christ) which, because the Son and the Father are one, is also *imitatio Dei* (imitation of God). It is to be holy as God himself is holy. But, as Gorman insists, "John does not present us merely with an ethic of commandment and imitation. It is better described as a spirituality of mutual indwelling

---

36. The latter is suggested by Pilate's pregnant statement as Jesus stands before him *on his way to the cross* for others: "Behold the Human One" (19:5). The former is expressed by Thomas' confession *on the basis of the cruciform marks* of the risen Son's body: "My Lord and my God!" (20:28).

37. Cf. Flemming, *Why Mission*, 68–69.

that makes possible the fulfilling of the obligation of imitation."[38] In other words, being sanctified in this sense is connected with the language of *theosis* to which we referred earlier. It is to be immersed by God into a process in which the disciples become like God by participating in God's own life-giving missional life, inhabiting and being inhabited by the particular God revealed now as cruciform.

The Life-Giving Spirit and Jesus' Death, Resurrection, and Ascension

To use the language of "being inhabited by God" assumes the third person of the Trinity, and to this point we have scarcely mentioned the Spirit. Although Jesus' baptism is not narrated in John's gospel, John the Baptist testifies that he has seen the Spirit descend *and remain* upon Jesus (1:32–34). In that scene, the Spirit comes primarily to reveal to John the Baptist who Jesus is, not to give Jesus divine power that he lacked.[39] However, as in the Synoptic Gospels, the language ("and remain on him") makes it clear that Jesus is inhabited by the life-giving Spirit throughout the gospel to the very point of his death when he "handed over the Spirit (19:30)." It is this same Holy Spirit that Jesus promises the Father will send in his name (14:26) or that he himself will send from the Father to his disciples (15:26). But this would only happen after Jesus was glorified (7:39)—after the single trajectory of Jesus "going to the Father" in his crucifixion, resurrection, and ascension. Jesus' "going to the Father" is the basis of the disciples becoming participants in his life-giving mission: "Very truly I say to you, the one who believes into me will do the works I am doing and will do even greater works than these[40] *because I am going to the Father*" (14:12). Hence, we are prepared for the connection John will make in chapter 20 between the risen Son's ascension to the Father and his bestowal of the Spirit on the disciples to equip them for participating in the life-giving mission of the Father and the Son. It is important to trace the way John leads up to that scene in the way that he narrates the death and resurrection of Jesus.

At his death John says that Jesus "bowed his head and handed over the Spirit (19:30)." As in the Synoptic Gospels, when the Son embraces death as the ultimate impurity, the Spirit exits his human body, but only so that this

---

38. Gorman, *Death of the Messiah*, 47.
39. Koester, *Word of Life*, 136.
40. Greater in number and range of location; cf. Thompson, *John*, 312.

same Spirit—whom Ezekiel had foreseen raising a dead, lifeless Israel in the valley of dry bones—would be freed to rush in and raise that very body from the dead.[41] Before we get to that part of the story, John's description of what happens immediately after Jesus dies is worth a brief exploration. Because the Jews did not want crucified bodies left on the cross over the Passover Sabbath, they asked Pilate to have the legs of those crucified broken so that they would die quickly and their bodies could be removed from the crosses (19:31–32). But since Jesus was already dead, they did not break his legs and John tells us what happens next:

> [34] Instead, one of the soldiers pierced his side with a spear, and immediately blood and water came out.... [36] For these things happened in order that the Scripture might be fulfilled (or filled with significance): "Not a bone of him will be broken." [37] And again, another Scripture says: "They will look on him whom they have pierced" (19:34, 36–37).

It is clear that John depicts Jesus' death as the death of the Passover Lamb since he is handed over to die at the very moment the slaughter of the Passover lambs begins (19:14–16) and he dies before sundown (19:31). In addition, the Scripture passage quoted in 19:36 comes from Exod 12:10 (LXX) (cf. Num 9:12), which refers to not breaking the bones of the Passover lamb.[42] Passover lambs do not necessarily function as a sin offering. Rather, their blood is used to signify the setting apart of a distinct/holy people who are delivered from slavery/death. Hence, first and foremost, the blood from the side of Jesus signifies that Jesus' willing embrace of death sets apart and gives life to others by delivering them from death (cf. 10:11–15). And yet, as we have seen, deliverance from death in John takes place by "the Lamb of God *taking away the Sin* of the world" (1:29) because sin is the enslav-

---

41. Once again, we need to be clear that in John's account, as in the Synoptic Gospels and much of the NT, the Spirit is not explicitly said to be the one who raises Jesus from the dead. In fact, Jesus' words in 2:19 and his claim to "have power (*exousia*) to take it (his life/*psychē*) up again" (10:17–18) might seem to indicate that he was the agent of his own resurrection. However, Jesus' earlier words in 6:63 that "it is the Spirit who makes alive" may suggest that the Spirit is the "power (*exousia*)" through which Jesus is enabled to take his life up again (cf. 1 Cor 6:14; Rom 6:4). Hence, it is not a large leap to imagine the Spirit as the agent through whom the Father raises Jesus in John. For further reflections along these lines in a wider biblical context, see my *1 & 2 Thessalonians*, 308–12.

42. John also uses suffering servant imagery from Isa 52:13—53:12 to depict the significance of Jesus' death (on which, see Bauckham, *Gospel of Glory*, 53–55) and portrays him as the paradigmatic righteous sufferer of Psalms (Ps 22:19 in John 19:24; Ps 69:22 in 19:28–29; Ps 34:19–20 in 19:36).

Section 2—Relocating Holiness in Jesus

ing antipathy toward God that leads to death (8:24). Hence, the sacrifice of Jesus as a Passover lamb who gives life by delivering from death is, in Johannine logic, also a sacrifice that removes sin as an enslaving power.[43]

The imagery of the water that flows from Jesus' side may also signify this aspect of Jesus' death, especially in light of the explicit connection made in v. 37 to Zech 12:10. Whoever is said to be pierced in the original context of this passage in Zechariah,[44] in the verses that follow, the inhabitants of Jerusalem appear to have been the ones who did the piercing and then mourn over what they have done (vv. 11–14). But then we hear good news from Zechariah: "On that day a fountain shall be opened for the house of David and the inhabitants of Jerusalem, *to cleanse them from sin and impurity*" (13:1). Taking into consideration this larger context of Zechariah, we may conclude that the water that flows from the side of this Holy One of God signifies a fountain cleansing away sin and impurity, both of which are on the side of, or lead to, death in John's gospel. Such cleansing that flows from the Holy One of God's embracing of death's ultimate impurity results in life flowing to others. This imagery of life flowing to others also prompts us to recall John's earlier connection between Jesus giving living water gushing up to the life of the new age (4:10, 14) and the life-giving Spirit to be given as a result of Jesus' glorification (7:37–39).[45] All of these images (Passover Lamb, cleansing fountain of water, the life-giving Spirit as living water) converge in this context to underscore the death of Jesus as the key beginning moment in his being glorified in order to bring life to a world gripped by darkness, sin, and death.

We dare not forget that the Holy One of God brings this life to the world precisely by allowing himself to be gripped by the darkest darkness of the tomb, by the sin enslaving those who nail him to the cross, and by death itself as the ultimate impurity. If, however, this cruciform obedience

---

43. Even if there are echoes of the suffering servant of Isaiah 53 who is likened to a lamb led to slaughter bearing the sins (plural) of many, John's presentation of the significance of Jesus' death differs significantly from the view that Jesus dies as a sacrifice that pays the penalty for individual human sins in a way that satisfies divine justice or placates divine anger (Koester, *Word of Life*, 115–17).

44. This is a complex and difficult issue involving first choosing what Hebrew text to translate and then how to translate the particular Hebrew text one has chosen. In John, however, Jesus is clearly the one who is pierced and thus understood (in some way) to be the referent of the Zechariah text.

45. I take the referent of one from whom rivers of living water flow in 7:38 to be Jesus rather than the one who believes in him (so Lincoln, *Gospel*, 255). For the alternative view, see Thompson, *John*, 175–76.

culminating in death is the end of the story, the world remains gripped by darkness, sin, and death. When we come to the end of chapter 19, this is what seems to be the case. All we have is a body wrapped in grave clothes that are scented with one hundred pounds of spices to ward off the stench of decay (19:39–42). The darkness seems to have overcome the light of the world because the one who is the resurrection and the life lies dead in the deep darkness and impurity of the tomb. But we know the rest of the story. We know that Mary Magdalene comes to the tomb "early on the first day of the week" (20:1), a signal that we as readers are to be on the lookout for signs of the new creation. With the stone rolled away, all Mary can do is draw what seems to be an obvious conclusion: a grave robbery has occurred and someone has taken Jesus' corpse (20:2). We also know that Peter and the beloved disciple discover the tomb to be empty with the grave clothes neatly folded, which at least seems to preclude a grave robbery and is the catalyst for the beloved disciple believing, although it is not clear exactly what he believes (20:3–10). Surprisingly, unlike in the Synoptic Gospels, there are no heavenly messengers announcing that Jesus has been raised from the dead. Or are there?

There are indeed angels in the tomb, but they apparently arrive after Peter and the beloved disciple go home. However, when Mary encounters them, they are effectively mute, just asking a silly question about why she is crying but not announcing a thing (20:11–13). And yet, while they say nothing of any consequence, their very presence and posture speaks volumes. Dressed in white and sitting silently at the head and foot of where Jesus' body had been placed, these essentially mute angels form the shape of the cherubim throne atop the Ark of the Covenant, the symbol of the Holy God's most focused presence during Israel's wanderings. Their silent testimony affirms that through his life-giving Spirit, the Father has been at work in this most unclean of places in raising the Son from the dead. Rather than being contaminated by death's impurity, the Holy One of God, the resurrection and the life, crosses the boundary into death defeating it from the inside out. In the resurrection of the Holy One of God—another key moment in Jesus being glorified in order to bring life to the world—the Triune God has swallowed up death and been enthroned in its very presence.

As one of the flock that belongs to the good shepherd who has laid down his life for his sheep (10:11–15), Mary recognizes the voice of that shepherd when he calls her by name (20:16; cf. 10:3–4). Although she wants to hold onto him, he tells her to stop clinging to him because he has "not

Section 2—Relocating Holiness in Jesus

yet ascended to the Father" and then orders her to go and tell his "brothers" that he is "going to ascend to my Father and your Father, my God and your God" (20:17). When the succeeding scene in 20:19–23 takes place, the clear implication is that he has indeed ascended to the Father—the final key moment in Jesus being glorified in order to bring life to the world.

> [19] Now, when it was evening *on that first day of the week*, and the doors were locked where the disciples were because they feared the Jews, Jesus came and stood in their midst and said to them, "*Shalom/Peace* to you all." [20] And after he said this, *he showed them his hands and side*. Then the disciples rejoiced when they saw the Lord. [21] Jesus said to them again, "*Shalom/Peace* to you all. Just as the Father has sent me, so I am sending you all." [22] And when he said this, *he breathed on them* and said, "Receive the Holy Spirit. [23] If you forgive the sins of any, they are forgiven them; if you retain them, they are retained."

Although the text does not explicitly mention Jesus' ascension, the movement of the narrative indicates that Jesus has ascended to the Father in order to become the conduit of the life-giving Spirit which he receives from the Father and had promised to send to his disciples. It is only by virtue of receiving the life-giving Spirit that comes from the Father through the Son that the disciples are sanctified; they are set apart and enabled to participate in the Triune God's life-giving mission to the world. Because his act of self-sanctification in his suffering and crucifixion is the key beginning moment of the Son's going to the Father to become the purveyor of the sanctifying Spirit, it is indeed the ground of, and ultimate means of, the Father sanctifying the disciples.

Before Jesus offers the Spirit to his disciples, however, he engages in two actions: the double offering of *shalom*/peace and the exhibition of his wounds. The latter is sandwiched between Jesus' first offering of *shalom* to his disciples and the second. Rather than coming with condemnation on his lips for the disciples' abandoning him in his arrest and death, Jesus comes with open arms that embody human and divine reconciliation, speaking words of peace that imply that the disciples are forgiven even before they ask to be. Jesus' showing his disciples the marks of his wounds in his hands and side may indeed constitute evidence for belief that Jesus is risen. But, *in light of the resurrection*—probably the seventh of the gospel's seven signs (2:18–19)—these wounds as markers of Jesus' selfless humiliation and death are the "ultimate manifestation of God's glory to the world,"[46] the unmistakable marks of divine life-giving power and presence in the face of death itself. They are a graphic illustration that the beginning moment of crucifixion stamps the whole process of Jesus' being glorified with the shape of the cross, thereby giving divine glory—the visible manifestation of holiness—a permanently cruciform character. To quote Bauckham on this point:

> They [these wounds] are that, of course, because they are the ultimate point to which the love of God—his *ḥesed*, his *charis*, his *agapē*—can go for our sake. This is the character of God that Moses heard on Sinai[47] now described in visible flesh on Golgotha. The paradox of the cross—honor in humiliation, visible splendor in disfigurement and death—exists to make us reckon with a love that is sufficient to resolve the paradox.[48]

In order for the disciples to receive the Spirit to empower them for participating in the life-giving mission of the Father and the Son, John says that Jesus "breathed (*enephysēsen*) on them" (20:22). This language resonates with the language of the wind/breath/Spirit coming in Ezekiel's valley of dry bones and "breathing upon" the bones to bring them to life (Ezek 37:9). But it more closely resonates with the creation language of Gen 2:7. There the holy God graciously breathed (*enephysēsen*) his breath/Spirit/life into a lifeless humanity (cf. Wis 15:11), thereby enabling humanity to represent his gracious presence (like priests) in his cosmic temple and to rule over it (like kings) in a way that creation would flourish with well-ordered life and reach its intended goal. Here, then, John presents the now glorified Son—who was with God from the beginning and the one through whom all things first came into existence—as breathing life into a new humanity "on that first day of the week," that first day of a new creation. But this now glorified Son is himself the prototypical human of this new creation who is more like Yahweh himself than the first Adam/human who *was made* into a "living being" (Gen 2:7; 1 Cor 15:45). This last Adam/human is so closely associated with the Spirit, the Lord and giver of life, that Paul can refer to

---

46. Bauckham, *Gospel of Glory*, 61.

47. This footnote is not in Bauckham's original text but it helps to know that Bauckham is here referring to these words of God's self-identification at Sinai: "The Lord, the Lord, a God merciful and gracious, slow to anger, and abounding in steadfast love and faithfulness" (Exod 34:6).

48. Bauckham, *Gospel of Glory*, 61.

Section 2—Relocating Holiness in Jesus

him as a "making-alive Spirit" (1 Cor 15:45; cf. 2 Cor 3:17–18). John's portrayal of this truly Human One breathing the Spirit of life into the disciples may be read as a graphic depiction of this Pauline conceptuality.

Now reborn from above (3:5–8), the disciples are prepared for the life of the new age, having both experienced the forgiving *shalom* the risen Christ announces in their midst and made by his breath/Spirit into a community through whom that *shalom* is to be embodied in its communal life and conveyed to the world.[49] Since the disciples are sent into the world "just as" Jesus was sent by the Father, the pattern of Jesus' mission provides a general pattern for the way the church is to convey the life-giving *shalom* of the new age to the world. Bringing healing to the physically disabled (the blind and lame), feeding the desperately hungry, reaching out to despised social and religious outsiders (like an impure Samaritan woman) with a word of invitation and hope would indeed fit this general pattern of engaging in the life-giving mission of the Father and the Son. This is the larger context within which we need to locate the specific task Jesus assigns to the disciples when he conveys the Spirit to them.[50] That specific task is the priestly role of administering the forgiveness of sins, thereby offering both human and divine reconciliation to a world whose sins keep *shalom* at bay. As representatives of the new humanity in a new age of *shalom*, they are to re-present the Holy God's gracious presence as priests making their new community, like Jesus' risen body itself (2:19–22), God's new temple. But the language John uses to describe their engagement in the mission of forgiveness moves beyond what priests did in the Jerusalem Temple. While priests oversaw and offered sacrifices for the forgiveness of sins and could then *announce* that sins had been forgiven, they would not be said to actually forgive sins. But Jesus says pointedly in this passage, "If you forgive/release the sins of any, they are forgiven/released for them; if you retain them, they are retained." Almost assuredly, the language in the second part of each of these clauses in the passive voice (they are forgiven/released/they are retained) is an example of the divine passive. In other words, the implied actor in the second part of each clause is God while the community of God's new creation people—not just a specific ordained order—is the actor in the first part of each clause.

Before trying to clarify the relationship between the community's action and God's action, we need more clarity on what is involved in the community's action of granting forgiveness. As was the case with Jesus,

---

49. Cf. the reflections of Hastings, *Missional God, Missional Church*, 127–28.
50. Cf. the comments of Gorman, *Abide and Go*, forthcoming.

this priestly community also has a prophetic function, (i.e., to confront the world with the truth about itself). This will require making discerning judgments about when and where people are committed to allegiances and practices that seem to promise life but in reality alienate them from God and each other, thereby entrapping them and others in death-bound circumstances. To those blinded to the effect that their own actions have in aiding and abetting racial, social, and economic injustice, to those who finally "feel fulfilled" in an adulterous relationship that is destroying their family, to those entrapped in the "simple pleasures" of pornography, to those whose (understandable) hatred toward violent people issues in calls for vengeance that perpetuate the cycle of violence—for the sake of all of these and many more, the church must engage in the life-giving practice of telling them the truth about their death-bound direction. The church must, in the Johannine sense, "retain" their sins which "involves exposing sin, identifying sin, and holding people to account for sin."[51] However, this is not the primary goal. "Retaining sins is a confrontational action that reaches its goal when the hearers recognize their accountability and are moved to change by embracing the release that comes through faith."[52] Hence, this confrontational action must be combined with words and deeds that convey the love and *shalom* of God that comes in Jesus.[53] When this happens the church becomes *the Spirit's instrument* of persuasion (16:8–11) to move people to recognize their accountability and trust the reality of divine forgiveness that comes to them in the form of human forgiveness enacted by the church. The (very human) church, then, really offers divine forgiveness that releases people from their entrapment to death-bound allegiances and practices and puts them on the road to abundant life.[54]

There is no doubt in all of this that God has acted and continues to act enabling the community to act. Or, to use language we used earlier, God has acted as the catalyst of his people's acting. Trying to go further than this and ferret out and even more clearly distinguish the action of the community from God's own action in this mission of forgiving/releasing and retaining sins is simply not necessary. We have already noted John's remarkable language of

51. Koester, *Word of Life*, 159.

52. Ibid., 160.

53. On the way John's gospel exemplifies how such confrontational words might be conveyed by the church in audience sensitive, contextually appropriate ways, see Flemming, *Recovering*, 118–20.

54. Cf. the comments of Koester, *Word of Life*, 159; Hastings, *Missional God, Missional Church*, 310–21.

Section 2—Relocating Holiness in Jesus

the mutual indwelling of the Son in the disciples and them in him, of their being in both the Father and the Son as they also share intimate life with one another in a unified corporate body. It is the very breath of the Son, the life-giving Spirit who comes from the Father that joins them intimately with the Father and the Son making them participants in/instruments of God's life-giving mission. Hence, as they participate in the Triune God's mission of offering forgiveness and reconciliation to each other and to the world through their cruciform witness of word and deed, they are not independent actors merely imitating Christ. John's image of Jesus as the vine and his disciples as branches illustrates in no uncertain terms that they can do nothing apart from "abiding" in Jesus (15:5). Sanctified and set apart with the breath of the Spirit both within them and among them as a corporate body, they together become an extension of Christ's own body into the world through which the reconciling, life-giving mission of the Holy God continues.[55] They become, in the words of Lincoln, "a bridgehead for God's continuing saving judgment of the world."[56] In doing so, they are becoming like God—being shaped into the *imago Dei*—by participating in God's own life-giving missional life, inhabiting and being inhabited by this particular God. As such, their missional pattern of life displays the essence of the Triune God to the world he loves; it displays the holiness of God in the flesh of a human community whose members love one another and God's world as God does. Since that flesh is always the flesh of a very culturally specific human community, they become "the cultural explication of God's identity."[57]

We see this clearly when we encounter the community of the risen Christ in the next book in the canon, the book of Acts. However, before moving to Acts, we will summarize what we have found regarding the relocation of holiness in Jesus in the gospels.

Section 2 Summary: Relocating Holiness in Jesus

We began this section by asking what happens when holiness—God's very essence, God's dangerous yet beneficent presence—is relocated in a Jew

---

55. For a more theologically detailed and nuanced argument that Christ's incarnation, life, death, resurrection and ascension was the *completed initiation* of the Triune God's saving work that now—*really and materially*—continues in the Spirit-inhabited corporate body of Christ, see my "Ecclesiology, Election," 247–65, esp. 263–65.

56. Lincoln, "Johannine Vision of the Church."

57. Rowe, *World*, 18.

from Nazareth. As we saw in John's gospel, Jesus is not just a human being from Galilee, although he is certainly that. He is God's audible Word, God's life-creating act of communication with God's world, the Son who was with God from the beginning and was God. In his flesh, God's own glory/holiness was made visible and as a result, the abundant life of the new age was made available to the world. And in his flesh, this divine glory took on a cruciform shape that explicates divine holiness in terms of the depths of a divine love that took the living God—the resurrection and the life—down into the darkness and impurity of the grave.

The impact of this dislocation of holiness as primarily separation from impurity and its relocation in the Spirit-inhabited, boundary-crossing Son of God is nothing less than a shakeup of cosmic proportions. Out of profound love for his rebellious world, in the person of Jesus, God himself entered into that world, setting into motion the end of the old creation and giving birth to a new one (2 Cor 5:17; Gal 6:15). By refusing to be cordoned off from impurity, God himself overhauled the whole "electrical system" that channeled his holiness in life-giving, beneficent ways. Especially by grasping *the ultimate impurity of the old cosmos*, by entering death itself in the person of the Spirit-inhabited Son, God changed the order and structure of that cosmos that had existed since humanity's garden rebellion. Therefore, any conception of purity or holiness relying *solely* on the old cosmic structure for its theological rationale is now of out step with God's own actions.

A conceptual pattern underlies all this that is similar to the pattern that undergirded OT conceptions of holiness; this is shown in three important respects. First, both the healing, life-giving activities of the Holy One of God (who is the very source of life) and the Father's raising of him by the life-giving Spirit demonstrates that "holiness at its source is [still] life itself—the antonym of death."[58] But now, paradoxically, this God's way of producing life is to directly confront death by entering into it and destroying it from the inside out. Second, the way that holiness is conceived is still based on the nature and structure of the cosmos, only now it is the nature and structure of the new cosmos whose microcosm is Christ's risen, cruciform body. That body remains marked by battle wounds, a vivid display of the life-giving pattern of faithful, redemptive and reconciling activity that characterized Christ's life and a permanent reminder of the depths "to

---

58. Harrington, *Holiness*, 179 (my addition of the word "still").

Section 2—Relocating Holiness in Jesus

which the love of God . . . can go for our sake."[59] Hence, Christ's risen body provides a new order or structure to the cosmos of which it is a microcosm, *a cross-shaped order*. Third—and this is closely connected with the last point—it is still God's own character or pattern of activity that defines the essence of holiness. In the face of forces of chaos that disorder God's good creation and a rebellious world who remains trapped by sin and alienated from the God of life, the essence of divine holiness remains a pattern of redemptive, reconciling life-giving activity directed toward offering healing and forgiveness, restoring justice and *shalom*, and ultimately bringing creation to its intended destiny. But it now bears the stamp of a particular human being, Israel's messianic representative, Jesus the Nazarene, through whom God continues his dream of bringing creation to its intended destiny through the agency of humanity. Therefore, the pattern of activity that now constitutes *both* divine and human holiness has an unmistakable cruciform shape manifest in faithfulness to God's life-giving, reconciling mission (*pistis*) expressed in costly, self-giving actions for others (*agapē*)—even and especially for those of the "world" in its rebellion against God.

So *this* is what happens when holiness gets relocated in a Jew from Nazareth. His missional life pattern reconfigures holiness in such a way that he turns out to be the visible *imago Dei*, the image/*eikōn* of the unseen Holy God (Col 1:15). And this brings us back to the way we concluded the last section. If God's means of (re)shaping his people into the *imago Dei*, of making them holy, is inseparable from—even primarily constituted by—their participation in, and witness to, the *missio Dei*, what happens when that *imago Dei* now has a visible form and human location, namely, Christ's risen, cruciform body? In this case, people are only reshaped into the *imago Dei* as they participate in it through the *corporate* body of the risen, cruciform Christ. That body, the locale of the new creation, is distinctly identified as its members' life together re-narrates a cruciform story analogous to that of Christ's in service to the *missio Dei*. Their holiness, then, is inseparable from, and derived from, their Spirit-enabled participation *in Christ's body*, a culturally specific human community, in and through which God is continuing his life-giving mission to bring creation to its intended destiny through the agency of humanity. As we will see in the next section, such missional communities, in their various social settings, become "the cultural explication of God's identity."[60]

59. Bauckham, *Gospel of Glory*, 61.
60. Rowe, *World*, 18.

SECTION 3

Other New Testament Witnesses

7

The Community of the Holy and Righteous One

Bearers of the Name of the Lord of All

> *"For there is no other name . . . "*
> *"This one is Lord of all . . . "*

Introduction

"THE STORY OF THE Church's beginnings is in reality the story of the mission of God. . . . In Acts the church's identity is formed only as it engages in mission."[1] So says Dean Flemming at the beginning of his chapter on the book of Acts in *Recovering the Full Mission of God*. In Acts, Luke presents the early church's life together as well as the lives of individual characters (e.g., Stephen, Peter, Paul) as a sort of re-narration of the cruciform story of Jesus he tells in his first volume.[2] Acts, in fact, opens in its first two verses by referring to the Gospel of Luke. Luke's first volume was about what Jesus *began* to do and teach (so NIV and RSV, not NRSV), with the implication that he himself continues to do and teach similar sorts of

---

1. Flemming, *Recovering*, 133.
2. In spite of challenges to it (e.g., Parsons and Pervo, *Rethinking*), I remain convinced that there is a rather clear narrative unity to Luke and Acts when they are read together (see the brief comments of Carroll, *Luke*, 9). Acts does indeed function canonically as an appropriate continuation of the fourfold gospel and as an indispensable introduction the Pauline corpus (e.g., Wall, *Acts*, 26–32). But in light of its many narrative connections with Luke, it also seems theologically appropriate to emphasize Acts' role as a continuation of the Third Gospel itself.

Section 3—Other New Testament Witnesses

things through his sent ones (apostles) whom he elected through the Holy Spirit (Acts 1:1–2).[3]

As we will see, however, God's mission goes forth through more people than simply the reconstituted original twelve (i.e., eleven plus Matthias).[4] Indeed, Luke depicts the whole community and individual characters (some not among these twelve) as participating in God's salvific mission in such a way that they become "the cultural explication of God's identity"[5] in various social settings. In other words, they become the embodiment of holiness itself, explicating the essence of who God is in ways appropriate to their own cultural location. They do so by engaging in the mission of God that has as its basis the living God's defeat of death from the inside out in raising Messiah Jesus from the dead.[6] Without that resurrection, there is no mission and therefore no church. Above all, then, the church in Acts participates in God's resurrection-generated mission as "witnesses to Jesus' resurrection." This entails verbally proclaiming Jesus' resurrection *and its implications for the world* (Acts 2:32–36).[7] It also entails embodying "the cruciform pattern that culminates in resurrection."[8] "[T]he main characters in Acts, to put it plainly, look like Jesus—and precisely in this way embody his life and carry it forth into the wider Greco-Roman world."[9] In this way, they offer a cultural explication of the identity and essence of the one who is indeed "Lord of all," and therefore, a cultural explication of the nature of holiness itself. In this chapter, we will focus less on the verbal proclamation of Jesus' resurrection than on the way the individual characters and communities as a whole embody a pattern of life through which

---

3. With the NIV and the RSV, I take the verb "began" (*ērxato*) to be emphatic, indicating that Jesus continues acting in the narrative that follows, rather than as an auxiliary verb with little effect as in the NRSV.

4. While the small band of original apostles begin as the primary "witnesses of the resurrection" in Acts (1:8), that language of "witness" is extended to others like Paul (22:15; 23:11; 26:16), Stephen (22:20), and "all the prophets" (10:43). Hence, the role of "witness" in Acts is broader than simply being a direct eyewitness of the resurrected Lord. As such, witnesses like the original apostles, Paul, and Stephen represent the whole missionally engaged church (cf. Flemming, *Recovering*, 135–36).

5. Rowe, *World*, 18.

6. Cf. Rowe, *World*, 121–23.

7. "[I]n his resurrection, God rejects the rejection of Jesus' lordship, authenticates his life—and death—as part of what it means to be the Lord of all, and extends this life into a mission of salvation in his name" (Ibid., 153).

8. Ibid., 121.

9. Ibid., 153.

God sanctifies/hallows his name "in Jerusalem, in all Judea and Samaria, and to the ends of the earth" (1:8).[10]

Holiness Terminology

We begin with a word about holiness terminology in Acts. The word "holy" is used most often (more than forty times) in reference to the Holy Spirit. In addition, in significant places Luke describes Jesus as in some way the unique embodiment of holiness. He is God's "Holy (*hosion*) One" (2:27; 13:35), the Lord's "holy (*hagion*) servant" (4:27, 30), "the Holy (*hagion*) and Righteous (*dikaion*) One" who—not surprisingly given the association of holiness with life—is also "the author of life" (3:14–15).[11] The followers of Jesus in the earliest Jerusalem community as well as in Lydda and Joppa are also explicitly called "holy ones/saints" (9:13; 26:10; 9:32; 9:41). Wherever the Holy Spirit is active among people and forms a community in the name of the Holy and Righteous One, they are considered to have been and remain "sanctified" (*hagiazō*); they are transformed and set apart as God's holy people who bear his name before a watching world (20:32: 26:18). As the early Jewish community comes to see, this even includes those from the nations/Gentiles whose blind eyes are opened so that they are enabled to switch lordships and receive forgiveness of sins (26:18). This all starts with the actions of the Triune God when the Holy and Righteous One receives the prophetically promised Holy Spirit from the Father and pours out that Spirit on Jews from around the world (2:33). It starts, that is, at Pentecost.

Pentecost through the Lens of Ezekiel

While other prophets also associated God's coming new age of salvation with the giving of the Spirit (e.g., Joel 2:28–3:1; Isa 32:15–17; 44:3; 59:21), earlier we discussed the way Ezekiel depicted Yahweh's restoration of Israel by means of the coming of the Spirit (Ezek 36:16–32; 37:1–14). Since Luke portrays Pentecost along the lines of the Lord's restoration of Israel, it will

---

10. This is not to say that verbal proclamation is less important in the way the characters participate in God's mission in Acts (see Flemming, *Recovering*, 137–45).

11. This latter phrase is probably to be taken as a reference to Jesus as the one who has originated the possibility new life for others in his life, death, resurrection and ascension (cf. Peterson, *Acts of the Apostles*, 176) rather than in the full Johannine sense of Jesus as the source of all created life.

Section 3—Other New Testament Witnesses

be helpful to recall some basic contours of our discussion of Ezekiel where Israel was depicted as in dire need of restoration and a transformation into a faithful covenant partner through whom God's mission could flow. As we saw, that transformative act involved God's Spirit and was presented as a life-giving "heart transplant" in chapter 36 and as a resurrection to new life (a "new creation") in chapter 37. Since Yahweh's name/reputation was inextricably and publicly linked to the way that Israel patterned its life together, this life-giving act of deliverance/transformation was the means by which he would sanctify or vindicate his holy name. The goal of all this was that Yahweh's own holiness would be displayed before the eyes of the nations through restored Israel's life together (Ezek 36:22–23) so that the nations might experience the life-giving blessing that flowed from acknowledging him as "the Lord," the One unique creator God.

Peter, of course, makes Joel 3:1–5 his primary "sermon text" (2:17–21). But this does not rule out discerning a pattern similar to that of Ezekiel's imagery of the Spirit's restoration of Israel at work in Acts as its story unfolds. With Matthias' election in chapter 1 signaling the restoration of the *twelve* apostles, the nucleus of the leadership of a restored Israel is in place (Luke 22:30). In Acts 2 there are Jews from "every nation under heaven" who had formerly been scattered throughout the Diaspora but were now living in Jerusalem (2:5–11). Hence, the stage is set for conceiving of what happens in Jerusalem as the "whole house of Israel" (Ezek 37:11//Acts 2:36) being re-gathered from the places where they had been scattered[12] and restored by the Spirit's coming. After Peter's speech to "the whole house of Israel," they are "cut to the heart" (2:37) and appropriately—at least as Peter describes it later in 15:8–9—receive a "cleansed heart" through the forgiveness of their sins as they receive the gift of the Holy Spirit.[13] This is analogous to the life-giving heart transplant Ezekiel had spoken about in 36:26–27.[14] In what follows in Acts, this transformative act of restoring a representative Israel ultimately results in representatives from the nations

---

12. They have—in terms roughly analogous to Ezekiel 36:24—been taken "from the nations," "gathered from all the countries," and brought "into [their] own land."

13. Recall Israel's self-diagnosis in Ezek 33:10 as they waste away in the valley of dry bones: "How our transgressions and *our sins* weigh on us! We waste away because of them. How can we live?"

14. "I will give you a new heart and *put a new spirit in you*. I will remove your stony heart from your body and replace it with a living one, and *I will give you my spirit* so that you may walk according to my regulations and carefully observe my case laws."

acknowledging Israel's God as "the Lord of all" when through this restored Israel, God displays his holiness before their eyes (cf. Ezek 36:22–23).

As in Ezekiel, God's name/reputation in Acts is inextricably and publicly linked to the way that restored Israel patterns its life together. Hence, their Spirit-empowered life together is intended to become the means by which Yahweh's name is sanctified/hallowed. It is just that Luke now uses that divine name—which comes over into Greek as *kyrios* ("Lord")[15]—to refer to the God of Israel (2:21) as well as to Jesus, the one who was crucified, raised and exalted to God's right hand (2:21 in light of 2:36).[16] In Acts 2, Peter's quotation of Joel 3:1–5 (LXX) is clearly marked out as what "*God says*" (v. 17) and concludes with the words from Joel that "whoever calls upon the name of the Lord (*kyrios*) will be saved" (v. 21), a clear reference to Yahweh in Joel's original context. That Jesus is now this Lord whose name is salvific is confirmed by Peter at the end of his speech in 2:36: "Therefore, let the whole house of Israel know with assurance that God has made this Jesus whom you yourselves crucified both Lord (*kyrios*) and Messiah."[17] Further, that Jesus is this Lord whose name is uniquely salvific is dramatically demonstrated in the narrative movement of Acts 4:10–12. In Acts the Lordship of "the God who made the world and all things in it . . . the Lord of heaven and earth" (17:24) is expressed in the Lordship of Jesus Christ who is "Lord of all" (10:36). Hence, to bear and use the name of the Lord, Jesus Christ, in the book of Acts is to bear and use the divine name of Israel's God. In doing so, the pattern of activity in which the community and individuals within it engage becomes inextricably and publicly linked to the way God has chosen to sanctify his name among the nations. God's holy name becomes sanctified as this community's life together and the actions of individuals with it become a display of God's own holiness with the ultimate outcome of the nations experiencing the life-giving blessing that flows from acknowledging Israel's God as "the Lord of all."

Hence, the importance of embodied and proclamatory witness in the Book of Acts to the activity, identity, and nature of the living and life-giving

---

15. It was the standard practice in the Septuagint and among many Greek-speaking Jews to use the word "Lord" (Greek: *kyrios*) as a reverent circumlocution for the divine name "Yahweh" (see my "Lord").

16. Regarding this practice in Luke's gospel, see Rowe, *Early Narrative Christology*; cf. my "Ripples." Regarding the practice in Acts, see my "Resurrection, Ascension;" Rowe, *World*, esp. 111–12.

17. That this verse refers to God confirming Jesus' identity in the face of death rather than God making him something he was not before, see Rowe, "Acts 2:36."

God can hardly be overestimated. Peter confirms this in his Pentecost speech in 2:32 when he maintains in no uncertain terms "This Jesus God raised up, and of this we are all witnesses." But Peter's whole argument fails if his audience does not grant their adherence to this one statement: "This Jesus God raised up." If this is true, it confirms Jesus' basic message that the kingdom of the living and life-giving God has drawn near since it would be a particular instance of one of its constitutive events (i.e., the resurrection of the dead).[18] However, he only supports this statement by saying: "of this we are all *witnesses*." At best, his argument to this point would have persuaded his Jerusalem audience that David had predicted the resurrection of the Messiah who was to come (vv. 25–31). But that *this crucified Jesus* had been the Messiah to whom David was referring and that God had actually raised him has its only support in the *public testimony* of those upon whom the Spirit had just fallen. That testimony is a re-embodiment—in their words and communal life—of God's coming kingdom that Jesus himself had announced and embodied. As such, it publicly attests to the truth that God raised Jesus, thereby vindicating his life, mission and identity as God's Holy One, Israel's Messiah—and therefore, the world's true Lord. We will focus first on the way this is manifest in the life of the earliest community in Jerusalem.

The Community of the Holy and Righteous One in Jerusalem

The pattern of the early Jerusalem community's life together witnesses to the life-giving God's resurrection of Jesus, and in doing so, also becomes the means by which God's name is sanctified/hallowed. While Luke never explicitly refers to the sanctification of God's name in Acts, he does so in his first volume in the first line of the pattern prayer Jesus gives to his disciples (11:2–4). In that passage, at the request of one of his disciples to teach them to pray, Jesus says to pray as follows:

> Father, may your name be sanctified.
>
> May your kingdom come.
>
> Continue giving to us day by day our bread for the day.[19]

---

18. Pannenberg, *Systematic Theology*, 337.

19. The meaning of the Greek word *epiousion* (for the day) is not completely clear and might also mean "for the coming day," "necessary," or perhaps "for the coming age."

And forgive/release for us our sins,

for we ourselves are forgiving/releasing [debts] for everyone indebted to us.

And do not bring us into an ordeal of testing.

Jesus' instructions are to say this corporate prayer (note the plural pronouns) *whenever* you (plural) pray (11:2). The word *whenever* (*hotan*) implies that, while corporate prayer can certainly be expanded beyond these words, this short pattern prayer in some form ought to be part of corporate, public prayer *whenever* Jesus' disciples pray together. Although we see the followers of Jesus engaging in corporate prayer often, especially in the early chapters of Acts (e.g., 1:14, 24–25; 2:42; 4:23–30; 6:4), there is never any explicit mention of them praying in this particular way that Jesus had taught them. If there is a narrative unity of Luke and Acts, however, we might reasonably expect that we are to imagine some form of this short pattern prayer being a part of the unstated content of the community's corporate prayers.[20] In any case, even if Luke never explicitly has them pray this pattern prayer, their early life together embodies aspects of it.

Beginning prayer with a petition that the divine name may be sanctified/hallowed is self-involving, particularly if we hear it with the language and conceptuality of Ezekiel in the background. That is, praying that God's name will be sanctified/hallowed involves those praying in the process by which God brings that about. Whatever else it means for God's name to be sanctified, it at least means that the praying community's life together and the actions of individuals within it will become a true display of God's own holiness or character so that proper honor is brought to his name/reputation.

This happens in the life of this early community as they embody other aspects of this pattern prayer, in particular the petition that God's kingdom come. Luke portrays the church as the restored Israel of the last days, embodying the eschatological Jubilee ("release") of God's coming reign that Jesus had announced in Luke 4 *and embodied* throughout the gospel narrative.[21] Recall that the effect of practicing a Jubilee year would

---

20. For example, the first time there is corporate prayer in Acts, the 120 are gathered in the upper room "constantly devoting themselves to (the) prayer" (1:14). The definite article ("the") comes before the word "prayer" in Greek, *possibly* signaling a particular prayer, the one that we might expect the community to be praying if they were following Jesus' earlier instructions in Luke 11:2.

21. For elaboration of the claim that Jubilee imagery was associated with expectations

Section 3—Other New Testament Witnesses

have been to keep the worst effects of economic misfortune and injustice from continuing into perpetuity in Israelite society. Although we have no evidence that Israel ever actually carried out a Jubilee year in any full sense, it was not forgotten, but rather came to be understood as characterizing God's coming eschatological kingdom of justice and *shalom*.[22] Luke pictures this community as an advance version of Jubilee where all debts are "released." They have "no needy person among them" (Acts 4:34; cf. Deut 15:4) and have "all things in common" (Acts 2:44, 4:32), suggesting that when a member of the community owed another member a debt, that debt was considered "released" (cf. Deut 15:2). Luke's pattern prayer makes the *basis* for the request for God to forgive sins (i.e., our debts to God) precisely the community's claim: "for we ourselves are forgiving/releasing [debts] for everyone indebted to us."

In addition, the community is portrayed as living out the petition to "Continue giving to us day by day our bread for the day" (cf., Acts 2:46 with reference to breaking bread and 6:1 with reference to the daily distribution of food). God's life-giving provision is shared as all have need so that there is no needy person in the community. This practice further marks the community as an advance version of the eschatological Jubilee community. Although Luke is not naïve about the difficulties such a community will continue to face (6:1f; 11:27f), the very reign/kingdom of God has *begun to come* in a community who embodies Jesus' pattern prayer and his programmatic Jubilee announcement in these ways. As such, the life of this community in Acts functions as a public testimony of God's in-breaking reign, and thus of God's vindicating resurrection of the crucified one who had proclaimed and embodied it. It distinguishes this community from others around it and simultaneously displays the character of their God as committed to just socioeconomic practices that allow life to flourish for all, not just the few who happen to be winning the economic game. Hence, this holy pattern of human life—made possible by the Christ-shaped, poured out Spirit—corroborates the verbal witness to Jesus' resurrection (cf. the

---

of God's eschatological reign and was particularly important in Jesus' articulation of that reign in Luke, see Ringe, *Jesus, Liberation*; Evans and Sanders, *Luke and Scripture*, 46–69, 84–92.

22. See, e.g., Isaiah 58 and 61 (both of which Jesus uses to characterize his ministry in Luke 4:18–19) and some of the writings in what are often referred to as the Dead Sea Scrolls (e.g., 11QMelch).

logic of 4:32–34), displays God's own holiness before the eyes of others, and thereby sanctifies or hallows his name/reputation.[23]

Re-narrating the Story of the Holy and Righteous One

Actions of Individual Characters in Acts

Engaging the Forces of Chaos

There are numerous parallels between the actions of Jesus in Luke's gospel and the actions of his followers in Acts. Like Jesus, they are involved in proclaiming good news about the kingdom of God (e.g., 8:4, 12) and especially about Jesus and his resurrection through which God confirmed him as Messiah and Lord (e.g., the paradigmatic sermons of Peter in Acts 2 and Paul in Acts 13 [note esp. 13:32]). As we have seen, to proclaim the latter was also to proclaim the good news that God's kingdom had broken into the world since resurrection was one of its constituent events. Like Jesus, they are also actively involved in God's work of reclaiming some for his reign from the forces of chaos. In his speech at Pentecost, Peter describes Jesus as having performed "signs and wonders" (Acts 2:22), which in Luke's gospel were salvific in nature and purpose. In Acts, not only do the original apostles do "signs/signs and wonders" in the name of the Lord Jesus that are similar to those of Jesus in Luke (2:43; 4:16, 22; 5:12), but so do others like Stephen (6:8), Philip (8:6, 13), and Paul and Barnabas (14:3; 15:12).

Acts explicitly uses "signs and wonders" to refer to God's actions through Jesus' followers that bring salvific restoration of bodies to health (3:1—4:22; 5:15–16; 8:7; cf. Luke 5:17–26; 7:22) and deliverance from "unclean spirits" (5:16; 8:7; cf. Luke 4:33, 36). And while at times Luke does not explicitly call such actions "signs and wonders" in their immediate context, it is clear that actions of Jesus' followers that parallel Jesus' salvific actions throughout Acts are precisely salvific, life-giving "signs and wonders" (e.g., 19:11). Particularly noteworthy in this regard are Peter's healing of

---

23. Luke's depiction of the community also draws on Hellenistic friendship language in a way that displays the community as a kind of utopia of friends. At the same time, however, it subverts the typical rules of "friendship" governing gift giving in that any gift given typically carries with it the expectation of some form of "payback." This circle of friends give with no expectation of return, in line with Jesus' own teaching (in addition to his model prayer, see Luke 6:30, 34–36; 12:33–34), some of which implies that such activity publicly displays the character of the Most High (esp. 6:35–36). Cf. Flemming, *Recovering*, 152–53.

a paralytic (9:32–35; cf. Luke 5:17–26) and raising a woman who had died (9:36–41; cf. Luke 8:40–42, 49–55; 7:11–16). Peter commands one to "rise" from his paralysis and another to "rise" from her death (9:34, 40–41), underscoring the life-giving (resurrection) character of both these acts. Paul's healing of a lame man (14:8–10) and raising a young man who died during his sermon (20:7–10) is worth mention here as well.

Having been "received" and "poured out" by the risen, ascended Son (2:33), the now Christ-shaped Holy Spirit who was at work in Jesus in Luke's gospel is at work in his followers. These followers of the Holy One of God, the Author of Life, recapitulate his story in the pages of Acts by engaging in battle against similar forces of chaos with which he did battle. Like him, they too become channels of the life-giving power of holiness overcoming the death-dealing forces of chaos rather than being threatened by them. They become participants in God's life-giving mission by becoming the channel of Jesus' continued activity. Like Jesus, they also faithfully endure persecution without retaliation because of their role in this mission (e.g., Stephen in chapter 7, numerous followers of Jesus in 8:1; Paul throughout his travels). In doing so, they become so closely associated with Jesus that Luke depicts persecuting Jesus' followers as equivalent to persecuting Jesus himself (9:4–5). What Jesus began to do (1:1), he is still doing, only now through his followers and his community as a whole. His story is being re-narrated through them.

Boundary Crossing

As we saw in the Synoptic Gospels, and to a lesser extent in John, another aspect of Jesus' story is the way he regularly crossed social and purity boundaries. In doing so he brought God's holy cleansing presence to bear on contaminated, debilitated, weak and isolated people, healing and rescuing them from the forces of chaos and reincorporating them into human community. We also saw that Jesus regularly ate with low status Jewish outsiders—those called "sinners" by others who operated with more stringent purity maps—essentially implying that they were *already* a part of his extended family *in order to* bring them to repentance and life. The implication was that Jesus was the locale of the holy, cleansing presence of God where "baptism with the Holy Spirit" neutralized impurity and reincorporated low status "sinners" and outsiders into God's own family. In addition, we saw how, on Jesus' purity map, engaging in an overall life pattern of participating in just, *shalom*-restoring, actions towards others and whole-hearted dedication/fidelity to God makes one "pure" inside and out. Crossing social and purity boundaries in the service of God's mission, then, was simply part and parcel of Jesus' *modus operandi*.

We learn at the beginning of Acts that crossing social boundaries will also characterize the mission in which the community who bears the name will participate (1:8). Becoming witnesses in Jerusalem and Judea is one thing, but going into Samaria (8:4–25) is quite another. While first-century Jews did not consider Samaritans to be Gentiles, they disdained them as "lost sheep" of Israel, religious heretics who claimed to worship Israel's God and follow Torah. The sentiment went both ways. Samaritans also despised Jews, considering themselves to be the true worshippers of the God of Israel. In Luke's gospel Jesus does not specifically engage in salvific mission to Samaritans (although see 9:51–56), and he continues to refer to them as "foreigners" (17:18). But he hints that they may indeed become part of the people he was forming around himself (10:30–37; 17:11–19). Hence, when Philip is forced out of Jerusalem by persecution and goes down into Samaria proclaiming the kingdom of God and engaging in salvific "signs and wonders," he is not only doing the kinds of things that Jesus did; he is doing them in a place that continues Jesus' pattern of crossing social boundaries to include marginalized outsiders into the community of restored Israel. Even though Philip is "full of the [Christ-shaped Holy] Spirit" (6:3) enabling him to participate in this Samaritan mission, and even though the Samaritans respond positively to his embodied proclamation (8:6–8; 14), it is not until Peter and John get there to verify what God is doing that the Samaritans receive the Holy Spirit as had the Jews at Pentecost (8:15–17). Here then, representatives from the community that bears the name of the Holy and Righteous One are engaged in a pattern of activity that crosses social boundaries, healing and rescuing marginalized outsiders from the debilitating forces of chaos (8:6–7), reclaiming them for the Kingdom of God and incorporating them into the community of God's restored people (8:12, 17). Even people from this marginalized community have been and remain "sanctified" (*hagiazō*), i.e., transformed and set apart as God's holy people who bear his name before a watching world (20:32: 26:18). Even if there might be some slight hesitation exhibited with Peter and John sent to verify things, Philip, Peter and John all become channels of God's reconciling activity. Through them God not only reconciles a despised people to himself, but in so doing also brings reconciliation—at least representatively—to two

Section 3—Other New Testament Witnesses

groups of people who were previously hostile toward one another. Luke's summary statement in 9:31 highlights this when he speaks of "*the* [one single] church throughout Judea, Galilee and Samaria" which "had peace" as its numbers increased.[24]

If the Samaritans were at best considered "lost sheep" by first-century Jews, they at least had some connection to Israel, claiming to worship Israel's one God and holding to their own version of the Pentateuch. They were not part of the wider Gentile world, which had a multiplicity of deities and—*from a Jewish perspective*—therefore, a multitude of polluting, unholy influences in their daily lives.[25] Hence, when God thrusts the representatives of his restored Israel out into that world to deal with what God is doing there, concerns about crossing social and purity boundaries intensify. This comes to the fore in chapter 10 when God's messenger appears to Cornelius, a Roman centurion in Caesarea, and tells him to send for Peter (10:3–6). Cornelius was a "god fearer"—a Gentile attracted to Israel's one God associated with a local synagogue but not a full-fledged (circumcised) proselyte (10:2, 22). When he sends for Peter, Peter is staying in Joppa at the house of "Simon the tanner" (9:43), perhaps a signal of his willingness to cross boundaries erected by more stringent purity maps that tended to keep some Jews on the margins of God's people.[26] But staying with a Jew who might pass on impurity is one thing; going into the house of a Gentile—much less having table fellowship with them—was quite another. According to the terms of many first century Jewish purity maps, going into Gentile dwellings and engaging in table fellowship with them were considered polluting,[27] and Peter's words in 10:28a seem to confirm that

---

24. The story of the Ethiopian eunuch that follows (8:26–40) is also a boundary crossing incident. It narrates the full inclusion of a man from God's scattered people into restored Israel. As sexually mutilated, he probably would have been denied full participation in God's people heretofore (Deut 23:2 LXX). Given the amount of emphasis Luke gives to the Cornelius events in chapters 10–15 regarding inclusion of the Gentiles, it is not likely he intends us to view the eunuch as a Gentile in whom the full inclusion of Gentiles begins (cf. L. Johnson, *Acts*, 158–59).

25. Gentiles were not unfamiliar with conceptions of impurity and pollution. Indeed, some aspects of their purity maps overlapped with that of purity maps in Judaism e.g., giving birth, having sex, and contact with a corpse were often seen as defiling (deSilva, *Honor, Patronage, Kinship & Purity*, 249–53).

26. Because their job required constant contact with the hides of dead animals, tanners were often regarded as likely transmitters of corpse impurity. Cf. Jesus staying at the house of Simon the leper (Mark 14:3; Matt 26:6).

27. deSilva, *Honor, Patronage, Kinship & Purity*, 286, n. 6.

this had reflected his own view prior to his vision earlier in the chapter (10:10–16; cf. 11:2–3).[28] But now having seen the vision from God, having heard Cornelius' story, having conversed with Gentiles on the way to Caesarea, and now standing in a Gentile's house with the whole household present, Peter begins to catch up with what God is doing when he says to those gathered there: "God has indeed shown to me that I am not to call any person common or unclean" (10:28b). He then goes on to narrate a telescoped version of the story of Jesus, the proclaimer of peace and the "Lord of all" in whose name salvation and life comes, here in the form of "forgiveness of sins" (10:34–43; cf. 11:14, 18). Even before he can finish speaking, the same Holy Spirit of Acts 2 is poured out on these Gentiles *precisely as Gentiles* (10:44–46) and they were subsequently "baptized in the name of Jesus Christ." In this account, we once again see a representative of the Holy and Righteous One functioning as a channel of God's reconciling activity. In spite of Peter's initial reluctance, he becomes a participant in God's boundary-crossing activity to reconcile even Gentiles to himself, and in so doing, initiating the reconciliation of his restored Israel to representatives from the Gentile world.

But incorporating Jews and Gentiles into the same community raises all sorts of questions. As the subsequent story makes clear, Peter's assertion that God has shown him that he is not to call any person "common or unclean" is not the last word on concerns about impurity and pollution; it is not a blanket solution to the difficulties created when major social/purity boundaries are crossed. Such concerns neither disappear nor become unimportant when Jews loyal to Torah who bear the divine name share a table with Gentiles who now bear the same name having—like the Jews of restored Israel—received the Holy Spirit and been baptized in the name of Jesus, "the Lord of all." In addition, since these Gentiles now bear the name of the Lord of all, how will their individual lives and their ecclesial life together hallow/sanctify that name, giving witness to the character of Israel's Holy God? If such concerns are raised when God's Holy Spirit comes upon Gentiles who are already "god fearers" influenced by their connection to local synagogues, they are exacerbated when Gentiles with no prior Jewish influence begin to respond to God and are formed into communities who bear the name. How are such communities to become an appropriate

---

28. In practice, there was some debate in the varied expressions of first century Judaism about how much and how close of contact a Jew might have with Gentiles and yet remain loyal to Torah.

"cultural explication of God's identity," an embodiment of God's holiness in a way that visibly participates in his salvific mission?

Communities of the Holy and Righteous One among the Nations

The Cornelius episode gives no details on how, or whether, this household comes to be a part of a larger mixed community who bears the name of the Lord of all. But we are soon introduced to a publicly identifiable, mixed community composed of both Gentiles and Jews located in the Syrian metropolis of Antioch (11:19–30). Started by messianic Diaspora Jews, it was discipled extensively by Barnabas and Saul. Luke depicts this community as similar to the community in Jerusalem, thus portraying them as "an authentic realization of the messianic people."[29] With great numbers being brought to the Lord of all (11:21, 24; cf. 2:41, 47) because the hand of the Lord was with them doing signs and wonders (11:21; cf. 4:30), and with the grace of God on the community (11:23; cf. 4:33), they also practiced economic sharing for the benefit of those in need. In this case, they freely shared their resources with the earliest Judean community (11:29–30). Given this description, it seems likely that this community, like that earliest community, was practicing table fellowship among all its members. If indeed Jews and Gentiles were eating together, it was a powerful public display of reconciliation between peoples formerly at odds with each other, an advance glimpse of the reconciliation between all peoples that is characteristic of creation's intended destiny. Whether or not this was happening, in Luke's initial depiction of this community, he says nothing regarding problems concerning purity boundaries within the community.

However, later in the story this community becomes the flash-point of controversy over boundary issues, more specifically over whether Gentiles who turn to Israel's God must also be circumcised and keep the Torah to be included in the holy people who bear his name (15:1, 5).[30] Paul and Barnabas' report about numerous Gentiles becoming part of identifiable communities in Asia Minor who bear the name of the Lord gives urgency to the

---

29. L. Johnson, *Acts*, 207.

30. This is not necessarily to equate the contention of "some *people* from Judea" in v. 1 which specifically has to do with salvation with the similar, but perhaps different, contention of "some *believers* from the Pharisees" in v. 5 which does not specifically mention salvation.

whole issue (15:3-4, 12). But their report about what God had done was not enough to settle the issue. Nor was Peter's report of what the Holy Spirit had done for the Gentile household of Cornelius (15:8-9). His contention that their hearts had been cleansed by faith and they had received the Holy Spirit was not the end of the matter. Even if Gentiles could become and remain part of the community of the Holy and Righteous One without being circumcised and keeping the whole Torah, what would mark them out publicly—individually and as local communities—as bearers of the name? This was a question of identity, but as such, it was thereby also decidedly a missional question. Issues of purity and concerns about pollution become part of James's solution precisely here, and James is the one to whom Luke gives the last word.

While some of the details of James's scriptural argument are complex, its general contours are clear enough.[31] He begins by assuming the reality of the reports of Paul and Barnabas and particularly that of Peter (Simeon), summing them all up as God's action of having taken "a people from among the Gentiles *for his name*" (15:14). He then builds a case showing how Scripture agrees with what God has done in restoring/rebuilding Israel (15:16) at Pentecost "in order that the rest of humanity might seek the Lord, indeed all the Gentiles over whom my name has been called" (15:17). Such scriptural language came to life in the home of a Gentile centurion when he and all his household were baptized as the name of the Lord of all, Jesus Christ (10:36, 48), was called over them. Since the name of this Lord is salvific, the implication of James's argument is that these Gentiles are already a part of a people on the way to salvation. Hence, contra the view expressed in 15:1, they do not need to be circumcised in accordance with the custom of Moses *to be saved*. But while James's argument verifies from Scripture that the Gentiles were supposed to turn to God for salvation when Israel was restored, there is no scriptural warrant in his argument that exempts them from circumcision or any other part of the Torah.[32] The question that remains open and to which James offers a solution might then be phrased as follows: Granted that the Holy Spirit has already marked out these Gentiles as a people on their way to salvation who now publicly bear the name of the

---

31. For more detailed treatment, see L. Johnson, *Acts*, 264-65.

32. James's scriptural argument privileges what God is seen to be doing through the Holy Spirit over what the proponents of the view in 15:1 might cite as clear scriptural texts to the contrary (e.g., Gen 17:14; Exod 12:46-49; Josh 5:1-7). Hermeneutically, his argument moves from what God is seen to be doing to Scripture's agreement with it, rather than vice-versa (L. Johnson, *Acts*, 264, 270-73).

Section 3—Other New Testament Witnesses

Lord, how will this Lord's name/character be hallowed/sanctified through its non-Jewish bearers? This is a question that ties the public identity of the Gentiles who have turned to Israel's God to the explication of that God's identity in a variety of cultural locations in the nations. Hence, it is at once a question of both identity and mission, and James proceeds to answer it using the language and categories of purity/impurity.

James's instructions to those Gentiles who are turning to God and thus become bearers of his name are "to abstain from the pollutions of idols, from sexual immorality, from that which is strangled, and from blood" (15:20). While the exact content and purpose of these admonitions that are referred to twice more in Acts (15:29; 21:25) remains debated, the general tenor of two of the commands remain consistent throughout—in particular, "to abstain from pollutions of idols/food sacrificed to idols and from sexual immorality." The other two unclean practices in the lists are also probably associated with practices at various temples and are therefore themselves "pollutions of idols."[33] As we saw earlier, idolatry and all its trappings were considered polluting since, in opposition to the living God of Israel, other gods belonged to the realm of death and decay (cf. Ezek 36:17–18, 25).[34] The OT and Second Temple Judaism commonly connected sexual immorality with idolatry. Such admonitions may indeed be rooted in Torah's requirements for proselytes and sojourners (Lev 17–18) that would help to enable and regulate the social interaction in mixed Christian communities of Jews and these Gentiles who were turning to God.[35] This, in itself—a community composed of Jews and Gentiles regularly eating together in a Greco-Roman city—would be a powerful public testimony to the reconciling power of God, as we noted above in regard to the mixed community at Antioch. But James's framing the issue from the outset with the language of God choosing a people from the Gentiles who would bear his name suggests that these purity practices may also have to do with the public identity of communities composed totally of Gentiles who bear the name of the Lord in the wider Greco-Roman world. Being the holy people of God who bear his name in such a context includes not only "*an inward purity of heart by faith (Acts 15:9), but also . . . public practices that demonstrate purity thereby bearing witness to the church's faithfulness to Israel's God.*"[36]

33. Barrett, *Acts*, 730–36.
34. See p. 29.
35. Cf. L. Johnson, *Acts*, 267; Wall, "Reading Paul with Acts," 134.
36. Ibid., 131 (Wall's emphasis).

The Community of the Holy and Righteous One

"Turning to the living and true God from idols" (to use similar language from Paul in 1 Thess 1:9) and bearing the name of that God would mean becoming a part of a particular community known for publicly visible actions of refusing to engage in—and thereby challenging the very intelligibility of—a variety of "commonsensical" practices constitutive of pagan culture. Refusing to honor (at least) the gods of traditional Greco-Roman religion meant refusing to engage in "normal" activities like public festivals, trade association meetings in temples, or various private celebrations (e.g., birthday parties, weddings) in local temples. Since the gods were seen as the city's benefactors, such a way of life might be conceived as bringing their wrath (e.g., earthquakes, floods, agricultural failure). Hence, such practices of "abstaining from the pollutions of idols," might be understood by others as threatening to destabilize the very fabric of pagan culture.[37] This is evident in Luke's narration of Paul's mission in Acts when upheaval follows Paul in city after city (e.g., 14:8–20; 16:16–24; 17:1–9) where their inhabitants intuit a serious threat to their pattern of life when visible communities start to form in line with Paul's preaching. For example, when a large group in Ephesus who had formerly attempted to manipulate the gods with magic became part of the community of believers and burned their magic books,[38] Demetrius was able to rightly intuit the threat that such a community who bore the name of the Lord of all might represent to the whole temple-based economic system associated with the goddess Artemis (19:23–41).[39] The reactions of pagans in these cities indicate their intuition that a public pattern of communal life characterized by "abstaining from the pollutions of idols" threatens the very fabric of their culture. Rowe says it this way:

> To see the potential for the Christian mission for cultural demise is to read it rightly. Indeed, this is but the flip side of the reality that

---

37. See especially Rowe's historically sophisticated treatment of the way Luke narrates this perceived threat in the Pauline mission in Acts (*World*, 17–51).

38. The value of which was enormous (fifty thousand coins of silver) because their practitioners could earn a great deal of money with their incantations. Hence, to destroy such books was to threaten the religious and economic fabric of culture, both of which were inextricably intertwined.

39. On this whole episode, see Rowe, *World*, 41–49. The town clerk's subsequent speech is a less accurate understanding of the Christian mission than the speech of Demetrius. As Rowe maintains, it "does nothing whatever to address Demetrius' business worries; it merely points to his skill with a mob as a spokesman for Roman order and the status quo" (*World*, 49).

Section 3—Other New Testament Witnesses

> God's identity receives new cultural explication in the formation of a community whose moral or metaphysical order requires an alternative way of life. "Abstaining from the pollutions of idols" (Acts 15:20) is essentially—not accidentally—related to the "taking out of a people for God's name (15:14)."[40]

Apart from a few moral philosophers (e.g., Musonius Rufus), the notion that free married males could have sexual relations outside of marriage was simply "commonsense." Rather than being categorized as "immoral," it was generally considered their "right." As noted above, first-century Jews readily made a connection between idolatry and sexual immorality.[41] Israel's idolatry/covenant unfaithfulness was rhetorically cast in terms of sexual immorality/adultery (e.g., Ezek 23; Hos 1:2), and in a sense, sexual immorality was a form or expression of idolatry. In cities to which this decree would have been delivered (e.g., Antioch, Lystra, Philippi, Thessalonica), the two were also concretely connected in a number of social settings (e.g., public festivals and banquets in the temples or private homes involving gluttony, drunkenness, and sex with prostitutes[42]). For the Gentiles turning to God to engage in such sexual immorality would make their individual lives and their communal life together indistinguishable from much of the society around them. It would, therefore, threaten their character as a community set apart from its culture as an instrument of the *missio Dei*. Such activity that treated others simply as objects to exploit for gratifying sexual lust and (if one was married) exhibited infidelity to one's spouse might reflect the character and activities of the gods in the Greco-Roman pantheon, but it would not reflect the character of the God to whom these Gentiles had turned.[43] For a whole community of free males to abstain from such activity in a social context like this would reflect the faithful and loving character of Israel's God exhibited most clearly in the story of

---

40. Ibid., 146.

41. Note that in 1 Corinthians, Paul uses the verb "flee" only twice, once with its referent as sexual immorality (6:18) and once with it as idolatry (10:14). Cf. Marcus, "Idolatry," 154–55.

42. For a more detailed description of this social background, see Winter, *After Paul Left Corinth*, 86–94.

43. Greco-Roman religion was not characterized by organized communities devoted to worshipping a particular god or goddess nor was there any expectation that one's life ought to be patterned after the character of any of the particular gods or goddesses to whom they might pay homage. In this sense, Christian and Jewish communities were anomalies.

the crucified Lord of all. It would have the effect of explicating the identity of the God to whom they had turned as faithful and as characterized by self-giving love rather than selfish exploitation of others. It would be one means through which God's name was sanctified/hallowed through the life together of those Gentiles who were bearing name of the Lord of all among their unbelieving counterparts.

In this section, we have explored what happens in Acts when Gentiles with little or no prior Jewish influence begin to respond to God and are formed into communities who bear the divine name. We have seen that Luke's depiction of the practices in which these communities are engaging, and/or are directed to engage, would mark them out as bearers of the name of Israel's God and display his identity to the nations. We saw that the church at Antioch continued to engage in economic sharing for those in need in a similar way as the Jerusalem community (11:29–30). In a typical Greco-Roman city, such sharing with no expectation of a "payback" would subvert the normal expectations of gift giving while reflecting the generous character of their God of self-giving love. We also noted that one effect of implementing the purity practices called for by James in mixed Jew and Gentile communities would have been to enable and facilitate table fellowship within the group. This practice would have given powerful public witness to the reconciliation desired and enabled by the God whose name they bore. In addition, their abstaining from all the trappings of the idolatry that permeated daily life in Greco-Roman cities would set these communities apart, marking them off as belonging to Israel's "living God" and displaying their loyalty to him. As we just saw, a community of free males choosing to abstain from sexual immorality essentially explicates the very essence of the God to whom they had turned as faithful and characterized by self-giving love. Such a pattern of life has a cruciform shape manifest in faithfulness to God's life-giving, reconciling mission (*pistis*) that is expressed in self-giving actions for others (*agapē*) and avoiding actions that exploit others for selfish reasons. As such these communities taken from the nations in order to bear the divine name among the nations are "sanctified" (*hagiazō*), i.e., transformed and set apart as God's holy people through whom the Triune God sanctifies/hallows his name (20:32: 26:18). Their life together is a re-narration of the story of God's "Holy and Righteous One."

Section 3—Other New Testament Witnesses

Conclusion

In this chapter, we have seen that the early church in Acts is a sanctified community where members of the nations/Gentiles who switch lordships and receive forgiveness of sins are welcome. With cleansed hearts accomplished by repentance, baptism, and the reception of the Holy Spirit, the whole community is empowered by the same Spirit as was their crucified Lord for participation in God's mission. In witnessing to the resurrection of Jesus, the individual characters and communities in Acts embody a pattern of life through which God sanctifies/hallows his name "in Jerusalem, in all Judea and Samaria, and to the ends of the earth" (1:8). In this way, they offer a cultural explication of the identity and essence of the one who is indeed "Lord of all," and therefore, a cultural explication of the nature of holiness itself. Acting publicly in his name in ways that parallel his own actions, they thereby embody the character of the Holy and Righteous One, displaying a pattern of redemptive and reconciling activity through which God's mission is being accomplished. They are, therefore, those who have been and remain sanctified by faith in Jesus (26:18); they are transformed and set apart as God's holy people through whom the Triune God sanctifies/hallows his name. Their identity as God's sanctified people is formed as they—out of faith in, and faithfulness to, the Lord of all—participate in and witness to the *missio Dei*.

8

Paul and New Creation
"Colonies of Cruciformity"

Introduction

IN OUR READING OF the gospels, we called attention to the theme of Christ's body as a new temple with Christ's resurrection as the catalyst for a new creation with a redrawn purity map corresponding to its new structures. In Acts we saw that Luke, while not using the terminology of the church as the "body of Christ" or of followers of Jesus being "in Christ," depicted the lives of individual characters and the communal life of the church as "re-narrating" a story analogous to that of Christ's in the service of the *missio Dei*, sharing in the holiness of the Holy and Righteous One as bearers of the divine name.[1] With this conceptuality from the gospels and Acts, we have already begun transitioning into the thought world of Paul's letters. In this chapter our focus will be on Paul and his new creation "colonies of cruciformity."[2] Although much of our time will be spent on one of those colonies, the one in Thessalonica, we will not hesitate to draw from passages in other letters, not least of which is Paul's "master story" about Jesus in Phil 2:6–11.[3]

---

1. Whether or not Luke knows the "body of Christ" conceptuality of Paul, the way he tells the story of the church in Acts might make such language appropriate to use for the church (e.g., note the implications of Acts 9:4–5). Cf. the comments of Rowe, *World*, 173.

2. This language comes from Gorman, *Cruciformity*, 349.

3. Recent, helpful treatments of holiness in Paul's letters include Brower, *Living as God's Holy People* and the essays on individual Pauline letters in Brower and Johnson,

Section 3—Other New Testament Witnesses

Paul's Master Story

Paul did not set out to write a story of Jesus, but there is a story of Jesus that theologically underpins his letters, a story whose basic pattern is similar to that of the gospels. To flesh this out, we turn to Paul's "master story" in Phil 2:6–11.[4] It is a story about Christ/Messiah

> [6] who, although he was in the form of God, did not consider this equality with God as something to be exploited. [7] Rather, he poured himself out by taking the form of a slave, by being born in the likeness of human beings. And being found in human form, [8] he humbled himself by becoming obedient all the way to death—even death on a cross.[9] Therefore God has indeed highly exalted him and granted to him the name that is above every name. [10] [God did this] so that at this name belonging to Jesus every knee should bow in heaven, and on earth, and under the earth, [11] and every tongue confess that Jesus, the Messiah, is Lord, leading to the glory of God the Father.

In this passage, Paul says that Jesus was equal with God, God in visible form. However, unlike the garden's first human pair who grasped at godlike status, Christ refused to exploit his status of (already) being equal to God. Instead, in a downward *divine* movement he emptied himself, lowering his status by taking the form of a slave and becoming fully human. Then, in a corresponding downward *human* movement, he humbled himself by becoming obedient all the way to a shameful death on a Roman cross. In other words, on both sides of the divine/human equation, the pattern of activity that characterized this one person has a self-emptying, cruciform character.

For Paul, then, Christ revealed the essence of God's own character as one who displays his power through his vulnerable love. He acted this way precisely *because* he was equal with God even though it would have been out of character for the way "normal divinity" was conceived in the Roman empire—or in any other empire for that matter. In this same act, Jesus showed the lengths to which God would go to carry out his life-giving

---

Holiness and Ecclesiology. Of the latter, even though it is not often cited directly here, Gorman's essay ("'You Shall Be Cruciform'") has been particularly influential on what follows.

4. The "master story" terminology again comes from Gorman (*Cruciformity*, 88) and the following interpretation of it is similar to his more detailed treatment in *Inhabiting*, 9–39.

mission by becoming human and sharing in the plight of his creation gone awry even to the point of sharing in death itself. In his downward human movement, Jesus also revealed the essence of what God intended for Israel and for all humans—faithful obedience to God the Father expressed in self-giving love for others. The inseparability of this faithful obedience and self-giving love is evident throughout Paul's letters. Note, for example, Gal 2:20b: "And the life which I am now living in the flesh, I am living by means of the *faithfulness* of the Son of God who *loved* me *by giving himself up [on the cross]* for me." Hence, as in the gospels, Jesus' mission of faithful obedience to God (the Father) expressed in self-giving love for others was the means by which God's dream of carrying out his life-giving mission through humanity begins to come to fruition, and this is good news indeed.

For Paul, the gospel—the "good news"—is not a propositional roadmap to show individuals how to get our particular sins forgiven and go to heaven when we die. It certainly does have implications for addressing the sins of individuals and Sin as a power, as well as our participation in the life of the new age/creation. But, first and foremost, the "good news" is the proclamation of Jesus' faithfulness to the point of death in self-giving love for others and God's subsequent vindication of him as the world's true Lord. (This may remind us of Peter's preaching in Acts 2:22–36 and 10:34–43).

Paul's good news is related to the pattern that we saw earlier in Isa 5:16b where the prophet says: "the Holy God displays himself as holy by his [and his people's] righteousness (*tsedhaqah/dikaiosynē*)." In this passage, Isaiah maintains that the way that the sovereign Lord displays himself to be holy (or is sanctified) is through his own pattern of activity as well as by his people's reflection of that activity in their public life. In Rom 1:16–17, Paul maintains that the righteousness of God (*dikaiosynē Theou*), God's saving justice/covenant faithfulness,[5] is revealed precisely in the gospel/good news. That saving justice of God *by which he displays his holiness*, is revealed in Jesus' own life of covenant faithfulness (i.e., fidelity to God and love toward others). Romans 3:21–22: "But now, apart from the Law, God's saving jus-

---

5. As I have noted elsewhere, I understand God's *dikaiosynē* in Paul's writings to refer primarily to "a pattern of liberating, justice-restoring activity whereby God, in faithfulness to Israel and the entire created order, reclaims and reveals his sovereignty over a world enslaved by the powers of Sin and Death in order to make right what is wrong with individuals, societies and the cosmos itself" ("Paul's 'Anti-Christology,'" 129, n. 16). God's acting in judgment may also be a part of this saving activity (cf. Brower, *Living as God's Holy People*, 7–10). As shorthand for this broader definition, I will use the language of "saving justice."

Section 3—Other New Testament Witnesses

tice (*dikaiosynē*) stands revealed ... the saving justice (*dikaiosynē*) of God revealed through the faithfulness of Jesus Christ[6] to all those exercising believing allegiance." This one man's *human* obedience (cf. Phil 2:8) that is constituted by a deed of saving justice (*dikaiōmatos*) simultaneously reveals *divine* saving justice (*dikaiosynē*) because it salvifically reverses Adam's disobedience together with its death-dealing effects and leads to "rectification (*dikaiōsin*) of life" for all (Rom 5:18–19). So then, the faithfulness (*pistis*) of Jesus reveals God's saving justice (*dikaiosynē*) because his obedient deed of saving justice (*dikaiōmatos*) is its human embodiment. Hence, both human righteousness and divine righteousness come to their fullest expression in the cruciform Messiah.[7] It is no wonder that Paul can say that the crucified Christ has become "*holiness*" for us from God (1 Cor 1:30) since the righteousness by which God displays his holiness is revealed in the story of the cruciform Christ. This connection between righteousness/saving justice (*dikaiosynē*) and holiness in the character of God revealed in Christ is crucial for Paul, and we will note this same connection in the life of the church later.

The goal of God's mission is expressed in Phil 2:10–11.[8] That goal is that every creature will bow the knee to the one true human, the incarnate Son, to whom the Father has given the divine name and who will exercise God's lordship over creation. (Gentiles acknowledging Jesus as "Lord of all" in Cornelius' house was a "preview of this coming attraction.") When Jesus' lordship is universally acknowledged, with every creature giving proper honor to their creator, creation will itself be "rectified" or "rightly" ordered. With God at the center and all of Babel's diverse voices now in rich harmony honoring the one true God, diverse people are not only reconciled to God but also at peace with each other. We saw an advance glimpse of this in Acts with Jews, Samaritans, and Gentiles reconciled when they acknowledged the Lordship of Jesus together. This is nothing short of the "new creation" Paul believed God had already begun to bring in the body of the risen, cruciform Son, the advance pattern of which was to be publicly displayed in the life of God's cruciform colonies (e.g., Rom 15:5–6). With

---

6. Taking the contested Greek phrase, *pistis Iēsou Christou*, as a subjective genitive that yields the translation, "faithfulness/fidelity of Christ." For a concise summary of the advantages of taking the phrase in this way, see Gorman, *Cruciformity*, 110–19.

7. For the connections made in this paragraph, see my "Paul's 'Anti-Christology,'" 129–30.

8. On this point, see my "Missional from First to Last."

this basic Pauline framework in mind, we turn now to focus on Paul's first letter to the Thessalonians.

Aspects of Holiness

Holiness as Derived from God/Spirit-Enabled

In 1 Thess 1:1, Paul describes this church as existing "in" or "by means of" the actions of God the Father and the Lord Jesus Christ. Paul usually does not describe a church as being "in God" (but cf. Col 3:3), but here he seems to be doing just that. Being "in" the Lord Jesus Christ"—by virtue of the close relationship between Jesus and the Father in Paul's writings—is simultaneously to be "in God the Father." Paul ends the body of 1 Thessalonians in 5:24 by affirming God's faithfulness to complete his work of sanctifying the Thessalonians. In the meantime, he highlights the Spirit's work in his proclamation that led to God initially electing them (1:5) and, borrowing Ezekiel's language from the valley of dry bones, he speaks of God "giving his Holy Spirit *into you all*" (4:8; cf. Ezek 37:6, 14), underscoring the Spirit's continuing activity *among* the community and *in* its members' individual bodies. God is continually breathing into them an ongoing supply of the cruciform Holy Spirit, God's own life-giving presence. Divine grace is not some "substance" God adds to peoples' lives; it is nothing other than the life-giving presence of God's very self.

It is "in the sphere of sanctification engendered by [this] Spirit" that the audience's ongoing salvation takes place (2 Thess 2:13, 16–17). That sphere is the network of relationships that constitutes the church—the risen body of the cruciform Christ in specific locales with all its ambiguities and problems. There the Spirit is active in sanctifying ways as the cruciform Lord encourages and strengthens the hearts/imaginations of those within it as they engage in cruciform practices for each other and for those outside the community (1 Thess 3:12–13). As we will see in more detail later, these Holy Spirit-enabled cruciform actions done by the whole community or the individuals within it become channels through which God not only continues God's mission, but also one means through which God continues their sanctification.

Located "in Christ," they are thereby located "in God." Since God's acts cannot be separated from God's being, their participation in this God's mission as the Holy Spirit is given "into" them entails a real participation in the Triune God's own being.[9] Paul depicts this community as holy and as continuing to be made holy as they participate in the *missio Dei*. This holiness is derived from God the Father in the sphere of Christ the Son, through the activity of the Holy Spirit.[10] It was this Spirit who was at work in Paul's proclamation giving it persuasive power as the channel through which God began the process of sanctifying the audience when he initially elected this church (1:5).

Holiness and Election in 1 Thessalonians: The Corporate and Public Nature of Holiness

We saw in the OT that God elects Israel *as a whole people,* rescuing and setting them apart—or "sanctifying" them—both because he loved them and so that they might become an instrument for his mission (Ps 105:6; Isa 41:8–10; 42:1; 49:1–7). Drawing on OT covenantal language about God's love for, and election of, Israel to be God's holy people (e.g., Deut 7:6; 14:2), Paul gives thanks for the Thessalonian church because, as he says, "We know God has elected *you all*" (1:4). Similarly, in 2 Thessalonians, he says that he is obliged to continue giving thanks to God for the same congregation who are "beloved by the Lord" because "God chose *you all* as first fruits leading to salvation" (2 Thess 2:13). Paul's plural pronouns and the OT background of his language indicate that God's election of these Gentiles in Thessalonica for holiness is a corporate election of a whole people, a people "in Christ," God's elect one. But they remain secondarily elect "in Christ," Israel's representative Messiah, God's primary Elect and Holy One (Luke 9:35; 23:35; Mark 1:24; John 6:68–69).[11] Individuals are only elect and holy "in Christ," i.e., as part of the publicly visible body of the risen cruciform Christ in a particular social location.

Holiness, therefore, is intensely personal but never private; it has an unavoidably *public* expression. As we saw in Acts, in the social settings of Paul's predominantly Gentile churches, switching lordships and living in singular faithfulness to the God of Israel makes the notion of a holy "invisible church" incoherent. Election and holiness are inextricably joined.

---

9. On the inseparability of God's actions and God's being, see Gunton, *Act and Being*. Since God's actions reveal who God actually is, participating in God's mission/actions is a real participation in God's being.

10. Cf. Gorman, "'You Shall Be Cruciform.'"

11. See my "Ecclesiology, Election," 250.

Paul and New Creation "Colonies of Cruciformity"

Hence, in 1 Thess 1:5–8, one of the reasons Paul gives for why he knows God had elected the Thessalonians was because the church body *as a whole* had become a *public* model,[12] exhibiting their "faithfulness" (*pistis*) toward God in the midst of the difficult social and political pressures we described in the last chapter as facing such Gentile churches (1 Thess 1:6–8; 2:14; 3:3). In "imitating" both the Lord and Paul (1:6), the Thessalonians were living out a pattern of life in their particular social context that was *analogous to*—not slavishly identical with—the Lord's faithful pattern of life and that which Paul displayed when he was with them (1 Thess 2:1–12).

Verse 8 fleshes this out, "For from you the message about the Lord has rung out not only in Macedonia and Achaia. But in every place your faithfulness (*pistis*) to God has gone forth." That is, not only had their oral proclamation[13] about God's mission in Jesus reverberated throughout the region, so had their faithful pattern of life. Speaking about the Lord's saving mission goes hand in hand with an observable pattern of life that reflects that mission. Paul refers to this life pattern throughout much of 1 and 2 Thessalonians (1 Thess 1:3, 8, 3:2, 5, 6, 7, 10; 2 Thess 1:3–4) with the term *pistis* (faith/faithfulness/fidelity). While this term certainly includes an element of trust and belief, it does not refer to some sort of inner trust or belief that a person somehow "trades" for a justified status or a ticket to heaven which then may *result in* outward faithfulness or "works." Rather, by definition, it includes an ongoing and costly turning away from the daily activities of honoring various (false) gods and goddesses to the living and true God. As 1:9 makes clear, this is a publicly observable action that gets people talking: "That is, [they are talking publicly about] how you all turned to God from idols to be enslaved to the living and true God."

Paul's description of this life pattern—this *pistis*—as enslavement (*douleuein*) to "the living and true God" (1 Thess 1:9) suggests an analogical relationship to Jesus' actions when he took the form of a slave (*doulos*) in becoming human and then demonstrated faithfulness to God in his obedience all the way to death on a cross out of love for others (Phil 2:6-8). Thus, Paul depicts the congregation as corporately displaying a pattern of missional faithfulness similar to that of Jesus. Their faithfulness (*pistis*)

---

12. In v. 7, Paul explicitly refers to "you all" becoming a *singular* model as a whole congregation (although he certainly expects each person to live an exemplary life).

13. This need not mean the Thessalonians were "street preaching." But others surely would have asked them about changes in their public behavior. In such conversations, naming Jesus as Lord and telling of his faithfulness to God's mission would have called their culture's idolatry into question, provoking the hostility of some.

Section 3—Other New Testament Witnesses

that is analogous to that of Jesus exhibits their participation in God's saving mission and may be characterized as an "*an initial and ongoing cruciformity, grounded in the faithfulness of Jesus the Messiah.*"[14] Engaging in this Spirit-enabled, cruciform pattern of life on an ongoing basis is the concrete form of their being "in Christ." Publicly participating in the life of Christ in this way is to participate in God's Elect, Holy One, the one whom Paul says has "become holiness (*hagiosmos*) for us from God" (1 Cor 1:30). Hence, their ongoing public pattern of life—their faithfulness (*pistis*)—re-presents the life of the cruciform risen Christ and marks them out as both holy and elect since they are "in" the Elect, Holy one of God.

In some of his other letters, Paul's imagery of the church as the "temple (*naos*) of God/the Holy Spirit" (1 Cor 3:16–17; 2 Cor 6:16; Eph 2:21) underscores the public nature of holiness. Public space in cities like Corinth and Thessalonica was dominated by a plethora of temples of various gods and goddesses. These temples (*naoi*) and the images (*eikones*) they housed were the primary public face of the god or goddess to whom they were "home." Hence, to refer to the Christian community as the temple of God/the Holy Spirit in a place like Corinth was to imply that their Spirit-enlivened life together functioned as the public face of the one Holy God of Israel. Indeed, it was to imply that their life together as that temple/sanctuary was the place where divine glory—God's holiness made visible—had come to dwell.[15]

To connect some dots with what we have already seen in this chapter and in our chapters on the gospels, since Jesus was the moveable sanctuary/temple (*naos*) of Israel's holy God, this community, whom Paul also depicts as the body of Christ (1 Cor 10:16–17; 12:12–31; Rom 12:4–5) is, like their Lord, the temple/sanctuary (*naos*) of the Holy God. To further extrapolate the connection, since Jesus is the very image of God (2 Cor 4:4) in whose face the glory of God is seen (2 Cor 4:6), the community who forms his body in the world is indeed the public image (*eikōn*) of the one God, God's public face where divine glory/holiness becomes visible. This holiness becomes visible in this community temple as they engage in a public pattern of activity that is analogous to the Lord's own faithfulness as instruments in God's saving mission.

---

14. Gorman, *Cruciformity*, 95, 387.

15. As such, one could argue that for Paul, the Holy Spirit indwelling the community is in some way identified with the long awaited returning Shekinah (glory or glorious presence of Yahweh) of Exod 40:34–38 and Ezek 43 (Wright, *Paul and the Faithfulness of God*, 712).

Paul and New Creation "Colonies of Cruciformity"

We may also note here a connection with the conceptuality of creation as temple in Genesis. Since the community's life together is the temple of the Holy God, they are also the beginning of the "new creation" (2 Cor 5:17; Gal 5:16). As the whole of the old creation was to be the temple of the creator God, the theater of his glory, the life of this community of the cruciform, risen Christ is to be a microcosm of the coming new creation, the temple of the Holy God that makes God's now cruciform glory/holiness publicly available in their specific locale.

In the contexts in the Pauline corpus where the church is described as God's temple, several features of the church's life together are emphasized through which God's cruciform glory is on display. In 1 Cor 3:16–17 Paul warns his audience that God will destroy anyone who defiles/destroys[16] God's holy temple by threatening its unity/integrity with selfish, status-seeking divisive actions. Hence, by implication, it is the presence of self-giving, loving actions on behalf of one another that contribute to the community's visible unity and become the "building material" of the temple of the Holy God in Corinth. A community that lives this way would stand out in a culture like that of Corinth, where it was simply "commonsense" for individuals to act in ways that brought them the most public status and honor. Its cruciform character would indeed be the theater of God's cruciform glory, God's visible holiness. As such it would function as the temple of the Holy God in Corinth, the public face of the community's Lord. No wonder then, that Paul was so upset with this community for the way their division and selfish, status seeking intra-communal life "defiled" the one true God's temple and smeared his face in public!

In 2 Cor 6:14—7:1, Paul calls the community "the temple of the living God," which, like Israel, is the "people of God" with the Holy God "dwelling and walking among" them (v. 16).[17] In this context Paul emphasizes the distinction of the community from its surroundings and calls for its "cleansing" and avoidance of what is "impure/unclean" and that which "pollutes." Paul does not specify here what would pollute or defile the community, but it would no doubt include some of the sexual behaviors he proscribes in 1 Corinthians (see e.g., 1 Cor 5; 6:12–20) as well as behaviors

---

16. On the wordplay involved in Paul's using one Greek term (*phtheirō*) in 1 Cor 3:17 to mean "defile" in the first part of the sentence and "destroy" in the second part, see Sampley, *1 Corinthians*, 831.

17. For a more extensive treatment of this passage in light of its OT background, see Wright, *Paul and the Faithfulness of God*, 713–15; cf., Adewuya, "People of God."

Section 3—Other New Testament Witnesses

that exploit others with injustice (e.g., 1 Cor 6:1–9a).[18] In 1 Cor 6:19–20, Paul uses temple of God imagery with reference to both individuals and the community to counter the tendency of some men in the community who are engaging in a very common social practice of having sex with prostitutes.[19] There Paul says: "Or don't you all know that your (plural) body is the temple of the Holy Spirit who is among you whom you all have from God and you don't belong to yourselves? Therefore, glorify God in your (plural) body." As we will see, behavior that exploited others as objects for sexual gratification would have been "defiling" on Paul's purity map and, therefore, totally incongruous in the life of a community that is the temple of the Holy God. For males in this society to avoid this sort of behavior that was understood to be their "right" would have been part of what it meant to be in the process of "perfecting holiness in the fear of God" (2 Cor 7:1). It would have made them as individuals, and the community of which they were a part, stand out in the culture of Corinth and would have publicly differentiated the face of their Holy God from the faces of the gods and goddesses whose temples lined the streets of Corinth.

Perhaps an even more striking characteristic of such new creation communities, however, would have been their public display of reconciliation between people formerly at odds with each other. The context of Eph 2:11–22 has to do with what God has done in Christ to reconcile two groups that were previously hostile toward each other (i.e., Gentiles and Jews). The imagery of this passage is arresting, particularly that of vv. 14–16, which speaks of Christ having "broken down the dividing wall[20] . . . [and] created one new humanity in himself by making peace so that he might reconcile both [groups] to God in one body through the cross, having put their hostility to death in himself (or by means of the cross)." This community now reconciled to God and to each other—the community elected by God in Christ, God's Elect One (Eph 1:4–6)[21]—is being joined together and "is

---

18. See the section below on "Holiness and Purity."

19. This language is usually taken as only referring to each individual's body as a temple of the Holy Spirit. But Paul's language suggests that there also remains a corporate aspect to this image (e.g., Levison, *Filled with the Spirit*, 294–300). This is not surprising in that in Paul's writings, the Holy Spirit is understood to dwell both *in* individuals and *among* the community as a whole. What follows in this paragraph assumes that the temple imagery applies to both individuals and the community as a whole in this context.

20. Possibly a reference to the wall in the Jerusalem temple that divided the court of the Gentiles from the inner area of the temple where only Jews could go.

21. On the nature of this election language in Eph 1:4–6, see my "Ecclesiology,

growing into a holy temple in the Lord," being built into "a dwelling place of God by means of the Spirit" (Eph 2:21–22). The *shalom*/peace that is presently reflected in this new humanity of the new creation powerfully testifies to the actions and essence of the peacemaking God who has made the church's corporate life together an exhibition of the gospel of peace.[22] Hence, publicly visible reconciliation and peace between previously hostile groups is characteristic of the holy temple that reflects the face of its particular God.

To sum up this section, we return to 1 Thessalonians where we saw that the reason Paul knew God had "elected" the community at Thessalonica, had set them apart as holy, is because their public life together mirrored Jesus' own life pattern of fidelity to God. Their ongoing public pattern of life—their *pistis* (faithfulness)—re-presents the life of the cruciform risen Christ and marks them out as both holy and elect since they are "in" the Elect, Holy one of God. Paul's metaphorical depiction of God's elect in Christ as his holy temple underscores the public and corporate nature of holiness. As beneficiaries of God's mission, Paul's communities were now expected to participate in it as publicly identifiable corporate bodies reflecting the face of their God. We turn now to explicate further the church's participation in that mission, and in particular its *mode* of participation.

Holiness and Righteousness/Saving Justice

We saw earlier that the connection between righteousness/saving justice (*dikaiosynē*) and holiness in the character of God revealed in Christ is crucial for Paul. The connection between the two is also crucial in the life of God's people. We can see this in both Romans and 1 Thessalonians.[23]

The language of being enslaved to God appears in both 1 Thessalonians (1:9) and in Romans 6 (v. 22). Romans 6 is best understood as a *definition of* (not a result of) the justification (*dikaiōsis*) by faith/faithfulness Paul speaks of in Romans 3–5.[24] In Romans 6 Paul is describing a justified people who have been rescued by the saving justice (*dikaiosynē*)

Election," 250.

22. Cf. Gorman, *Becoming the Gospel*, 189–92.

23. Here again, for this section on Romans I have adapted material from my "Paul's 'Anti-Christology,'" 130–31.

24. Gorman, *Inhabiting*, 73–79; cf. Campbell's comments on the language of Rom 6:7–8 which implicitly move in a similar direction (*Deliverance*, 825–27).

Section 3—Other New Testament Witnesses

of God (Rom 1:16–17) from the chaotic progression of enslavement that he rehearses in Rom 1:18–32. As such, they have been rectified/justified/liberated (*dikaioō*) from their enslavement to the powers of Sin and Death (6:7) and reconciled to God and each other by God's justice-restoring mission (5:1, 10–11). They are no longer to present themselves to the power of Sin as "weapons of injustice/unrighteousness (*adikia*)" but, rather, to present themselves as "weapons of saving justice/righteousness (*dikaiosynē*) to God" (6:13). As such they become weapons for God through which his saving justice is channeled;[25] they become God's means of continuing his mission to reclaim his cosmos from the chaos of Rom 1:18–32. Paul goes on in 6:18–22 to connect this language to the language of holiness:

> [18] Now having been freed from Sin, you all have been enslaved to saving justice/righteousness (*dikaiosynēn*)[19] . . . For just as you all presented your members as slaves to impurity resulting in lawlessness leading to more lawlessness, so now present yourselves as slaves to saving justice/righteousness leading to holiness/sanctification (*hagiosmon*). [20] For when you all used to be slaves of Sin, you all were "free" with respect to saving justice/righteousness. [21] So what benefit did you have then from the things of which you are now ashamed? The result of these things is death! [22] But now, since you have been freed from Sin and enslaved to God, the benefit you all have leads to holiness/sanctification (*hagiosmon*), the result of which is the life of the new age!

In this passage, the pattern of life for a justified/rectified people is enslavement to God/God's saving justice (*dikaiosynē*) that leads to, and is constitutive of, holiness/sanctification (*hagiosmos*). In essence, they become the very saving justice (*dikaiosynē*) of God (cf., 2 Cor 5:21), the weapon(s) through which the Spirit continues God's life-giving invasion of the world. Having been liberated by God's life-giving mission, as they participate in this mission they are a set-apart people, the holy/sanctified people of God.

When we return to 1 Thessalonians with its heavy emphasis on holiness and its similar language early in the letter about being "enslaved to the living and true God" (1:9), we might have expected to see the term saving justice (*dikaiosynē*) throughout. But Paul never uses it and only once uses a word in the "righteousness" word family (*dikaiōs*, 2:10). The relative absence of words, however, does not necessarily signal that the theme is absent.

---

25. Similarly, Jewett, *Romans*, 411.

Paul and New Creation "Colonies of Cruciformity"

At least one aspect of the good news that the Thessalonians heard (1:5) would have been that God's saving justice (*dikaiosynē*) was revealed in Jesus' life of covenant faithfulness (i.e., his fidelity to God and love toward others). As noted, in Phil 2:6–11, Jesus' faithful obedience to God and his self-emptying love for others are on display in one single action—his death on the cross. This connection between fidelity to God and love for others is as inseparable in the lives of those elect "in Christ" as it was in Jesus' own life. Note, for example, Gal 5:6: "For in Christ Jesus neither circumcision nor uncircumcision counts for anything. What counts is faithfulness (*pistis*) being concretely worked out through loving actions (*agapē*)." Christ's risen, cruciform body (i.e., the church) is the microcosm of the new creation where the structures of the old cosmos (e.g., circumcision/uncircumcision) are now irrelevant. Faithfulness to God joined with cruciform love for others constitutes this new creation's (Gal 6:15) fundamental cross-shaped structuring principle, or as one might say, its new purity map.[26]

In 1 Thess 2:1–9, Paul recounts the "sort of people" (1:5c) he and his companions were in Thessalonica as they engaged in concrete, costly actions for the good of the Thessalonians as they faithfully proclaimed the gospel. *Simultaneously* displaying *both* their fidelity (*pistis*) to the God who called them to proclaim the gospel (vv. 1–6) and cruciform actions of love (*agapē*) toward others (vv. 7–9), they exhibited the very pattern of the good news they proclaimed (1:5c). They "became the gospel."[27] Paul goes on in 2:10 to characterize this pattern of activity as "*holy (hosiōs)* and righteous (*dikaiōs*)" and "blameless" (2:10). In Israel's scriptural tradition, God can also be described as "righteous and holy" (Deut 32:4b) with humans created to reflect that character. Humans were created by God "to rule the world in holiness (*hosiotēs*) and righteousness" (*dikaiosynē*, Wis 9:3). Hence, in "putting on the new humanity, created in accordance with God in true righteousness (*dikaiosynē*) and holiness (*hosiotēs*, Eph 4:24)," we are restored into God's own image as we begin to reflect his divine character. Paul's own personal example among the Thessalonians sews together righteousness and holiness and functions as "a living exegesis of what divine righteousness and holiness looks like when reflected by human beings, i.e.,

---

26. We will enlarge on this point later in this chapter.

27. Gorman has recently developed this missional theme in Paul at length (*Becoming the Gospel*) and his treatment of 1 Thess moves along similar lines as this chapter (63–105).

Section 3—Other New Testament Witnesses

fidelity toward God that is simultaneously costly love for others."[28] This personal example was not lost on the Thessalonians. Their lives also are characterized by fidelity to God and love for others (1:3; 3:6), and therefore reflect divine righteousness (*dikaiosynē*) and holiness (*hosiotēs*) in their particular social setting.

Paul's imagery in 1 Thess 5:8 moves in a similar direction and reminds us of the holy warfare language of Romans 6: "But since we belong to the day, let's remain self-controlled now that we've put on a breastplate of faithfulness and love and a helmet, which is hope for salvation." Here, Paul implies that he and the Thessalonians are involved in some sort of ongoing "war" and that faithfulness and love together constitute one *singular* piece of defensive armor. As the primary contours of a cruciform mindset, they can be distinguished but not separated. Nor are they some sort of static qualities; both fidelity and love can continue to develop and grow (1 Thess 3:10, 12; 2 Thess 1:3) and are the primary *mode* in which God's elect participate in God's life-giving invasion of the world.

In Isa 59:17, the source for Paul's imagery in 1 Thess 5:8, the prophet describes God on a mission to rescue his helpless people from their own idolatry and injustice by saying that he "put on saving justice (*dikaiosynē*) like a breastplate and placed a helmet of salvation on his head." In Isaiah the breastplate of saving justice (*dikaiosynē*) is part of the divine warrior's armor as he engages in his rescue mission, and Paul has the church wearing similar armor in 1 Thess 5:8. However, unlike Eph 6:14, which maintains the original wording of Isaiah's "breastplate of saving justice (*dikaiosynē*)," here in 1 Thessalonians Paul has the church as a whole wearing the *singular* breastplate of faithfulness (*pistis*) and love (*agapē*). Like Paul's language in 1 Thess 2:10, this suggests that when divine righteousness/saving justice (*dikaiosynē*) is embodied by a human community, it takes the form of fidelity (*pistis*) to God and loving cruciform actions (*agapē*) for others.

In putting on the breastplate of fidelity toward God and love toward others, the church becomes "the righteousness/saving justice (*dikaiosynē*) of God in [Christ]" (2 Cor 5:21). Or one might say, it becomes the gospel in which God's righteousness/saving justice (*dikaiosynē*) is revealed (Rom 1:17). In line with the patterns we have seen in Isaiah and Ezekiel, embodying this divine righteousness/saving justice (*dikaiosynē*) becomes a public display of God's holiness. God's giving his Spirit into the Thessalonian church (1 Thess 4:8//Ezek 37:6, 14), making them blameless in holiness in

---

28. A. Johnson, *1 & 2 Thessalonians*, 233.

the *parousia* (3:13), is not for their sake alone. It is so that the now cruciform Lord might *manifest his holiness by means of their life together* before the eyes of the "nations/Gentiles who do not acknowledge God" (4:8//Ezek 36:23).

In this section, we have seen that even if explicit "righteousness/justice" terminology is not common in 1 Thessalonians, its conceptuality is not absent. In fact, its emphasis on holiness provides a fruitful context for fleshing out the connection between righteousness/justice and holiness that we have seen elsewhere. The God revealed on the cross is a "missional, justifying, justice-making God [who] creates a missional, justified, justice-making people."[29] When the elect human community is enabled by the Spirit to reflect divine righteousness/saving justice through their faithfulness to God and cruciform, loving actions for others, they thereby also reflect God's holiness. They become the means by which the triune God reveals his own holiness to the (currently) non-elect, the holy channel through which he continues his saving, justice-making mission and calls others to join it.

Holiness and the Pursuit of Peace

Immediately after mentioning the divine warrior's "helmet of salvation," Isaiah goes on to describe his taking vengeance on his adversaries, clothed with a "garment of vengeance" (Isa 59:17b–18). Paul echoes this language in 2 Thess 1:5–8 and speaks about the Lord's "giving vengeance (*ekdikēsin*)" against those who oppose him when he is revealed (2 Thess 1:7–8). Those who continue in opposing his saving mission will experience God's saving justice (*dikaiosynē*) as judgment. However, Paul never depicts "vengeance" as being a part of the wardrobe of those in his colonies of cruciformity. Paul never depicts them as becoming a channel through which *that* part of God's saving mission is enacted—whatever form such "vengeance" ultimately takes.[30] Echoing Isa 59:17b–18, Rom 12:19 makes this perfectly clear: "'Vengeance is mine; I will repay,' says the Lord" (cf. also Deut 32:35).

Wearing the singular breastplate of faithfulness and love by which they embody divine saving justice, this community has essentially "presented their members as weapons of saving justice to God" (Rom 6:13).

---

29. Gorman, *Becoming the Gospel*, 9.

30. For some reflections on Revelation's imagery regarding the form of God's ultimate judgment, see the next chapter.

Section 3—Other New Testament Witnesses

But they are not weapons that destroy. They have been delivered by God's invasive, life-giving mission in order to be enlisted in that same mission. In essence, they become God's "weapons" for continuing his mission. In the words of Willard Swartley, they have been "enlisted, yes at baptism, in the warfare of peacemaking."[31] As I have said elsewhere, "When holiness itself was dislocated and then relocated in a crucified Nazarene, the 'holiness' of holy war was also dislocated away from destructive exclusionary violence and relocated in nonviolent actions of peacemaking."[32] Hence, for those "in Christ," *holy* warfare in this new cosmos can only be the nonviolent "warfare" of peacemaking—at least in principle.[33]

Peacemaking is a decidedly missional activity constitutive of holiness itself because it is constitutive of the God revealed in the cruciform Christ. This God is the "God of peace,"[34] the agent of sanctification (1 Thess 5:23) whose actions in Christ sought to create peace between himself and human beings (e.g., Rom 5:1; Col 1:20) as well as peace among human beings themselves (e.g., Eph 2:14–16). Peace, in this sense, is not primarily a psychological state (i.e., "peace of mind"). It is more so a social reality characterized by the lack of hostility between persons and groups of persons, an overall state of well-being, the full *shalom* that God intends for creation when it reaches its intended goal. To seek peace in this sense is indeed to be a participant in God's mission on behalf of his creation.[35]

This pursuit of peace involves seeking peaceful relationships among those who are within the church and peaceful relationships with those outside the church. Anyone who has read 1 Corinthians (or ever been a part of a church themselves!) will immediately recognize that peaceful relationships among those "in Christ" is not at all automatic. As in churches today, in Paul's churches divisive issues and/or potentially divisive issues were common and often complex.[36] A key ingredient in the way he addressed such

---

31. Swartley, *Covenant of Peace*, 245.

32. A. Johnson, *1 & 2 Thessalonians*, 237.

33. Once again, this "in principle" represents my ongoing caveat to a total pacifism. While I do not think that war can ever be "holy," it might be possible that in some very limited situations, some use of force is the *least unholy* option available in the situation. See my earlier, admittedly somewhat ambivalent, reflections on pp. 17–18.

34. The phrase "God of peace" is apparently Paul's own creation and thoroughly undergirds Paul's ethics (Swartley, *Covenant of Peace*, 210–11).

35. Again, see Gorman's more detailed development of this missional theme in *Becoming the Gospel*, 142–211.

36. For example, Paul addresses issues that seem to have already divided the church

issues was to exhort others to act in accordance with his own cruciform example of seeking the interests of others rather than his own (Phil 2:4) by giving up that to which he was "rightfully" entitled (e.g., 1 Cor 6:7; 8:9–13; 9:1–27; 10:23–24; 14:18–19; Rom 14:15–21; 2 Thess 3:7–9). In essence, this requires those "in Christ" to exhibit a mindset ("a pattern of thinking, acting, and feeling"[37]) that is appropriate for those whose corporate body is a re-presentation of the cruciform, risen Christ (Phil 2:5). In the midst of these difficult situations, as well as in less conflict-charged situations, Paul counsels his congregations to continue seeking intra-communal peace and to engage in practices that will sustain such peaceful relationships (e.g., Rom 14:19; 1 Thess 5:12–12).

This is always easier said than done and presupposes the initial and ongoing transformation of those "in Christ" (on which, see below). It is "the Lord himself who engenders peace" whom Paul can call upon to be at work in the community to grant the community peaceful internal relationships (2 Thess 3:16). So even when tensions among brothers and sisters remain, the Lord's work in transforming them and their intra-communal relational networks continues. Indeed, since the fruit of the Spirit that God continually supplies to the church (1 Thess 4:8) includes peace (Gal 5:22), and since the faithful God who will sanctify them completely is none other than "the God of peace, himself" (1 Thess 5:23), there is every reason for Paul to expect that peaceful relationships can and should characterize the church's present life together. But God will not bring this about unilaterally; *God will be at work through their efforts* to maintain peaceful relationships in the community. Since the Lord's own character/activity defines holiness, and that very character is marked by peace, it is only by pursuing peace with each other that those "in Christ" will be able to reflect this God's character to one another and to those outside their community. Hence, the holiness/sanctification of the whole community depends on God's transforming work that happens in and through its members *continuing to pursue* right relations with their brothers and sisters.

Paul also calls for practices that would facilitate peaceful relationships with those *outside* the church (e.g., 1 Thess 5:15; Rom 12:17–21). When writing to the Thessalonians who are experiencing extreme social pressure

---

in 1 Cor 1:10–12; 3:3–4; 6:1–8; 11:17–31; 14:1–40; Phil 4:2–3. If division has not already occurred, Paul addresses other issues that have the potential for causing division in places like 1 Cor 5; 8:1—11:1; Rom 14:1–23; 2 Thess 3:6–16.

37. Fowl's language in translating Phil 2:5 (*Philippians*, 88).

Section 3—Other New Testament Witnesses

from others in Thessalonica, Paul strikingly directs them to see to it that "no one repays evil for evil but always seek the good for each other *and for all*" (1 Thess 5:15). Seeking the good not just for one another but "for all" virtually defines the cruciform love that Paul prays will increase and flourish in the congregation in 1 Thess 3:12. There he prays that the Lord would enable the Thessalonians "to increase and flourish in love for one another *and for all*" that leads to their community being "blameless in holiness" at the Lord's coming (1 Thess 3:12–13). Acting this way would mark them off as a distinctive community and would extend God's peace to those perpetuating evil against them. It would concretely display God's own character/holiness because it would reflect the way he acted toward enemies (cf. Luke 6:35–36), a way of acting that explicated the nature of divine justice as the restoration of *shalom*/peace as in Romans 5 (esp. vv.1, 10).[38] They would thereby become an instrument of God's love through which the God of peace is at work to change violent enemies (like Paul himself had been at one time) into his own children, to restore justice by reconciling them to himself *and* to their victims.[39] With their corporate life simultaneously displaying what God means by peace and justice, they would, therefore, become one channel of what Rom 5:1–10 might call God's justification of the ungodly. That is precisely what the Christian community in southern Bangladesh became in their particular social setting (see pp. xv–xvi). As God's elect, they bore the consequences within themselves of God's current wrath being poured out on their persecutors manifest in latter's rebellion and ignorance. In doing so, like their Lord, they became a channel of God's reconciling love through which the God of peace worked to change their (ungodly) violent enemies into his own children, and brothers and sisters of their former victims.

Such reconciliation between people and God and between people formerly alienated from each other is a mark of the new creation in Paul's colonies of cruciformity, an advance peek into the window of creation reaching its intended destiny. Faithfully *pursuing* such peace—not necessarily successfully attaining it (Rom 12:18)[40]—belongs to the essence of holiness. It is a "critical marker of ecclesial identity—not as an ethical principle but

---

38. See the insightful reflections along these lines in Gorman, *Inhabiting*, 129–60.

39. Cf. Swartley, *Covenant of Peace*, 211–16.

40. Seeking the good of one's enemies and confronting them with the mercies/restorative justice of God may do little more than bring on more suffering for the church (see comments on 2 Thess 1:6 in my *1 & 2 Thessalonians*, 168-69).

as a sign of the presence of Jesus [through the Spirit] and of the church's fellowship with him."[41] It is not just another task on the church's "to do" list. Rather it is a Spirit-enabled activity apart from which the church ceases to truly be the church. In and through the church's pursuit of peace, the God of peace not only continues his life-giving rectifying and reconciling mission, he continues his work to bring about the church's complete sanctification making it the one, holy church it is called to be. Hence, pursuing peace with everyone is constitutive of—or a necessary condition for—"the holiness without which no one will see the Lord" (Heb 12:14; NRSV).[42]

But holiness is not only about actively engaging in particular practices. As we have already seen in the chapter on Acts, for a community to be God's holy people, they must also avoid certain practices. Throughout his letters, Paul also counsels his hearers to avoid certain practices, particularly ones that are out of bounds with the cross-shaped "purity map" of the new creation.

Holiness and Purity: Faith and Love as the Cross-Shaped "Purity Map" of the New Creation

In the risen cruciform body of Christ, the microcosm of the new creation, the structures of the old cosmos are no longer relevant. But Paul still sees the world through the lens of purity/impurity, where impurity is a polluting force that can detrimentally impact individuals and the whole network of relations in which they live. We saw hints of this earlier in 1 Cor 3:16–17, where Paul warned his audience that God will destroy anyone who defiles/destroys God's holy temple by threatening its unity/integrity with selfish, status-seeking divisive actions,[43] and in 2 Cor 6:14—7:1, where Paul exhorts the Corinthian community as "the temple of the living God" to avoid what is "impure/unclean" and that which "pollutes." Hence, while this microcosm of the new creation has its own structures, it is not without a purity map. While there remains some overlap with the purity map of the old creation (particularly regarding issues of sexual immorality), the contours of the new creation's purity map are cross-shaped along the lines of fidelity to God and cruciform love for others.

---

41. Gorman, "Lord of Peace," 238.

42. On which, see Thomas, "Perfection of Christ," 308–10.

43. Such actions are "defiling" because they are the opposite of cruciform actions of love for others.

Section 3—Other New Testament Witnesses

We see a good example of the way these contours work regarding sexual immorality in 1 Thess 4:3–8. Whatever the historical specifics of the situation,[44] Paul's main concern is to counsel self-control in sexual matters, prohibiting any form of sexual immorality (for Paul, any sexual relationship outside of marriage). In the chapter on Acts, we described the widespread "commonsense" assumption in the Greco-Roman world that free males—married or not—had the "right" to have to have sex with various sexual partners. We saw how the "decree" from James and the Jerusalem church, in line with general Jewish assumptions reflecting the purity map of the old creation, connected such behavior with idolatry. If the "Gentiles turning to God" were to continue to engage in such activity, it would not only make fellowship with Jewish believers difficult, it would make them indistinguishable from much of the society around them. Such uncontrolled sexual behavior would not reflect the character of the faithful God to whom they had turned and would, therefore, threaten their character as a community set apart from its culture as an instrument of the *missio Dei*.

Since the Thessalonians were among those "Gentiles turning to God" (1 Thess 1:9) away from the idolatry of their culture, Paul had similar concerns in the situation reflected in 1 Thess 4:3–8. However, to be a little more specific about the situation reflected here, Paul claims that acting with the sort of lustful passion characteristic of Gentiles who do not acknowledge God would result in wronging or exploiting a brother or sister (4:6). Hence, the main issue appears to be the possibility of intra-communal sexual immorality, which Paul characterizes as "impurity," (4:7) suggesting that it has a contagious, polluting potential for the community as a whole.

Such exploitative behavior—whether in the first or twenty-first century—is the opposite of cruciform love for others. It is an idolatrous form of self-love that gives allegiance to one's own sexual fulfillment rather than to the God who created humans as sexual beings.[45] Like other forms of idolatry, it ultimately has destructive consequences, and not just for those directly involved in it. Particularly when it occurs within a local church, its destructive impact radiates throughout the community in multiple directions. The resulting pain and broken relationships may continue long into the future and continue to generate more pain and more broken relationships. In

---

44. On which, see the discussion in my *1 & 2 Thessalonians*, 107–12.

45. Like other Second Temple Jews, Paul understood *porneia*/sexual immorality as an expression of idolatry (on which, see my *1 & 2 Thessalonians*, 108). Cf. Gorman, *Inhabiting*, 127.

Paul's letters, this sort of "impurity" continues to be a dynamic, contagious force able to infiltrate and pollute entire relational networks (e.g., 1 Cor 5; 6:12–20). The resulting brokenness and pain is the opposite of the *shalom* that God, through the giving of the Spirit, is attempting to bring about in the church as part and parcel of their sanctification. Hence, Paul insists that "God did not call us to impurity" (4:7)—to live in a sphere which is contaminated by practices that violate the new creation's cross-shaped structure of fidelity to God (*pistis*) and cruciform love for others (*agape*). Rather, God called us "[to live] in the sphere of sanctification" (4:7).

Contamination of the holy sphere with practices (not just those that are sexual in nature) that violate the new creation's cross-shaped structure release "contagious impurities" of various sorts within the community to do their infiltrating, destructive work, compromising the *shalom* of the community and thereby its holiness. Avoiding such practices, therefore, is a *necessary condition*[46] for God to continue his sanctifying work and bring it to completion with the audience "blamelessly" reflecting his holy character.

Holy Practices and God's Sanctification of Our Imagination

Paul does not use "inner" anthropological terms like "heart" or "mind" in overly precise ways. In general, however, he uses such terms to refer to the inner aspect of a person's intentions, dispositions, and cognitive judgments.[47] Such terms refer broadly to one's framework for making cognitive and volitional judgments and construals about the world and they roughly correspond to the way I will use the term "imagination." Our imagination usually functions invisibly at an unacknowledged level shaping our intentions and dispositions and the practices that flow out of them. It is not, however, a disembodied "mental" or "spiritual" faculty. Rather, if recent work by psychologists and neuroscientists is on track, what I am calling "imagination" is physically embedded in the neural network of our brain and each of us is socially embedded within a network of relationships.[48]

---

46. *Necessary*, but *not sufficient*, since Paul clearly understands sanctification as involving more than the avoidance of certain practices, sexual or otherwise.

47. See my *1 & 2 Thessalonians*, 97.

48. For accessible introductions to this work by psychologists and neuroscientists in light of its theological and ecclesial implications, see Brown and Strawn, *Physical Nature*; Green, *Body*.

Section 3—Other New Testament Witnesses

As we engage in concrete physical practices and various forms of social interactions, our neural networks are physically "rewired," thereby reshaping—even transforming—our imaginations.[49]

Unless they were already connected with a synagogue, Gentiles in Paul's churches had not previously associated honoring a god or goddess with either joining a community with singular allegiance to that deity or patterning their lives after that deity's character. In addition, their "commonsense" notions of divinity focused primarily on raw power, and their social lives were typically consumed with maximizing the honor and status others might attribute to them. So it would have required no less than a "conversion of the imagination"[50] for them to join a community whose members were to pattern their lives after the power-in-weakness, self-lowering character of the Lord they honored. For the Thessalonians, the Spirit began this transformation of their imaginations through their social interaction with Paul, Silas and Timothy who both proclaimed the good news about the cruciform Lord to them (1 Thess 1:5) and modeled his faithful, cruciform life before them (1 Thess 2:1–12). In the prolonged presence of others in such a mentoring relationship, we unconsciously begin to mimic their mannerisms, facial expressions, behavior, and even their dispositions and ways of thinking.[51] Such social interactions with Paul and his companions became the Spirit's channel for "rewiring" or sanctifying the neural networks of the Thessalonians so that the "commonsense" of the ancient culture of honor and status would no longer be the unacknowledged, embedded framework undergirding their dispositions and practices. Engaging in these social interactions within this ecclesial framework was the only way the Thessalonians could begin to discern what faithfulness to the living and true God entailed and how they might enact such loyalty in their particular cultural context.

This "sanctification of their imaginations"[52] was an ongoing process that, as Paul's wish to "make complete the things lacking in [the Thessalonians'] faithfulness" (1 Thess 3:10) suggests, was incomplete when he wrote the letter. Such language is probably not referring to those in the

---

49. See Markham, *Rewired*. Markham essentially equates conversion and sanctification, arguing that conversion/sanctification is a continual, life-long process involving both biological and social aspects (68–72).

50. This phrase is from Hays, "Conversion of the Imagination."

51. Brown and Strawn, *Physical Nature*, 78–82.

52. On this language, see my "Sanctification of the Imagination."

community being *intentionally* disloyal to God, but rather, to *a lack in their ability to discern* how their fidelity to God ought to be embodied in the variety of circumstances that might come up in their daily lives.[53] The community was constantly bombarded with conceptions of "normal divinity" not just in the plethora of local temples, but also on coins, statues, altars etc. Such conceptions could not accommodate notions of shame, vulnerability, and suffering. They were at odds with the cruciform pattern of true divine glory seen in the face of Jesus (2 Cor 4:6). They could easily creep back unintentionally into the community's conception of the God to whom they had turned, underwriting a pattern of life at odds with this cruciform God's character. But as the Thessalonians' imagination is continually transformed into a progressively more cruciform shape, that which is "lacking in their faithfulness" will be made complete because they become increasingly proficient in discerning and carrying out God's will in a variety of circumstances. Paul expresses this idea in Rom 12:2 when he urges his hearers to be continually transformed by the renewing of their mind *in order that* they can then discern God's good will.[54]

With his prayer in 3:11–13, Paul makes the sanctification of the church's imagination a public concern (not a private matter between the individual and God) for "all the brothers and sisters" hearing the letter:

> [11] Now may our God and Father himself and our Lord Jesus clear our way to you all. [12] And may the Lord enable you *to increase and flourish in love* for one another and for all just as we [were enabled by the Lord to increase and flourish in love] for you all [13] *in order that* he might *strengthen your hearts* to be *blameless in holiness* in the presence of our God and Father in the royal coming of our Lord Jesus with all his holy ones.

Here Paul specifically focuses on the Lord enabling the audience's loving practices to increase, some of which are directed toward "all," even those outside the community who may be persecuting them. As we saw earlier, such loving actions for "all" would extend God's peace to those perpetuating evil against the community, making them an instrument of God's love

---

53. The verb in 1 Thess 3:10 translated as "make complete" (*katartizō*) is often used in educational contexts referring to the teacher completing the student's instruction so that the student might live fully as an adult (cf. Luke 6:40). See comments on this verse in my *1 & 2 Thessalonians*, 91.

54. Phil 1:9–10 moves in a similar direction in that the audience's increase in loving practices is connected to their heightened ability to discern how best to live in fidelity to God so that they are blameless on the day of the Lord (cf. Wagner, "Working," 257–74).

Section 3—Other New Testament Witnesses

through which he carries out his reconciling mission. Paul's prayer assumes an initiating divine action (enabling the increase in loving practices) which is followed by a responsive human action (engaging in cruciform practices). This initiating activity followed by God's taking up and incorporating faithful human response into his purposes and activity is the paradigmatic theological pattern we have seen in the biblical story since Genesis 18.

The prayer also assumes a reciprocal movement *from* their being engaged in grace-enabled, cruciform practices *to* (or for the goal of) strengthening their hearts/imaginations to be blameless in holiness at the Lord's royal coming. That is, Paul is depicting the Lord as sanctifying the Thessalonians' hearts/imaginations *in the context of*, or even *by means of*, their own grace-enabled concrete practices in a way that continues their initial transformation. Hence, the Lord works among the Thessalonians to sanctify their imaginations in a similar way as God worked through Israel's divinely enabled Torah practices as one means of continuing their sanctification. In other words, participation in concretely physical practices through which God continues his mission is one means God uses to enable his elect people to "unlearn" what passes for "commonsense" in their culture and replace it with "cruciform" sense. It is one avenue through which the Spirit "hardwires" the new creation's pattern and structure into the minds and bodies of those "in Christ."

A brief story might help to clarify what we are saying in this section. In a discussion of what ecclesial holiness means, a pastor from Guyana offered the following example. One of his church's outdoor worship services was interrupted by a man who was being chased by second man wielding a pitchfork. The latter was screaming threats to murder the former because he had stolen his chicken. Placing their very bodies in harm's way out of love for both men, the entire worshipping assembly moved between these men, keeping the second man from making good on his threats. As they were doing so, they began a conversation with both men. After clarifying what the dispute was about, they were able to bring about reconciliation between them and restore justice in the situation regarding the chicken. Enabled by the Spirit, these church members moved as one body—the body of the risen, cruciform Christ—to become a channel of God's *shalom* and restorative justice in this moment and thereby to display the character of the Holy God in their unique social setting. Perhaps this movement was the Spirit's channel for initiating the conversion of one or both these men's imagination. But participating in it as a member of the church no doubt had a sanctifying effect on the imaginations of the participants. In a culture in which violent retribution against someone who wronged you was "commonsense," participating in such a social interaction comprised of this sort of concrete, physical act would began to "rewire" one's neural network with "cruciform sense." This ecclesial action—which literally required a network of communal relations to be carried out—was enabled by the Holy Spirit. In turn, the Spirit worked through their grace-enabled actions to shape and transform, indeed, to continue simultaneously sanctifying both the imaginations of persons within that assembly and its corporate imagination as a whole.[55]

Grace-enabled participation in the *missio Dei* within an ecclesial framework is one means by which God sanctifies the "old cosmos-shaped" imagination of his elect community and transforms it into a "new-creation imagination." Therefore, God's means of carrying out his will to sanctify his elect community and the entire self of each person in it (1 Thess 4:3; 5:23[56])—of (re)shaping a whole people into the *imago Dei*—is inseparable from, or even primarily constituted by, participation in the *missio Dei*.

Summary: Holiness and the *Missio Dei* in Paul's Colonies of Cruciformity

There are other aspects of holiness that could be emphasized in Paul's letters (e.g., the connection between holiness and work).[57] However, by focusing on 1 Thessalonians with briefer forays into Paul's other letters, enough has been said to see the major aspects of holiness and its connection with the mission of God in these letters. A short recap of these aspects is in order.

First, we saw that human holiness is always derived from God the Father in the sphere of Christ the Son, through the activity of the Holy Spirit. Since the church is located "in Christ," and thereby "in God," with the Holy Spirit being continuously given "into" it, its members' participation in this Triune God's mission entails a real participation in his activity/being (i.e.,

---

55. The *exact mechanics* of *how* the Spirit works to enable and transform persons and communities is not clear. *That* the Spirit does work in the midst of, and even by means of, self-giving actions requiring an ecclesial framework has been the main focus of this section.

56. For a fuller discussion of the language of God sanctifying "his elect community and the entire self of each person in it," see my comments on 1 Thess 5:23 in *1 & 2 Thessalonians*, 156–59.

57. On which see, my *1 & 2 Thessalonians*, 249–55.

Section 3—Other New Testament Witnesses

in his holiness).[58] Second, while holiness is intensely personal, it is not a private matter to be worked out by individuals in some "invisible church." Rather, it is necessarily public and corporate, on display in a visible community whose public pattern of life re-presents the life of the cruciform risen Christ, thereby making them instruments of God's mission and marking them out as both holy and elect. Third, the mode in which the church participates in God's mission—the mode of the church's embodiment of divine saving justice through which God's holiness is displayed to those not currently elect—is faithfulness to God and cruciform loving actions for others. Fourth, faithfully pursuing peace, both inside the church and with those outside it, belongs to the essence of holiness since the God who sanctifies is "the God of peace" whose character the church is to reflect. Fifth, for those participating in God's mission, purity is still important. Avoiding practices that violate the new creation's cross-shaped structure by releasing destructive, *shalom*-compromising "contagious impurities" within the community is a *necessary condition* for God to continue his sanctifying work. Finally, Spirit-initiated and -enabled participation in God's mission in the form of concrete, physical cruciform practices is one way the Spirit works to continue sanctifying the imaginations of persons within a local assembly and thereby simultaneously sanctify its corporate imagination as a whole. Hence, God's means of (re)shaping us into the *imago Dei*, of making us holy, is inseparable from—and primarily constituted by—our participation in, and witness to, the *missio Dei* whose ultimate goal is to bring creation to its intended destiny.

It is time now to move on to the final book of the New Testament, the book in which creation's intended destiny is most fully on display.

---

58. As we noted above, since God's actions reveal who God actually is, participating in God's mission/actions is a real participation in God's being.

9

Revelation, Holiness, and Mission

Introduction

WE BEGAN THIS BOOK with a question: what does holiness/sanctification have to do with the *missio Dei* (i.e., the mission of God in the world)? The answer we have given to this question—at least as it relates to *God's rescue mission of the world*—has been that for both Israel and the Church, to be sanctified is to be graciously taken up into, and set apart for witness to and active participation in, the saving, reconciling, life-giving purposes of the missional God, whose ultimate desire and mission is to bring his good creation to its intended goal.

But how can one square this vision of holiness and God's ultimate desire for his creation with the last book of the Bible?[1] Popular escapist interpretations of Revelation abound (e.g., the *Left Behind* series) where the book is understood to provide a literal roadmap of God's plan to whisk the church out of the world in a secret rapture to a heavenly party while everyone else is left to suffer unspeakable devastation and horror before the earth itself is utterly destroyed. This is the general plot line of a particular (very faulty) scheme of interpretation that originated in the early nineteenth century and is overlaid onto not just Revelation, but the Bible as a whole (i.e., popular Dispensationalism).[2] Such an escapist framework for approaching

---

1. For the basic structure, socio-political background, and theological orientation to the way I read Revelation, see esp. Bauckham, *The Theology of the Book of Revelation*. For accessible introductions to Revelation, see Gorman, *Reading Revelation Responsibly*; Koester, *Revelation and the End of all Things*, and esp. for a lay level audience, Boone, *Answers for Chicken Little*.

2. For a further description and critique of this interpretive scheme, see my *1 & 2*

Section 3—Other New Testament Witnesses

Scripture is at odds with our missional approach that explicates holiness as costly participation in God's mission to bring his good creation to its ultimate goal of brimming with fruitful life and *shalom*. At first glance, with the plethora of terrifying images and planet-wide scenes of divine judgment and destruction, it may seem as though an escapist interpretation of Revelation might be warranted. A closer look, however, demonstrates just the opposite. We will see that Revelation does indeed display a similar pattern to what we have seen in other biblical books regarding holiness and participation in the saving, reconciling, life-giving purposes of the missional God. Revelation, in fact, is a missional text through and through designed not to equip the church to be ready to escape in a secret rapture, but to participate in God's rescue mission by "following the Lamb into the new creation."[3]

A Brief Orientation to the World of the Seven Churches and John's Purpose for Writing

John's way of communicating using apocalyptic symbols can sometimes be bewildering, but as the book's first word and title (revelation) indicate, his purpose is to reveal, not conceal. His book is sent out in the form of a letter to seven first-century urban churches in Asia Minor in the larger Roman Empire, where social, economic, and political life was pervaded by a "civil religion." People were expected to pay proper homage to the traditional gods and goddesses and also to demonstrate their loyalty to the empire and its emperors though the imperial cult. As we saw in the chapter on Acts, this would happen in daily activities like public festivals, trade-association meetings in temples, or private celebrations (e.g., birthday parties, weddings) in the local temples which dominated public space in these cities. Since the traditional gods/goddesses were seen as a city's benefactors, refusing to participate in these "normal" activities might be understood as bringing divine wrath (e.g., earthquakes, volcanic eruptions, food shortages, foreign invasions) down on the city or, at the very least, destabilizing the culture. In the imperial cult in Asia Minor, the expectation of honoring these traditional gods extended to the deified Caesars and the

---

Thessalonians, 288–305; Gorman, *Reading Revelation Responsibly*, 70–73.

3. The words in quotes come from the subtitle of Gorman's, *Reading Revelation Responsibly: Uncivil Worship and Witness, Following the Lamb into the New Creation*. This book is a thoroughly missional reading of Revelation. See also Flemming, "Revelation and the *Missio Dei*."

"divinely sanctioned" empire of Rome. If those outside the churches in the seven cities concluded that Christians were refusing to give proper honor/worship to these deified Caesars and the "divinely sanctioned" empire they embodied, they might have understood these Christians as a threat to the peace and security of the city and the empire as a whole, *even if Christians never intended any such thing*. The result would, no doubt, have been *local* persecution of some sort, most probably in the form of social ostracism, verbal harassment, possible political sanctions, financial hardship, and even sporadic physical violence (e.g., Rev 2:10; 3:10).

While there was most likely no "official" persecution from the Roman Empire itself in the first century, such local pressure/persecution could be difficult to navigate, as the churches of Smyrna and Philadelphia knew all too well (Rev 2:8–11; 3:7–13). For the churches of Pergamum, Thyatira, Sardis, and Laodicea (Rev 2:12—3:6; 3:14–22), making some accommodation to the values of Rome's imperial culture might indeed have been an enticing way to lessen such local pressure/persecution. But in John's view, for these churches to accommodate to such values would involve them in a whole system of idolatry that violated first-commandment faithfulness and immersed them in allegiance to an exploitative economic and political system. Hence, using the symbolism of apocalyptic literature, John writes to the churches of Asia Minor to reveal the way things really are when seen "from the heavenly perspective."[4] That is, contrary to appearances: the power embodied in an empire and/or its leaders who have claimed ultimate—even divine—authority to rule and exploit many is not attractive but positively "beastly" in nature; those who suffer the consequences of prophetically witnessing against such rule (i.e., being "conquered" by this beast) do not suffer ultimate defeat but will share in God's new creation; such prophetic witness to God's mission to rescue the world from the beast and its allies is the role of the church in the first century (and the twenty-first century!). John puts his revelation in the form of a letter and employs apocalyptic symbolism to issue a prophetic call to those in the churches to "come out of Babylon" (18:4) by embodying a distinct way of life that resists the idolatrous system of Roman social, economic, and political values and verbally witnessing to the truth about its idolatry.

John's Revelation, then, is a prophetic call to holiness and might be "regarded as a vision of the fulfillment of the first three petitions of the Lord's Prayer: 'Your name be hallowed, your kingdom come, your will be

---

4. Bauckham, *Theology*, 7.

done, on earth as it is in heaven' (Matt 6:9–10)."[5] The problem for John and his first-century audience was clear: They "lived in a world in which God's name was not hallowed, his will was not done, and evil ruled through the oppression and exploitation of the Roman system of power."[6] It was a world that was far from the cosmic sanctuary God had created it to become through the agency of humanity. The vast majority of humans had failed to give proper honor/glory to their creator (cf. Rom 1:21–23), much less re-present his gracious presence to each other (like priests) in his cosmic temple and rule over it (like kings) in a way that creation would flourish with well-ordered life (Gen 1:28; 2:15). The world was—and is—not yet the "place in which the reign of God is visible and unchallenged, and his holiness is palpable, unthreatened, and pervasive."[7] It had—and has—not yet become the "theatre of his glory" (i.e., of his visible holiness) and thus was—and is—not yet flourishing with the abundant life engendered by God's pervasive, immediate holiness.

What, then, is John's vision of how God's name becomes hallowed, God's kingdom comes, and God's will be done on earth as in heaven? How does John envision the world becoming God's cosmic sanctuary saturated with his life-giving holiness that he had always intended it to become through the agency of his human priestly kings? To answer this question, we start where John does, with his vision of the heavenly throne room, the "place in which the reign of God is visible and unchallenged, and his holiness is palpable, unthreatened, and pervasive."[8]

The Heavenly Throne Room and the Slaughtered Lamb

When John is invited into the heavenly throne room in chapter 4, he is given a sneak peek of creation rightly ordered as all of heaven's creaturely inhabitants (the twenty-four elders and the four living creatures) continuously give the Creator proper glory/honor (4:8–11). Here there is *shalom*, overall well-being, as God's name is hallowed, his reign is uncontested, and his will is being done. Here, the words from the four living creatures who resemble Isaiah's (equally strange looking) seraphim (Isa 6:2) echo day

5. Ibid., 40.
6. Ibid.
7. Levenson, *Creation*, 86.
8. Ibid.

Revelation, Holiness, and Mission

and night through heaven's halls. Using the seraphim's words, they affirm that in heaven God's holiness is "palpable, unthreatened, and pervasive"[9] when they say: "Holy, holy, holy is the Lord, God Almighty" (4:8). And yet, the words they use next seem to signal their knowledge that while this is indeed the case in heaven, things remain amiss on the earth. In Isaiah, after the seraphim cry out to one another, "Holy, holy, holy is the Lord of hosts," they go on to say "the whole earth is full of his glory (*doxa*)" (Isa 6:3). Here, however, in the words of the four living creatures, there is the conspicuous absence of any affirmation that the earth is full of the Holy God's glory (*doxa*), his visible holiness. Rather, after affirming his holiness, they simply continue with a further description of the one on heaven's throne as "the one who was and who is and who is coming" (Rev 4:8). This language—which echoes the language of the burning bush in reference to God's name (Exod 3:14)—repeats John's opening description of God in 1:4. Such language implies that the creator God in the heavenly throne room is not satisfied with the way things are on the earth. For this God "is coming" to make things right so that the whole earth will be full of his glory (i.e., his visible holiness pervading a Spirit-saturated new creation).

Although we get little detailed description of this coming One, it is clear that the throne is occupied and that beauty emanates from its occupant (4:2). In the next chapter we are introduced to what is arguably the central image of the whole book, namely, the slaughtered Lamb who shares the throne with, and thus shares the identity of, the one on heaven's throne.[10] Hence, the one whom the four living creatures describe as "holy to the max" shares an identity with the Lamb who bears the marks of slaughter, the one whose faithful, obedient witness led to his death on a shameful cross. This shared identity is underscored when the twenty-four elders (and probably the four living creatures) and the myriads of angels sing praises to the Lamb with words that echo the praises they give to the Holy Creator God in chapter 4 (5:9, 12) and then when every creature in the cosmos gives *the same praise at the same time to both* the one seated on the throne and to the Lamb (5:13). The Lamb, of course, is none other than the risen, exalted, and yet *forever cruciform*[11] Christ. The way he exercises

---

9. Ibid.

10. The pattern of the slaughtered Lamb/Jesus sharing the identity of the creator God is embedded in Revelation's language in a variety of ways (see Bauckham, *Theology*, 54–65; Gorman, *Reading Revelation Responsibly*, 102–15, esp. 110–11).

11. The effect of the verb tense John uses to refer to the *slaughtered* Lamb is that it emphasizes, like Paul's "stamped forever with the legacy of crucifixion" language (1 Cor

Section 3—Other New Testament Witnesses

his messianic power as "the Lion of the tribe of Judah" (5:5)—the very way he "conquers"—is through his sacrificial death in faithfulness to God for the sake of others. The Lamb, then, not only redefines the nature of true power, he reconfigures what it means to be the almighty, thrice holy God. In other words, in the Lamb, the God who is on the throne and is coming to make things right is reconfigured Christologically.[12] Hence, it is the pattern of Lamb-like activity—the pattern of the cruciform and risen Christ designated as "the Holy One" in 3:7—that also reconfigures divine holiness, of what it means to be holy to the max.

But what, according to Revelation, is Lamb-like activity? Revelation highlights three aspects of Christ's actions, all of which are in the service of establishing the kingdom of God on earth: (1) His faithful witness in word and deed to the truth that Israel's God is the one true god of creation and history resulting in (2) his sacrificial, liberating death bringing about a new exodus for an international people, a priestly kingdom in the service of this one true God; (3) his activity as judge at the Parousia.[13] For our purposes in this chapter, we will focus on the first two.

First, we consider Christ's faithful witness in word and deed. The first descriptor of Jesus in Revelation is "the faithful witness" (1:5), a designation that appears again in slightly altered form in 3:14 as "the faithful and true witness." Given the association of the word "witness" in Revelation with the language of the "word of God" (1:2, 9; 6:9), the witness given clearly has a verbal component and is prophetic in character. But since it can also be associated with "keeping the commandments of God" (12:17), faithful practices are also involved. Hence, Jesus' faithful witness in Revelation should be understood as involving witness *in word and deed* to the truth that Israel's God is the one true god of creation and history. In terms more specific to Revelation itself, we could say that "[i]t is primarily Jesus' and his followers' witness to the true God and his righteousness, which exposes the falsehood of idolatry and the evil of those who worship the beast."[14] As John's very next descriptor of Jesus in 1:5 ("the firstborn from the dead") implies, this sort of faithful witness in Revelation's world is likely to result in

---

1:23; 2:2; cf. Mark 16:6), that this risen, exalted One continues to bear the marks of pain and shame into the very life and identity of the Triune God, and therefore reveals that God's very nature is cruciform.

12. On which, see Gorman, *Reading Revelation Responsibly*, 102–15.

13. Cf. Bauckham, *Theology*, 67–73.

14. Ibid., 72–73.

death, as is confirmed by the death of "Antipas, my *faithful witness*" (2:13). It is Christ's faithful witness in word and deed—in Pauline terms, his "obedience to the point of death"—that reaches its culmination in the second aspect of Christ's work highlighted in Revelation, his sacrificial death for the sake of others.[15]

Shortly after introducing the imagery of Christ as slaughtered Lamb, John says more specifically: "You were slaughtered and by means of your blood you purchased for God those from every tribe and tongue and people and nation and you made them a kingdom and priests for our God" (5:9). Here, John metaphorically depicts Jesus' death as the slaughter of a Passover lamb whose sacrificial death "ransoms" people in a new exodus,[16] thereby creating an international people with the same vocation that was supposed to characterize Israel, and indeed all of humanity in the first place, i.e., being mediators of God's presence (priests) and rule (kings) for the sake of others (cf. Exod 19:6). Revelation's addressees in the seven churches were characterized in precisely this way when John refers to them as having been "loosed from our sins by means of his [Christ's] blood" and made "a kingdom, priests for his God and Father" (1:5). They are, therefore, depicted as sharing in the character and vocation of the risen, cruciform Christ who is himself portrayed in 1:13 in both royal and (high) priestly garments.[17] The sacrifice that Christ as high priest offered was that of his faithful testimony in word and deed that led to his own sacrificial death that liberated others. In this way, he mediated the holy, life-giving presence of God to others. In John's vision, those who have been liberated in this way and made a kingdom of priests for this thrice holy, life-giving God are called to offer an analogous sacrifice. That is, they are called to offer faithful testimony in word and deed that will—at least potentially—become *part* of the way God draws others to repent and confess his rule, thereby liberating them from slavery to the beastly system in a new exodus.

We will see this most clearly in the story of the two witnesses in chapter 11. However, between here and there we have to endure vivid—even gruesome—scenes of God's judgment on an idolatrous and unjust world

---

15. For the basic content of this paragraph, cf. Flemming, *Recovering*, 234.

16. Rev 5:9 may also allude to Isaiah's Suffering Servant who is also depicted as a sacrificial lamb (Isa 53:7), perhaps as a way of portraying Jesus as the Passover lamb of Deutero-Isaiah's new exodus (Bauckham, *Theology*, 71).

17. The "golden sash" is the royal emblem of a king (cf. "the ruler of the kings of the earth," 1:5). The "long robe (*podērē*)" is part of the holy vestments which Aaron, as high priest, wears (Exod 28:4).

SECTION 3—OTHER NEW TESTAMENT WITNESSES

in chapters 6, 8, and 9. Before we can see the fuller picture of the role of God's people in God's mission in Revelation, we need to address a question that some might imagine poses a serious problem for the argument we have been making in this chapter: How do these scenes of judgment work in Revelation's own logic to facilitate God's rescue mission and further his ultimate missional purpose of making the whole earth that he loves "full of his glory" (i.e., his "palpable, unthreatened, and pervasive"[18] holiness)?

Judgment Visions and Holiness

The vivid imagery used in the judgment scenes of Revelation is unmatched in Scripture, but those scenes share a common biblical pattern to which we called attention in chapter 1. As we saw in the story of Sodom, while judgment and destruction clearly come from God, it is not God's original intent for the way he would deal with his creatures. But God's judgment against persistent opposition to his life-giving purposes is a manifestation of his loving sovereignty over his creation, his refusal to allow human beings to go on indefinitely treating others as less than the images of God they are and thereby become more and more beastly and dehumanized themselves. Sodom becomes a kind of cipher in the biblical story for people and empires (like Egypt and Babylon) that engage in such dehumanizing, beastly behavior and oppose God's people and/or purposes. It is not surprising, then, that the city in which God's two (paradigmatic) faithful witnesses are opposed and killed by the beast who arises over and over in ever new incarnations (11:7) is symbolically called "Sodom and Egypt" (Rev 11:8).[19]

The first two series of vivid judgment imagery come in chapters 6 and 8–9. While this imagery must be taken seriously, there is no more warrant for taking it literally than there is for insisting that Jesus is literally a wooly lamb and has a sharp sword for a tongue. These vivid scenes may indeed symbolize punishment on those who oppose God and God's people, but Revelation's own structure and words indicate that punishment is *not the*

---

18. Levenson, *Creation*, 86.

19. The language of "over and over again" is implied by the present tense participle form of the Greek word for "arise" in 11:7. Like the "man of lawlessness" in 2 Thess 2:3–12, the beast in Revelation represents the pinnacle of unredeemed life "in Adam." This is life so far from what humanity should be that it can properly be called "beastly" (see my "Paul's 'Anti-Christology'").

primary function of these first two series of judgments.[20] Revelation 9:20–21 functions as a summary statement, indicating that the essential purpose of these judgments had been *to bring about repentance* for idolatry and the resulting unjust/immoral actions that spring from it:[21]

> The rest of humanity who were not killed by these plagues *did not repent* of the works of their hands so that they would not worship demons and idols of gold, silver, bronze, stone, and wood which can't see, hear, or walk. And they *did not repent* of their murders, sorceries, fornication, or thefts.

For the *shalom* that characterizes a centered heaven to also pervade life on earth, for God's kingdom to come, humans would have to repent of their idolatry and give the creator God and the Lamb proper glory/honor (Rev 14:6–7), thereby centering their lives on the life-giving God. In other words, something like Phil 2:10–11 would have to take place. For that to happen, however, a humanity gone awry into enslavement would have to be shaken loose from its false securities; people would have to experience the chaos for which they cast their vote in their idolatrous lifestyle *as the destructive chaos that it actually is*. The judgment scenes leading up to 9:20–21 are essentially John's way of depicting God allowing humans to experience his wrath in the form of injustice, violence, and death that results when God's creatures and creation is not centered around his will and purposes. John is making a similar point as is Paul in Rom 1:18–32, but he does so with "apocalyptically enlarged" images whose effect is to evoke a sense of unease in those who encounter them and *draw them to repentance*—especially

---

20. The extreme vividness of the language in these chapters makes it unsettling that John traces such destruction and death directly or indirectly to God. The Lamb opens the seals leading to the judgment scenes associated with the seals (6:1). The angels who stand before God are given trumpets (either by God or with God's permission) and blow them, initiating the plagues that follow (e.g., 8:2, 6–7). But in the larger theological context of the NT and of Revelation itself, God is not unaffected by the chaos he allows his creatures to experience as a result of their idolatrous choices. Rather, God has acted in a slaughtered Lamb, absorbing the effects of those choices (i.e., injustice, violence, and death) into the very throne itself in order to purge the world of those effects. The Lamb is "worthy to open the scroll" (5:9) only *because* he himself has experienced the very effects of the divine wrath that cannot but characterize a world centered on idolatrous embodiments of the divine.

21. The "plagues" connected with the blowing of the seven trumpets in chapters 8–9 are partially modeled on the plagues against the Egyptians and, thus, also symbolize God acting in Exodus-like ways to bring deliverance to his people in the midst of trying to bring their oppressors to repentance.

Section 3—Other New Testament Witnesses

hearers from the seven churches, which are often called to repentance (2:5, 16, 21; 3:3, 19). As Yahweh's lesson to Abraham in Genesis 18 made clear, the "way of the Lord" is not simply characterized by quantifiable retributive justice. *As his initial move* to rectify situations of injustice, *God does not desire to destroy* those involved in that injustice,[22] but rather to extend his mercy as far as is possible if there remains any real possibility for repentance and change in the situation.

In John's vision, such warning judgments alone do not finally bring about repentance (9:20–21). For God's kingdom to come, for his will to be done on earth as it is in heaven, for God's name to be hallowed by an idolatrous human race finally giving proper honor and glory to God, for God's holiness to become "palpable, unthreatened, and pervasive"[23] on earth so that the world becomes his cosmic sanctuary, something else has to happen. John begins to clarify that something else in chapter 11.

"The Revelation" in Revelation: How the World Becomes God's Cosmic Sanctuary

The primary revelation in the book of Revelation has to do with the role that God's people have to play in God's kingdom and the world becoming God's sanctuary. One can trace the path of the scroll that John eats in chapter 10 along the route that we are told John's revelation comes in 1:1. The first time we encounter this scroll, it is "in the right hand of the one seated upon the throne" and is "sealed with seven seals" (5:1). This scroll contains the revelation spoken about in 1:1 that originates with God (the one on the throne in 5:1), who gives it to Jesus Christ (5:7), who then sends the now unsealed scroll through an angel to John (10:8).[24] John is told to eat this scroll containing that revelation and then to prophesy. What comes from John's mouth after he eats the scroll reveals to the servants/slaves of Christ (cf. 1:1) their missional role in bringing the nations to repentance by

---

22. Note that unlike the complete destruction of Sodom, these first two series of warning judgments are partial in their impact (one-fourth, 6:8; one-third, 8:7–12).

23. Levenson, *Creation and the Persistence*, 86.

24. Since John uses a different word for the scroll in 10:4 (*biblaridion*/little scroll) than he does in 5:1 (*biblion*/scroll), some argue that this precludes them from being the same scroll. However, in 10:8 John refers to the little scroll of 10:4 with the same word he uses in 5:1, indicating that he uses these two words (*biblion* and *biblaridion*) interchangeably.

communicating it in the symbolic imagery of the measuring of the temple and the story of the two witnesses in chapter 11.

In 11:1–2 John is given a measuring rod and told to measure the "temple/inner sanctuary (*naos*) of God," the altar and those worshipping there. But he is told not to measure the court outside the sanctuary because it will be given over to the nations who will trample on the holy city for forty-two months. Although the Jerusalem Temple was no longer standing at the time he writes, John appears to be using it as a symbolic way of referring to the faithful, holy people of God (cf. 1 Cor 3:16; 2 Cor 6:16; Eph 2:20; 1 Pet 2:5). In other words, this inner sanctuary he is told to measure is not a literal building, but is a metaphor for a community of people (cf. 3:12 where the faithful will become "a pillar in the inner sanctuary [*naos*] of God"). The inner court (*naos*) of the Jerusalem Temple where the altar stood was the court of priests and hence, is a good way to symbolize the faithful community redeemed by the Lamb and made to be priests for God (1:6; 5:10). Not only their vocation as priests, but also the close proximity of the court of priests to the Holy Place and the Holy of Holies in the Jerusalem Temple tends to highlight the holiness of the community symbolized by this image and the practices in which they engage. The metaphor of the "holy city" upon which the gentiles/nations will trample represents this same community (cf. the association of the church as the "bridegroom of the Lamb" [19:7] with "the holy city" [21:9–10]). Their "being measured" in the midst of "being trampled" for three and a half years (i.e., a divinely limited amount of time) symbolizes that even in the midst of severe persecution brought on by their faithful testimony, God will preserve and vindicate the community.[25] This is essentially the condensed version of what follows next, the story of the two witnesses.

Since all seven churches were earlier identified as lampstands (1:20), when the two witnesses are called "the two lampstands" (11:4), there can be little doubt that they symbolize the church. Given that both the first and the second Jerusalem Temple included lampstands as a part of their primary furniture, the imagery of vv. 1–2 dovetails well into this story of the two witnesses. In addition, their identification as "two olive trees," an OT image that refers to a Davidic prince and a high priest (two "anointed" ones, Zech 4:14), corroborates the identity of these two witnesses as a reference to the

---

25. Less clear is the meaning of "the outer court." It may symbolize faithless Christians, unbelievers in general, or possibly the church experiencing bodily persecution outwardly while its inner essence (represented by the inner court) is preserved.

Section 3—Other New Testament Witnesses

people of God/the church as "kings and priests" (cf. Rev 1:6; 5:10). Hence, the two witnesses in 11:3–13 symbolize the church as engaging it its mediatorial priestly role *precisely through its prophetic witness* to, and challenge of, the nations who are in captivity to their idolatrous commitments. With powers like Moses and Elijah (11:6), both of whom confronted idolatry as prophets *par excellence*, they confront their own world of pagan idolatry by speaking fiery words of truth (11:5) in the face of the falsehood that claims the beast's rule as divinely ordained. Their clothing (i.e., sackcloth, v. 3) is particularly appropriate for situations of mourning and repentance and thus signals that their fiery words of truth are for the purpose of calling those who hear them to repentance. But the imperial beast who demands the loyalty and adoration reserved for God alone—this beast who arises over and over from the abyss in ever new incarnations of what amounts to human rule turned beastly—cannot tolerate such truth to be spoken and therefore "conquers" the two witnesses by killing them (11:7). Like their Lord, the high priest *par excellence*, they speak prophetically out of faithfulness to God for the sake of freeing others from their idolatrous commitments, calling people to repentance and loyalty to the one God.[26] Like their Lord, they are killed and shamed[27] by beastly human rule so that it appears that the beast has once again triumphed. Hence, like their high priestly Lord, these priests paradoxically offer themselves as a sacrifice on the altar of faithfulness to God for the sake of others as a result of their prophetic witness to the truth. Like their Lord, after a short period, the Spirit of life who blew through Ezekiel's valley of dry bones raises them bodily from the dead as they "stand on their feet" (cf. Ezek 37:5, 10) and ascend to heaven in a cloud (11:11–12, cf. Acts 1:9).

Their enemies, presumably the very ones who had shamed and killed them who come from "peoples and tribes and tongues and nations" (11:9), watch as they ascend (11:12). In other words, those who remain candidates for redemption by the blood of the Lamb (5:9) are depicted as watching the vindication of God's people. Prior to the blowing of the seventh trumpet announcing the arrival of the kingdom of God in 11:15, a further warning

---

26. This is essentially the same role for the church that the Fourth Gospel describes as "retaining sins," the life-giving practice of telling the world the truth about their death-bound direction in order that they might turn and be released from their entrapment (see pp. 100–101).

27. Crucifixion was the most shameful way to die in the Roman Empire. The shame for the two witnesses is underscored by the fact that their corpses remained unburied and exposed (11:9).

judgment comes in the form of a great earthquake (11:13). But the numbers John uses here depict only a minority who are destroyed. For example, *only* one tenth of the city falls, a *merciful reversal* of a prophetic pattern where it is only a tenth part of a city that remains standing as a result of God's judgment (Isa 6:13) or only a tenth of those who march out who return (Amos 5:3). Only seven thousand people in this Sodom-like city are killed in God's judgment, a *merciful reversal* of the number of those in the remnant who had not bowed the knee to Baal in 1 Kgs 19:14–18 (a *minority* of seven thousand). The implication is that the *vast majority* of those from "peoples, tribes, tongues, and nations" (11:9) repent and "give glory/honor to the God of heaven" (11:13). In this case, it is when a warning judgment is combined with the faithful prophetic testimony, death, and vindication of the two witnesses that the vast majority of those in the nations are brought to repentance so that the angel can blow the seventh trumpet to announce the arrival of the kingdom of God (11:15).[28]

This story is *the* revelation in the book of Revelation. The new revelation for the churches is that their missional vocation as holy priests of God—their mediatorial role of representing God to the nations in their particular cultural setting—will be carried out primarily through their faithful prophetic witness, and their life, death, and public vindication will be instrumental in bringing about the repentance of the nations. Hence, the new revelation is precisely the opposite of the logic of a "secret rapture" theology. God's kingdom does not come through his saving an elect/holy people that acknowledges his lordship by whisking them out of a rebellious world so that he can then extinguish all the rebels. Rather, it arrives only after God's holy people suffer and/or die in sacrificially fulfilling their missional vocation of prophetically challenging the idolatry of their day by witnessing to the rule of God with their deeds and words and are then vindicated by God. In addition to God showing up in the earthquake for final judgment, this is instrumental in bringing the vast majority of those from every people, tribe, tongue, and nation to acknowledge God's rule. The minority who still refuse to do so would appear to be the ones who are destroyed by that final judgment. God's holy people have been redeemed from the nations (5:9) in order to participate in God's mission by their prophetic witness to all the nations (11:3–13).

28. "Not the faithful majority, but the faithless minority are spared, so that they may come to repentance and faith. Thanks to the witness of the witnesses, the judgment is actually salvific" (Bauckham, *Theology*, 87). The basic outline of the argument in this paragraph and the following one comes from Bauckham, *Theology*, 84–88.

Section 3—Other New Testament Witnesses

We might have expected Revelation to end in 11:19. After all, while God is still described as "the one who is and was," he is no longer the one "who is to come" since he has now shown up with both salvation and judgment and "taken his great power and begun to reign" (v. 17). The kingdom of God has now arrived on earth as it is in heaven. But Revelation does not end here because it does not tell a story that develops in linear fashion. Rather, in what follows, we get the story of the two witnesses projected onto the big screen, so to speak.

Alternate Endings on the Big Screen Version of the Story of the Two Witnesses

In Hollywood-like fashion, we see a number of possible "alternative endings" to the story of the two witnesses, indicating that there is nothing *automatic* about the prophetic witness of God's people resulting in salvation for the vast majority of humanity. The scenes in chapters 12–22 project the paradigmatic story of the two witnesses onto the big screen following a similar—albeit not identical—pattern, but these scenes offer alternative ways the story might end. There remain choices to be made by the inhabitants of the earth and even by those among God's people (e.g., Rev 18:4), and the scenes in the last half of Revelation display the potential consequences of those choices as alternative endings to the story.

Chapter 12 portrays a cosmic battle between God's forces and a great red Dragon/Satan and his forces. In chapter 13, this Dragon becomes incarnate in the beast and, with the aid of the false prophet, leads astray the inhabitants of the earth into slavery. In this beastly system there is no hiding where one's true loyalties lie since one is publicly marked either as a slave to the beast (13:16–17) or as belonging to God (14:1). As with the two witnesses, the beast does battle with God's "holy ones" and conquers them (13:7). After the beast has his day in chapter 13, we discover that, like the two witnesses who die in the beast's conquest, the defeat of the holy ones is actually their victory when we see them *standing* with the Lamb on Mount Zion, raised/vindicated by God (14:1).[29] They are depicted as a holy army whose census we have already seen taken (7:4–8), resulting in 144,000 who are ready to follow the "lion of the tribe of Judah."[30] Not surprisingly, since

---

29. Cf. the language where the two witnesses are raised/vindicated after Ezekiel's life-giving Spirit enters into them: "and they *stood* on their feet" (11:11).

30. On this army of martyrs, see Bauckham, *Theology*, 76–80.

this lion turns out to be a Lamb who conquers by sacrificially giving his life, this army who "follows the Lamb wherever he goes" (14:4) conquers in a Lamb-like way by the *blameless* sacrifice of their lives in their determination to speak the truth in the face of the power of the beast (14:4–5).[31] While they too had been enslaved to the beastly system, they are now "redeemed from the earth" (14:3). They are publicly marked out as God's holy, *priestly* people who—like Aaron, who wears the name of God on his turban as high priest (Exod 28:36–38)—have the singular name (YHWH) that belongs to the Lamb and his Father written on their foreheads (14:1). They have been missionally faithful in their costly battle with the beast, actively participating in the saving, reconciling, life-giving purposes of the missional God. By doing so, they have become Lamb-like, and therefore holy, like the thrice-holy God. Reshaped into the *imago Dei*, they now stand vindicated before the inhabitants of the earth.

This pattern we see in 13:1—14:5, then, is similar to the story of the two witnesses. But now the story is projected onto the big screen where these witnesses are depicted as 144,000 strong. Numbers in Revelation often function essentially as adjectives, telling us more about the nature of something or someone than about actual quantity.[32] In this case, 144,000 works like an adjective that describes the nature of this group as the almost unimaginably large (by first-century standards anyway) full people of God (12 x 12 x 1000).[33] It is clear that John's use of this number should not be understood as a way of numerically limiting God's people since they are, after all, said to be "firstfruits for God and the Lamb" (14:4). The language of "firstfruits" suggests that there is a far greater harvest to come from among the mass of human beings from whom the 144,000 have been redeemed (14:4). And so, as in the story of the two witnesses, after their faithful prophetic witness in their battle against the beast and his enslaving system, followed by their vindication with the Lamb on Mount Zion, the rest of

---

31. The Greek word translated "blameless" (*amōmoi*) in 14:5 is often used to describe sacrificial animals without defect or blemish.

32. Gorman, *Reading*, 17–19.

33. Twelve is a number symbolizing God's people, and 1,000 symbolizes a very large number. In this case, since there were twelve tribes of Israel and twelve apostles, 144 has special significance as a symbol for all of God's people and multiplying it by 1,000 to arrive at 144,000 suggests that this holy army of martyrs symbolizes the fullness of an unimaginably large people of God, a multitude no one could count (as the alternative description of this same group in 7:9 would have it).

Section 3—Other New Testament Witnesses

the inhabitants of the earth are offered "an eternal gospel"—that which is forever good news—in 14:6–7:

> ⁶ Then I saw another angel flying in mid-heaven with an eternal gospel to proclaim to the inhabitants of the earth—to every nation, and tribe, and tongue, and people—⁷ saying with a loud voice: "Fear/revere God and give him glory/honor because the hour of his judgment has come. Worship the One who made the heaven, the earth, the sea, and the springs of water."

Now that the beast and empire have been revealed for the beastly realities they are—and now with the missionally faithful and vindicated holy people of God displaying corporately the image of the Lamb they have followed—how will the rest of the inhabitants of the earth respond?

The rest of Revelation does not unfold in a linear fashion. Rather, there are two side-by-side alternative endings that open up in the last half of the book, making the future of the earth's inhabitants not set in stone but somehow dependent on their response to the witness and vindication of the Lamb's followers. One possibility seems to be that they can accept the testimony of God's faithful witnesses, as the majority seems to do in 11:13, and thereby become part of the large grain harvest as the Son of Man gathers his people (14:14–16) who give proper honor to God's name as they are gathered by the glassy sea (15:2–4) and participate in the marriage supper of the Lamb (19:5–9). However, a second possible ending looms. The majority could choose to reject that testimony, refuse to repent (e.g., 16:9, 11), and suffer ultimate judgment for persisting in their idolatrous lifestyle of loyalty to the beast (14:9–11), thereby becoming part of the grape harvest of judgment (14:17–20) meted out in seven final bowls of wrath that bring about the destruction of the Sodom-like "Babylon the Great" (chapters 16–18). If they do so, they would suffer final defeat by the rider on the white horse (Christ) that ends their opposition to God and his purposes (19:11–21).

Their response will be remain ambiguous, even into chapters 20–22. The famous "millennium" passage (20:1–10) illustrates this ambiguity. This passage has received far more attention from interpreters than is warranted by its overall importance in Revelation itself, and perhaps more so even than other parts of Revelation, much in these verses remains unclear. Hence, one ought to be cautious about holding too tightly to any particular interpretation of these verses. For our purposes, it is enough to highlight the similarity—albeit with some clear and important differences—of the pattern that we see in these verses and the paradigmatic pattern of the story of the two witnesses. First, though, we will identify the clear differences. In the story of the two witnesses it is the beast who arises over and over again from the abyss, the incarnation of the dragon/Satan, who does battle against the witnesses and "conquers" them. In this chapter, there is no human (beastly) incarnation of the dragon because the beast is assumed to be in the lake of fire (20:10; 19:20).[34] In addition, unlike the story of the two witnesses or the 144,000, there is a thousand-year period (read: a really long time) in which there is no opposition of any kind to God's people and purposes.

We see a certain similarity in this text to an aspect of the story of the 144,000, and therefore derivatively, a similarity to the story of the two witnesses. This text draws out and prolongs what happens when God's people (represented heretofore by the two witnesses and the 144,000) are publicly vindicated. While other interpretations are possible, v. 4 most likely pictures one group, namely, the martyrs (who in this context also represent all God's people who have been faithful witnesses in opposing the dragon's beastly incarnation [v. 4] whether or not they were killed in doing so).[35] These, then, would be the same group as the 144,000 who stand with the Lamb on Mt. Zion in chapter 14 and follow him wherever he goes; those who give honor to God by the glassy sea (15:2-4); those who are part of the "armies of heaven" clothed with pure white linen who ride into battle with the Lamb (19:14); those who have paradoxically "conquered" through their faithful death and who have now received their promised crown signaling their share in Christ's reign (3:21). They would be those whom the two witnesses represent in the story in chapter 11. Like the two witnesses who oppose the beast, are killed by him, and are then brought to life by an Ezekiel-like "spirit of life" (11:11), those in v. 4 have clearly opposed the beast, have been killed, and have "come to life" in a resurrection, as did Jesus (20:4; cf. 2:8). They now have crowns and are said to "reign with Christ," signaling their vindication before the nations. Like God's people throughout this book (and throughout Scripture) they are said to be "priests of God" and kings who reign with Christ for a thousand years, most likely on earth (20:6; cf. 5:10). But to whom would they be priestly mediators and over whom would they reign? Verse 8 mentions nations "at the four corners of the earth" whom Satan is released to deceive, indicating the continued

---

34. Here, the scene in chapter 20 does presume something of a linear progression following the events of 19:20.

35. On which, see Koester, *Revelation*, 771-73.

Section 3—Other New Testament Witnesses

presence of "inhabitants of the earth." Might the implication be that other nations remain, ones who are not "at the four corners of the earth"—the vast majority of nations—over whom God's faithful witnesses somehow "reign" and to whom they become priests on behalf of God/Christ?

Answering this last question in the affirmative may simply be pushing John's imagery too far. But if we press the similarities among the tale of the two witnesses, the 144,000 in the army of martyrs, and the scene related here in chapter 20, the millennial priests and kings are the missionally faithful *and now vindicated* people of God who corporately display the image of the Lamb they have followed. They would appear before the eyes of the nations for a millennium as "exhibit A" of humanity now reshaped into the *imago Dei*, humanity made entirely holy.

In that case, this whole millennial scene depicts God's extreme mercy. Christ is apparently personally present on earth, with his vindicated people acting as his vice-regents and priests in an environment where, for "a thousand years," there is no opposition to God and his purposes. One might imagine that during that time, the majority of the nations—like the majority in the story of the two witnesses—who have seen the public vindication of God's people and the destruction of all human incarnations of the dragon will know assuredly that the hour of God's judgment has come and will heed the proclamation of the eternal gospel by giving proper honor and worship to their creator (14:7). In such a scenario they would have "a thousand years" to experience Christ's reign and the reflection of God's holy character through his priests/"holy ones" in a way completely unhindered by evil. The result of this would be that the vast majority of people (all except "the nations" on the very periphery of earth) begin "giving glory/honor to the God of heaven" (11:13) and thereby become a part of "the camp of the holy ones, that is, the beloved city" (v. 9). The text clearly does not say all this explicitly, but there is a "narrative gap" that it leaves open. Filling it with these sorts of images would: (1) signal a staggering wideness in God's mercy that would be congruent with imagining God's faithful and vindicated people as being the first fruits of a much greater harvest to come (14:4); and (2) graphically depict *the Lord's way of doing justice as leading with compassion and mercy*, extending that mercy as far as is possible if there remains any real possibility for repentance and change in the situation.[36]

---

36. See our earlier comments on the Sodom episode (pp. 13–17).

Even if we fill this narrative gap with such images, verses 7–10 continue to hold open the possibility that such amazing grace can still be refused. Even after such a very long time, when Satan is released and continues his deceptive ways, a large number from the periphery ("like the sands of the sea") continue to refuse to give proper honor and worship to their creator and join this deceiver in one last attack on these "holy ones/the beloved city" (v. 9; cf. "the holy city" in 11:2 and 21:10). But there is no real battle. Fire simply comes down from heaven and consumes them, Satan is thrown into the lake of fire, and that is that (v. 10). Everything and everyone that opposes God's people and purposes for his cosmos is simply consumed. In addition, in the judgment scene immediately following, all the dead whose names are not written in the book of life—and we are given no indication as to how many this might be—suffer the "second death, the lake of fire," the ultimate exclusion from God's new creation (vv. 11–15). God's mercy may be wider than we can imagine, but all persistent and defiant opposition to God's purposes will be destroyed.

In chapters 21–22, we encounter a more detailed description of the "camp of the holy ones," the "beloved city," when we are introduced to the "new Jerusalem," an image that represents both God's holy people and the holy place in which they dwell.[37] But even in this imagery we encounter a certain ambiguity when we try to nail down the ultimate fate of those whose final destiny we might have presumed had already been decided. For example, we are told that "the nations/gentiles walk by means of its [the New Jerusalem's] light," that "the kings of the earth bring their glory into it,"[38] that "they bring the glory and honor of the nations into it" (21:24, 26), and that the leaves on the tree of life are "for the healing of the nations" (22:2). The last time the "kings of the earth" were mentioned was in 19:19, where they were allied with the beast in making war against the rider on the white horse (i.e., Jesus) and were among the rest who were "killed by the sword of the one seated on the white horse that came forth from his mouth" (19:21). The last explicit mention of "the nations" was in 20:8, where the ones at the four corners of the earth were deceived by, and allied with, Satan against the people of God and were consumed by heavenly fire. Both the kings of the earth and the nations appear again here in ways that indicate

37. On which, see Bauckham, *Theology*, 132–40; cf. Middleton, *New Heaven*, 172, n. 34.

38. I.e., "the best of human workmanship that has been developed throughout history . . . transformed into means of glorifying the God of Israel" (Middleton, *New Heaven*, 173).

Section 3—Other New Testament Witnesses

that they give proper honor/glory to their creator and share in his healing/*shalom*. This suggests that we are dealing here with another possible ending that is an alternative to the nations and their leaders finally opposing the Lamb and his followers (19:11–21) and God's final purposes for his creation (20:7–10). At the very least, as the final image of God's purposes for his creation, this indicates that God's ultimate will is for the salvation of the nations as we see, for example, depicted in Isaiah's earlier prophetic vision in 2:2–4:

> ² In days to come the mountain of the Lord's house shall be established as the highest of the mountains, and shall be raised above the hills; all the nations shall stream to it. ³ Many peoples shall come and say, "Come, let us go up to the mountain of the Lord, to the house of the God of Jacob; that he may teach us his ways and that we may walk in his paths." For out of Zion shall go forth instruction, and the word of the Lord from Jerusalem. ⁴ He shall judge between the nations, and shall arbitrate for many peoples; they shall beat their swords into plowshares, and their spears into pruning hooks; nation shall not lift up sword against nation, neither shall they learn war any more. (NRSV)

In this section, we have proposed that chapters 12–22 project the basic story line of the tale of the two witnesses onto the big screen in its cosmic significance. We have seen how the visions are not fixed advance predictions to which even God himself is bound. Rather, they offer different possibilities to the way things end for the nations/peoples of the earth depending on their response to the faithful, prophetic witness *and vindication* of God's holy people.

As we conclude this section, it is important to reemphasize that Revelation's new revelation for the seven churches is that their missional vocation as holy priests of God—their faithful prophetic life, death, and vindication—has cosmic significance given its great potential for being instrumental in bringing about the repentance of the nations. Fulfilling this missional vocation is "following the Lamb wherever he goes" and thus reflecting the image of the cruciform Son, who is himself the image of the thrice-holy creator God. During the time of God's rescue mission, it is the way redeemed human beings reflect the holiness of God. In the book of Revelation, then, divine and human holiness remains associated with a particular (cruciform) pattern of activity effecting the saving, reconciling mission of the Triune God, whose ultimate desire is to draw all into the abundant, Spirit-saturated life of the new creation that is richly depicted in the imagery of Revelation 21–22.

God's Cosmic Sanctuary of Holiness: Creation Entirely Sanctified

In Revelation 21–22, John portrays God's reign coming in its fullness[39] with the image of a renewed creation and the descent of the New Jerusalem. Here the Holy God "pitches a tent," or "tabernacles" (cf. John 1:14), among his diverse people(s), and his divine presence heals and transforms both God's people(s) as well as God's creation.[40] God has fully dealt with the sin and guilt of human beings and rescued his creation from the resulting devastating consequences of that sin. Not only is there no sin, suffering, or death (21:4), there is no capacity for these chaotic evil forces to ever re-emerge (21:1).[41] The curse that the original pair had brought on all of creation (Gen 3:17) is now reversed (Rev 22:3), bringing a fitting resolution to that (very large) sub-plot of Scripture dealing with God's rescue operation.

But, as we said at the beginning of the book, these final chapters in Revelation move beyond this rescue mission sub-plot by offering the most detailed depiction of the resolution of Scripture's main plot, namely, God's mission to bring his creation to its intended goal. Here God's original garden creation with only two inhabitants has become a bustling city bursting with fruitful life, and the diverse peoples of the world living in harmony with God and each other (21:3).[42] Creation's curse has not simply been reversed (22:3); the rich abundant life that characterized Eden is now available—*but exponentially so*—in this new creation where God's reign is unchallenged:

---

39. As we have seen, at various points in Revelation's non-linear unfolding, John proclaims that the Kingdom of God has come in fullness (11:15, 19:6). In 22:1–5 he recapitulates that claim by using the imagery of the *"throne of God and of the Lamb"* which is now among his people on a redeemed earth.

40. On "New Jerusalem" referring to both people and place, again see Bauckham, *Theology*, 132–40.

41. This is implied by the absence of the sea in the new earth. The sea symbolizes chaos in the ancient world and in Revelation itself (note that the first beast in Revelation emerges *from the sea* in 13:1).

42. John's vision of the richly diverse and uncountable multitude "from every nation, tribes, peoples, and languages" in 7:9–17 is an advance picture of these same reconciled and redeemed people(s).

Section 3—Other New Testament Witnesses

> ¹ And he (the angel) showed me the river of the water of life as clear as crystal coming out from the throne of God and of the Lamb ² and flowing through Main Street. On each side of the river was the tree of life making twelve kinds of fruits, yielding its fruit each month and the leaves of the true are for the healing of the nations (22:1–2).

John is dependent on Ezekiel's portrait of restored Jerusalem for much of his imagery in chapters 21–22, including the imagery in these two verses. For example, in Ezek 47:1–11 the prophet's vision includes a river that flows out from beneath the temple that makes stagnant, dead waters fresh and bursting with new life. The messenger in Ezekiel goes on in v. 12 to say:

> [B]ut on both banks of the river will grow up all kinds of fruit-bearing trees. Their leaves won't wither, and their fruitfulness won't wane. They will produce fruit in every month, because their water comes from the sanctuary. Their fruit will be for eating, their leaves for healing.

The river in Gen 2:10 that flowed out of Eden (where God was immediately present) to water the garden so that it could continue providing life for its inhabitants appears in modified form in both Ezekiel's vision and in Revelation. Given the connection between holiness and life, it is not surprising that in Ezekiel the river flows out from the sanctuary, the *most holy place*, of the restored temple where God is understood to be invisibly enthroned.⁴³ In Revelation, however, there is no temple because God is—once again as in Genesis prior to the fall—immediately present to this garden city's inhabitants. The river containing the water of life flows directly from "the throne of God and of the Lamb" (22:1). The implication is that unlimited life flows directly and immediately from the Holy God, the source of all life, when God's reign is unchallenged throughout the cosmos. John, then, emphasizes that the life flowing from this river comes from the direct, unmediated presence of God rather than from a restored temple. But he goes even further when he turns Ezekiel's reference to fruit trees lining the river into the garden's "tree of life" on each side of the river, which produces a diverse assortment of fruit. While aspects of this imagery are not completely clear,⁴⁴ it underscores the abundance and variety of flour-

---

43. Ezekiel differentiates the sanctuary (Heb: *miqdash*; Gk: *hagiōn*) from the temple at large (Heb: *bayit*; Gk: *oikos*).

44. E.g., by using the singular "tree," is John suggesting only one tree that somehow is on both sides of the river or does the term function collectively indicating a whole forest

ishing life. The garden city's inhabitants once again experience God's direct holy presence *as blessing*—as generating unlimited capacity for fruitful life (Gen 1:22, 28; 2:7) and the means of sustaining it (Gen 1:29–30). Since the chaos and disorder the first human pair had unleashed has now been decisively dealt with, the garden city's inhabitants can once again access the fruit of this tree of life which, unlike the one in Genesis, produces a diverse assortment of fruit/life fitting for an expanded Eden.

Unlike the leaves on Ezekiel's trees that are simply said to be "for healing," the leaves on John's tree of life are said to be "for the healing *of the nations*." This is fitting since this New Jerusalem is populated with inhabitants "from every nation, tribes, peoples, and languages" (7:9), so that all the nations have become God's covenant peoples (Rev 21:3) with whom he dwells directly. God now has diverse peoples representing his gracious presence throughout the whole of his cosmic temple rather than one homogenized, Babel-like humanity refusing to disperse voluntarily to carry out their creational mandate.

In Genesis, the first time we hear of God "sanctifying" something—setting it apart or making it holy—the purpose of the action is so that well-ordered life can flourish. *Holiness at the very beginning of Scripture is explicitly connected with blessing and life.* Hence, not surprisingly, flourishing life and *shalom* characterize this New Jerusalem—almost by definition—since the entirety of the renewed creation is soaked with God's unmediated holy, life-giving presence/glory (21:11, 22; 22:3–5; cf. 1 Cor 15:28) making all of it God's now completed holy temple/sanctuary. Like the interior of the inner sanctuary of the most holy place in the first temple (1 Kgs 6:19–20), the New Jerusalem is a perfect cube (21:16). The New Jerusalem is depicted as God's most holy place/sanctuary. The whole cosmos has become God's sanctuary in which his name is hallowed, his reign unchallenged, and his holiness is "palpable, unthreatened, and pervasive."[45] Unlike Ezekiel's restored Jerusalem dominated by a restored temple, there is no need for a temple in this New Jerusalem (Rev. 21:22–23), no need to mark off "sacred" from "profane" space, because the city and people as a whole are permeated by the holy presence of God and the Lamb.

---

of "trees of life?" And does/do the tree/trees produce one kind of fruit for each month of the year or twelve different kinds of fruit each month making for an amazing variety of 144 different kinds of fruit?

45. Levenson, *Creation*, 86.

Section 3—Other New Testament Witnesses

The Holy Spirit is only mentioned tangentially in these chapters (22:17). But as we have seen in other parts of Scripture, the Spirit/breath of God is particularly associated with the giving of life (as also in 11:11). Hence, it is not too much of a stretch to describe the New Jerusalem's flourishing life that is permeated by the holy presence of God and the Lamb as the Spirit-saturated life of the new creation.[46] Like Paul's "spiritual body" in 1 Cor 15:44–46—a human body raised from the dead and totally permeated by the Spirit, fitting it for the new creation—the whole cosmos reaches its intended destiny of being "entirely sanctified."[47]

Now that creation has reached its intended goal of bursting forth with abundant life because the holy God dwells directly with his holy people in a completely holy place,[48] what is left for God's holy people to do? To put it sharply, what is the role of God's holy people now that God's rescue operation is over so that there is no longer any need to participate in, or witness to, God's *saving, reconciling* purposes? We could answer with the words of the Westminster Shorter Catechism: "to glorify God and enjoy him forever." To this, most of us would say a hearty "amen." But what exactly does giving God glory/honor mean? In this new creation, do God's holy people simply surround the throne voicing ceaseless praise while they enjoy the glorious glow of God's presence? Since that seemed to be what went on in heaven around the throne in chapters 4–5, it is certainly *part* of what God's holy people are to do now that heaven's glory has come to earth. Admittedly we are getting into somewhat speculative territory here, but is there more to it than this? If we do not imagine this "new creation" in terms of some sort of unchanging static perfection, but in terms of continuing and unhindered robust flourishing, what might this "more" include?

Rev 22:3b–5 describes the role of God's people in this new creation using the same priestly and royal categories of 1:6:

> [3b] The throne of God and of the Lamb will be in it. And his servants will worship him [as priests] [4] and they will see his face with his name on their foreheads [like the high priest]. [5] There is no night

---

46. The rhetorical patterns in Revelation suggest that when the Risen Christ/Lamb is referred to, the Spirit is also present. For example, what the risen Christ says to the seven churches is what the Spirit is saying (2:7, 11, 17, etc.). In addition, the Lamb has seven horns and eyes that "are the seven spirits [read: the Holy Spirit] of God" (5:6).

47. For this understanding of the meaning of "spiritual body," see my "Turning the World." On the conceptuality of creation being "entirely sanctified," see Hamner and Johnson, "Holy Mission."

48. This last phrase is from Thomas, "A Holy God."

so they have no need for a lamp's light or the sun's light because the Lord God will shine over them. And they will *reign* forever and ever.

In Exod 28:36–38 the high priest Aaron wears a turban on his forehead with a golden plate on which "Holy to/for Yahweh" is engraved. Here God's holy people have the name of the Lord *directly* on their foreheads. This suggests that in this new creation, they are all "high priests" but serve and worship God in an even more intimate way than Israel's high priests, the only ones who could enter the Holy of Holies in the sanctuary—and then only once a year. But now the renewed creation has become God's entirely sanctified cosmic sanctuary, and these high priests are themselves entirely holy. Hence, unlike Moses who could not see God's face directly (Exod 33:18–23)[49] and unlike the first human pair who had the good sense to hide themselves from the face of God in the garden after their disobedience (Gen 3:8), these holy high priests see God face to face in all his glory/visible holiness. Since there are no non-priests on behalf of whom priestly service might be conducted in worship of God, perhaps the role of these high priests is to reflect the glory/image of the Holy God to each other ceaselessly. The role of these priests, however, is also to reign forever. Since there are no "non-kings" over whom they might reign in this new creation, what might this royal language imply?

Richard Middleton's language may help us articulate what being priestly *kings* in this new creation might entail. After the earth is full of God's eschatological presence and the cosmic temple of creation has been brought to its intended destiny, God's redeemed humans are indeed "powerful, living images of the one true God" but are they still "called to manifest God's presence by their active cultural development of the earth"? What if, by their "obedient exercise of power, humanity as *imago Dei* continues to function like a prism, refracting the pure light of God into a rainbow of cultural activities that scintillate with the creator's glory throughout the earth"?[50] Perhaps something like this is being suggested by John's language of the kings of the earth bringing their glory into the New Jerusalem (21:24). Perhaps we are to take such language as depicting "the best of human workmanship that has been developed throughout history . . . transformed into means of glorifying

---

49. In the sense of seeing the fullness of God's very self, i.e., his glory/visible holiness (see pp. 8–9).

50. This modified language comes from Middleton, *New Heaven*, 49.

Section 3—Other New Testament Witnesses

the God of Israel."⁵¹ When every human being in this cosmic sanctuary has been shaped by the Holy Spirit into the image of the cruciform Son, thereby becoming truly human and completely holy, any such cultural activities in which they engage would be wholly for the sake of others, for creation as a whole, and for bringing honor to God. Might we imagine that the rich and vast diversity of experiences, talents, and knowledge of people from every nation, tribe, people, and language throughout the centuries become some of the "raw material" through which "the pure light of God [is refracted] into [that] rainbow of cultural activities that scintillate with the creator's glory throughout the earth"?[52] If so, as God's vice-regents, they would indeed be reflecting/sharing God's gracious rule over this new creation, contributing to its flourishing with well-ordered abundant life.

Any examples we might give here would be pure speculation . . . but here goes. What if everyone who has ever played in any production of "Les Miserables" joins together in a "cosmic" production that celebrates God's liberating activity and human participation in it throughout history? What if the world joins together to hear a cosmic production of Handel's "Messiah" performed by history's very best musicians and every creature in heaven and earth and under the earth, human and animal alike, rises for the Hallelujah Chorus? And what if Jenny, my Downs Syndrome cousin who loved to sing in church, has a solo in the production? What if the best architects and builders in human history join together to build unimaginably beautiful cosmic stages on which such productions are performed? What if they build the most magnificent cosmic stages on which Irish step dancers not only perform "River Dance" for the complete delight of formerly disabled and orphaned children in Calcutta, but teach them how to join the dance? Or what if the architects and builders build magnificent cosmic stadiums where the best Brazilian soccer teams ever showcase the beauty of the game they love? What if those who have had the uncanny ability to communicate with horses or dogs ("horse/dog whispers") teach all the rest of redeemed humanity how to communicate with the lion and the lamb who are lying down together? Random thoughts that are pure speculation arising from my own limited experience? No doubt. But such musings are one way of imagining how the truly human exercise of power and blessing from God might be a

---

51. Ibid., 173. Alternatively, such language may simply mean that the kings of the earth give proper honor to the Father and the Lamb, confessing their lordship over creation.

52. Language again modified from Middleton, *New Heaven*, 49.

way of sharing in his reign over a redeemed cosmos and a reflection of his life-giving presence to others and to the whole of redeemed creation.

Revelation, Holiness and Mission: Summary and Conclusion

In this chapter, we have seen that Revelation is indeed a missional text designed to equip the church to participate in God's rescue mission as his royal and priestly people. Revelation's new revelation for the churches is that their missional vocation as holy priests of God—their mediatorial role of representing God to the nations in their particular cultural setting—will be carried out primarily through their faithful prophetic witness, and their life, death, *and public vindication* may be instrumental in bringing about the repentance of the nations. Fulfilling this missional vocation is "following the Lamb wherever he goes" since, like their high priestly Lord, these priests paradoxically offer themselves as a sacrifice on the altar of faithfulness to God for the sake of others as a result of their prophetic witness to the truth. In this way, God's holy people in Revelation come to reflect the image of the cruciform Son, who is himself the image of the thrice-holy creator God. During the time of God's rescue mission, this is the way redeemed human beings are restored into the *imago Dei* and thereby reflect God's holiness. So then, in Revelation, God's means of (re)shaping humans into the *imago Dei*, of making us holy, remains inseparable from—indeed, primarily constituted by—our participation in, and witness to, the *missio Dei*. Hence, divine and human holiness in the Bible's last book remains associated with a particular (cruciform) pattern of activity effecting the saving, reconciling mission of the Triune God, whose ultimate desire is to draw all into the abundant, Spirit-saturated life of the new creation.

We concluded by reflecting on the role of God's holy people after God's rescue operation is over. We suggested that as priests and kings who continue to represent God's holy presence and rule to each other and to all of redeemed creation, their engagement in various forms of cultural activities unhindered by opposition from evil/chaos continues to participate in God's main mission of bringing creation to its intended destiny of forever flourishing with profusely abundant life. At the beginning of the biblical story, God dreamed of bringing his creation to this intended goal through the agency of humanity. In the end we have a glimpse of the fulfillment of this dream, but only a glimpse of the way that fulfillment *begins*.

Conclusion

Holiness and the *Missio Dei* in
Twenty-First Century North America

Introduction

WE ARE NOW READY to pull together the book's various strands and themes, and reflect theologically and missionally on their significance. In the first section, I will summarize the scriptural patterns regarding holiness and God's mission that are highlighted throughout the book. The next section will illustrate how one might flesh out in contemporary ways some of these scriptural patterns in the church's ongoing participation in God's mission in a North American context. In a final section, I will briefly suggest other issues that could occupy the church's missional attention in the North American context and return to the overall thesis of the book in the context of these issues.

Holiness and God's Mission: Scriptural Patterns

In section one of this book, chapters 1–3, we focused on holiness and the *missio Dei* in the OT. We described God's mission as being to engender life in all its fullness for his whole creation so that it becomes his holy sanctuary, soaked with his unmediated presence/glory. His dream was to accomplish this through the agency of humanity, through whom his life-giving mission would go forth. Humanity's task was to re-present his gracious presence

Conclusion

(like priests) in his cosmic temple and rule over it (like kings) in a way that creation would flourish with well-ordered life and reach its intended destiny. But after God's mission was sidetracked with the events in the garden, the flood, and the debacle at the tower of Babel, God chose Abraham's family to model the "way of the LORD" to those around them. That "way" was to lead with compassion and mercy even toward perpetrators of injustice, but to work to engender restorative justice in order to reinstate *shalom* in a chaotic and disordered world. In this sovereign, loving choice of Abraham, God's mission would henceforth go through that one family, namely, Israel. His mission would still maintain its essential character of engendering life in all its fullness. But now, God's mission would be directed first toward bringing fullness of life for Israel, and only then, through Israel, engendering that same fullness of life for the nations and creation as a whole.

God's initial sanctification of Israel made it possible for them to engage in practices guided by their "employee manual" (i.e., Torah) through which God would continue their sanctification, conforming their minds, bodies, and communal life to his own life-giving patterns. God's ultimate sanctifying aim was to restore Israel as a people into the *imago Dei*. This restoration was to be constituted by the corporate formation of a distinct and public people whose obedient actions would be one means God would use to conform them to his holy life-giving patterns, thereby shaping them into his set-apart missional instrument. Therefore, God's means of (re)shaping Israel into the *imago Dei* was inseparable from—and largely constituted by—their participation in, and witness to, the *missio Dei*. Therefore, both divine and human holiness in the OT is associated with a particular pattern of activity affecting the life-giving, missional purposes of Israel's holy God.

Like the Church in subsequent centuries, however, rather than reflecting this pattern of activity in their life together, Israel often displayed a way of life that looked more like that of the idolatrous nations around them, a way of life that at times even had Sodom and Egypt-like characteristics. Prophets like Isaiah and Jeremiah called for repentance, but the people failed to respond and went into exile. Even then, however, Ezekiel articulates visions of what God might do to rescue and transform his people with a "heart transplant" so that their life together would display Yahweh's own holiness before the nations of the world. But after the people of God returned to their own land, their life fell far short of the transformation articulated by the prophets, and it became clear that something had to change if Israel was going to become the display people God intended them to be.

Conclusion

The second section, chapters 4–6, focused on the change that happened. That is, Yahweh's own holiness was relocated in a particular human being, Israel's messianic representative, Jesus the Nazarene, through whom God realized his dream of carrying out his life-giving mission through humanity. Jesus became "the Holy One of God," Yahweh's moveable temple/tabernacle permeated by God's Holy Spirit and thereby the primary location of Yahweh's life-giving, beneficent holiness. However, rather than separating himself from all that was unclean, this Spirit-inhabited Son intentionally crossed purity boundaries, bringing God's holy cleansing presence to bear on contaminated, debilitated, weak, and isolated bodies, healing and rescuing them from death-dealing forces of chaos and reincorporating them into human community. Refusing to be cordoned off even from *the ultimate impurity of death itself*, God, in the flesh of Jesus, made his own glory, or holiness, visible in cruciform shape. He then vindicated Jesus' whole pattern of life by raising him from the dead through the life-giving Spirit. As a result, the abundant life of the new age was made available to the world, and the order and structure of the cosmos that had existed since humanity's garden rebellion was changed.

This was an act of love in which God himself entered into creation, setting into motion the end of the old creation and giving birth to a new one, thereby "rewiring" the "electrical system" that channeled his holiness in beneficent, life-giving ways. "Holiness at its source [was still] life itself—the antonym of death."[1] It was still conceived as being based on the nature and order of the cosmos. But now the risen cruciform body of Christ—the body marked by battle wounds revealing the depths of God's love—had become the microcosm of that cosmos, giving this new cosmos *a cross-shaped order*. As a result, God's own character or pattern of activity still defines the essence of both divine and human holiness. However, it now has an unmistakable cruciform shape manifest in faithfulness to God's life-giving, reconciling mission (*pistis*) expressed in costly, self-giving actions for others (*agapē*). This truly human Nazarene, then, this moveable temple/tabernacle of God in whom holiness is relocated, is the visible *imago Dei*, whose risen cruciform body is now on public display in the corporate life of those who are "in Christ."

At the beginning of the third section, chapters 7–9, we observed the Spirit-empowered, sanctified communities and individual characters in Acts witnessing to the resurrection of Jesus, embodying a pattern of life

---

1. Harrington, *Holiness*, 179 (my addition of the words "was still").

through which God sanctifies, or hallows, his name by means of those who bear that name (i.e., the name of the Lord Jesus). These early Christians acted publicly in the name of the Lord Jesus, the Holy and Righteous One, in ways that paralleled his own actions. The Spirit formed their identity as they embodied Jesus' character by displaying a missional pattern of redemptive and reconciling activity. Sharing in the holiness of this Holy and Righteous One as bearers of his divine name, they became a cultural explication of the identity and essence of "the Lord of all" in a variety of social settings, a cultural explication of the divine identity and thus of the nature of holiness itself.

This conceptuality in Acts of the communal life of the church—essentially "re-narrating" a story analogous to that of Christ's in the service of the *missio Dei* and thereby sharing in his holiness—also characterized Paul's cruciform communities. Our foray into Paul's letters indicated that human holiness is always derived from God, as people are an ongoing part of the corporate body of Christ in which the Holy Spirit is being continuously supplied to them, enabling them to participate publicly in God's mission. As humans participate in the Triune God's mission, they truly participate in his own activity and his being, and thereby in his holiness. The church participates in that divine mission through its faithfulness to God and its cruciform love for others through which God continues his work of *saving justice* and his *pursuit of peace/shalom* in the world, thereby displaying the essence of God's character/holiness. This Spirit-initiated and Spirit-enabled participation in God's mission in the form of concrete, physical, cruciform practices is one way the Spirit works to continue sanctifying the imaginations of his people and drawing others into that body. However, if such sanctifying work is to continue, practices that violate the new creation's cross-shaped structure by releasing destructive, *shalom*-compromising "contagious impurities" within the community must be avoided.

Finally, we saw that Revelation describes both the role of God's people in God's rescue mission and their continuing role of participating in bringing God's new creation to its intended destiny of flourishing forever with profusely abundant life. In God's rescue mission, the vocation of God's people is to function in the mediatorial role of priests, representing God to those around them in their particular cultural settings, primarily through their faithful prophetic witness with the hope that their life, death, and public vindication will be instrumental in bringing the nations to repentance. As a result of their prophetic witness to the truth, these priests

Conclusion

paradoxically offer themselves as a sacrifice on the altar of faithfulness to God out of love for others as did their high-priestly Lord. As they fulfill their missional vocation in this way, God's holy people "follow the Lamb wherever he goes" and thus come to reflect the image of the cruciform Son, who is himself the image of the thrice-holy creator God. Once again—during the time of God's rescue mission—God's primary means of reshaping us into the *imago Dei*, of making us holy, is via our participation in, and witness to, the *missio Dei*. As such, divine and human holiness both take on a cruciform shape in Revelation: a costly pattern of activity effecting the saving, reconciling mission of the Triune God. God's ultimate desire is to draw all into the abundant, Spirit-saturated life of the new creation where he dwells directly with his people in a holy place, with his redeemed people functioning as the priests and kings he made them to be at the beginning of the biblical story. When God's *rescue* mission is over, we suggested that the people of God may continue representing God's holy presence and rule to one another and to all of redeemed creation by engaging in various forms of rich cultural activities unhindered by opposition from evil and chaos. Hence, they continue participating in God's main mission of bringing creation to its intended dynamic destiny of flourishing forever with profusely abundant life.

We began the book with a story about a persecuted Christian community in Bangladesh. In their peaceful response of seeking the good even for their enemies, they became a channel of God's love, a visible display of his holy character, through which the God of peace worked to change violent enemies into his own children, restoring justice by reconciling them to himself and to their former victims. Their life-giving actions in sharing clean water with their enemies who had denied it to them and their children reflect the life-giving patterns of God's holiness, simultaneously displaying God's holy character of peace and justice. Being a part of a community participating in God's mission in this way, especially when it results in such visible reconciliation, is one means God uses to continue the initial transformation of the community itself. It is a major component in the way God continues the sanctification of their corporate and individual imaginations, enabling this community to "unlearn" patterns of retaliatory actions that pass for "commonsense" in their (and our!) culture and replace them with "cruciform" sense. Such concretely physical and social interactions within this ecclesial framework become a primary means the Spirit uses to "hardwire" the new creation's pattern and structure into the very neural networks of those "in Christ."

At this point, it will be helpful to recall that recent work by psychologists and neuroscientists suggests that what I am calling "imagination" is physically embedded in the neural network of our brain, and that each of us is socially embedded within a network of relationships.[2] As we engage in concrete physical practices and various forms of social interactions, our neural networks are physically "rewired," thereby reshaping—even transforming—our imaginations.[3] When such practices and social interactions are directed toward participation in God's life-giving mission, we might call the resulting physical rewiring of our neural networks the ongoing sanctification of our imaginations, forming us increasingly into the image of the cruciform Christ, who is himself the image of the unseen God. This is quite literally transformative participation in the life of God. The story of the Bangladesh community, then, offers a good example of the way participating in the *missio Dei* is a primary means through which God makes his people holy by reshaping them in Christ by the Spirit into the *imago Dei*, whereby they become the public face and temple of the Triune God in their particular social context.

I assume that most people who will be reading this book belong to churches in my own social context of North America, one that is very different from that of Bangladesh. Hence, before concluding the book, I want to offer an example of one way of participating in God's mission in the North American context through which God continues sanctifying Christians, both personally as individuals and corporately as local bodies of Christ. My hope is that this example will function to illustrate how one might flesh out in contemporary ways some of the patterns of Scripture regarding holiness and the *missio Dei* highlighted in this book.

Participating in God's Mission in North America: Payday Lending, Poverty and the Injustice Just around the Corner

> Patricia, a retired nursing home aide, encountered medical issues and decided it was best to move closer to her family in Northern Wisconsin. To do so, Patricia had to pay double rent for one

---

2. On which, see Brown and Strawn, *Physical Nature*; Green, *Body*.

3. Once again, see esp. Markham who argues that conversion/sanctification is a continual, life-long process involving both biological and social aspects (*Rewired*, 68–72).

Conclusion

month and rent a small moving truck. This was more than she could afford on her small monthly disability income. Since her other family members were also struggling financially, she sought out cash from payday lenders to help her cover moving-related expenses. Patricia took out three loans: two for $200, and another for $150. The total interest for these loans totaling $550 amounted to $123.50, resulting in her having to pay back $673.50 ($550 principal plus $123.50 in interest) to fully retire the debt. With her limited disability check, she was unable to afford to pay more than the interest on the loans. For nearly two years, Patricia continued to pay the finance charges each month. Patricia paid over $2,700 in interest only and not one penny toward the principal balance of $550.[4]

Jennifer Trogdon is a mother of five, four with special needs. Her husband works at a fast food restaurant making a little more than minimum wage. She is on disability. The thirty-nine-year-old Springfield woman says her family is trapped, struggling to break free from payday and car title loans. "It started off with a vehicle repair," she said. "You don't qualify for a loan at the bank so you take out this payday loan. They explain it to you and you think it's not going to be a problem paying back, but you really don't comprehend it fully. And not having any other option, what else are you supposed to do?"[5]

These sorts of stories are repeated over and over again right around the corner from where almost every reader of this book lives. I pass five or six payday loan companies driving from home to my seminary office, each advertising "EZ Cash" or "Fast Cash." Although suburban areas are not without such companies, most of these over twenty thousand loan shops in the United States are in areas with relatively high rates of poverty, and they intentionally target low-income borrowers.[6] On average, a payday loan customer takes out nine loans per year from these companies, which make most of their income from churning out loan after loan to existing borrow-

---

4. Patricia's story is taken directly from a website associated with The Center for Responsible Lending (http://www.responsiblelending.org/allies/faith-and-credit/Modern-Day-Usury-The-Payday-Loan-Trap.pdf). This particular website provides a good discussion guide for churches about the injustice of typical payday loan practices and tips for how to mobilize churches to combat them.

5. Rehwald, "Springfield Church," para. 1–3.

6. The numbers regarding these loan shops and their practices in this paragraph come from the website associated with the Center for Responsible Lending referred to in n. 4.

ers' loan accounts, trapping them in a cycle of debt. Households with access to these short-term loans are often forced into being late paying other bills, making their credit history even worse, and they tend to delay needed medical services and purchase of prescription drugs. With worsening health, it becomes more difficult to keep a steady job, and thus they sink deeper and deeper into the cycle of debt, poverty, and bad health. While there are clearly many other contributing causes of poverty in such communities, payday lending practices are part of a complex web of injustice—one form of the forces of chaos—engulfing such communities, inhibiting the ability of those who live in them to flourish with *shalom*, the rightly ordered, abundant life God desires for his creatures and his whole creation.

As we have seen throughout this book, holiness is not something limited to the "religious" sphere. Being holy is about being engaged in a pattern of activity as a part of a community in the messiness and particularity of that community's social context. The messiness and complexity of a social context inflicted with the injustice of payday loan practices has clear analogies to the social context of the most vulnerable poor in ancient Israel that led to prohibitions against usury (e.g., Exod 22:25; Lev 25:35–37; Ps 15:5; Ezek 18:5, 8, 13; Neh 5:3–11).[7] In discussing God's commands to Israel to set aside Sabbath years and/or the Jubilee year, we saw that this ritual marking of time would have built life-giving patterns of economic justice into Israel's communal life. Actually carrying out these commands would have distinguished Israel from the nations and simultaneously displayed the character of their God as committed to just socioeconomic practices that allow life to flourish for all, not just for the few who happen to be winning the economic game. Clearly, the economic and diverse religious and social context in North America is light years away from that of ancient Israel. However, there are certainly ways the church might attempt to address the payday loan issue that would mark us out as publicly recognizable communities reflecting the holy character of our particular God and his commitment to saving justice and *shalom*.

To begin with, we should recognize that this is not just an issue with which those outside church communities struggle; many low-income brothers and sisters in Christ are victims of these predatory loan practices. At the very least, local churches might begin to explore whether people within their own congregations are such victims, finding ways to allow

---

7. On which, see Biddle, "Biblical Prohibition." The whole issue of *Interpretation* in which Biddle's article appears is devoted to the topic of usury.

Conclusion

them to speak openly, honestly, and without shame about these sorts of debt traps. Inviting people like Patricia and Jennifer to tell their stories to their Christian sisters and brothers would inform many of us in the church about the real human effects of injustice just around the corner—effects we tend to ignore or about which we are simply unaware. Hearing such visceral stories face-to-face affects us more than just hearing abstract facts and figures about payday loan practices. As we hear such stories our brains internally simulate the actions and emotions we are hearing about in the story, assimilating them into our perspectives and ways of behaving. Hearing people like Patricia and Jennifer share their stories—and framing them with the hearing of Scripture passages regarding the prohibition of usury—has the potential of rewiring our very neural networks in transformative ways that move us to behave differently and respond concretely.[8]

One concrete response might be modeled after that of the Worship Center Christian Church in Birmingham, Alabama.[9] After educating the congregation on the issue, the church leaders took a special offering and paid off $41,000 of payday loan debt for both members and non-members of their church who had reported their indebtedness following a sermon dealing with the issue. They followed it up with financial counseling and financial workshops to help these borrowers avoid repeating the cycle.

Another creative response might look like that of the University Heights Baptist Church of Springfield, Missouri.[10] After becoming aware of the issue, church members educated themselves about it not only by reading books and watching videos, but also by attending a poverty simulation and by riding city buses. There is little question that these sorts of concrete physical practices and social interactions had a transformative impact on their imaginations, particularly regarding the way they thought about the working poor. They raised $6,000, with the goal of raising another $14,000, and set up an account called "University Hope" at a local credit union. People like Jennifer can borrow small loans from the credit union with no credit check because the money in the University Hope account functions as collateral for such loans. In fact, Jennifer did borrow $573 from the program in order to finally pay off an original payday loan of $500—after

---

8. On the shaping impact of stories at the level of our neural networks, see the brief discussion in Brown and Strawn, *Physical Nature*, 82–85.

9. Based on Garrison, "Deep in Debt?"

10. Based on Rehwald, "Springfield Church," para. 14–26. The Wesley Memorial United Methodist Church in Richmond, Virginia has a similar partnership with the Virginia United Methodist Credit Union (Robbins, "Churches Step In").

spending a couple of thousand dollars over two years desperately trying to retire the debt.

Among other possible responses, churches with more resources that have few, if any, members entrapped in the injustice of payday loan practices might partner with other churches that are located in lower-income areas where such injustice is rampant. Often there will not only be socio-economic differences between churches in these sorts of partnerships, but also racial and ethnic differences. Great care would have to be taken to insure that the partnership is truly mutually transforming, where members work together and learn from one another to guard against the whole endeavor becoming a thinly veiled way for those with more resources and power to construct an outlet to alleviate a guilty conscience.[11] If such a true partnership could be formed, not only could economic injustice be reduced, but when Christians with different socio-economic, racial, and ethnic backgrounds hear one another's stories and work together to participate in God's mission, such social engagement has the potential of contributing to reconciliation between members of Christ's own body, transforming the way we look at our world. It also has the potential of becoming one means whereby God continues the sanctification of all our imaginations together so that our life together in and as the body of Christ becomes a glimpse of the final reconciliation and peace characterizing creation's intended destiny in the face of rising racial and ethnic tension in the United States.

In responding to this issue, either as a single local church or in partnership with other churches or community organizations, after addressing the needs of Christian brothers and sisters, the ultimate goal would be to find a way to make low-cost loans available to those outside the church who are being exploited by payday loan companies. In doing so, churches would be reflecting the generosity and justice of the holy God to those who do not know him. In attempting to address one aspect of the injustice that robs communities of the *shalom* that God intends for creation and his creatures, churches would be participating in God's mission to bring his creation to its intended destiny. In engaging in such concrete physical actions and the social relationships that go along with it, God continues his transforming, sanctifying activity of shaping us in ways that increasingly reflect the image of his Son.

---

11. The problem that arises in Acts 6 in the early Jubilee community between the "Hellenists" and the "Hebrews" illustrates the ongoing challenge of addressing difference and power dynamics within the body of Christ.

CONCLUSION

If other local churches followed the lead of the two local churches we mentioned above and began creatively responding to this pervasive injustice in our communities, it would offer a picture of a different way of organizing economic life to those who control the power to change things in North American cities. By providing a visible witness to a viable alternative, such Spirit-enabled, embodied action would no doubt give more credence to churches speaking out publicly against such practices. Even if local churches do not have the financial resources to respond in these ways, they should publicly exercise their prophetic role of telling the truth to civic leaders, legislators, and even the owners of payday loan shops about the death-bound direction of these practices. This would mean calling them to eliminate, or at least heavily regulate, payday loaning in ways that keep the worst abuses at bay. This is one way the church might exercise its Johannine role of "retaining sins" (i.e., confronting and exposing this exploitation for the injustice and sin that it is). While it may seem farfetched, perhaps with the Spirit at work in, with, and under such efforts, we might even dare to imagine that a coalition of Christian business people and members of a particular community could persuade a local owner of one of these loan shops to reallocate his or her resources in ways that actually give life to the community while still resulting in a reasonable profit for the owner. If so, even the owner could receive the divine forgiveness that releases him or her from entrapment to death-bound allegiances and practices, and that puts them on the road to abundant life. Paying attention to these sorts of "mundane" matters may seem like the church has left the "religious" sphere. However, through such efforts, the Spirit continues to shapes us into Christ's own body in which we become "the saving justice of God," through which the holy God displays his holiness for the purpose of drawing all into the abundant, Spirit-saturated life of *shalom* that characterizes the new creation.

Concluding Reflections

The church working to combat predatory loan practices is just one example of the ways in which God is at work in the church to continue shaping us into Christ's image—and therefore into the *imago Dei*—as we participate in his mission. Once again, this is quite literally transformative participation in the life of the Triune God. Space prohibits developing other extended examples that would flesh out the patterns of Scripture regarding holiness and the *missio Dei* highlighted in this book. Such examples of churches engaged in mission in North America (not to mention throughout the world!), whereby they become the embodiment of God's own holiness in their communities, would be too numerous to name. But just for starters, in the North American context one might mention the way numerous churches are addressing such situations as the following:

- the injustices experienced by immigrants in our society, not to mention women and children refugees at our southern border who have fled from violence but are forced to live in prison-like conditions *even though they have never broken any laws*;
- pornography, a contemporary manifestation of the dynamic force of impurity that infiltrates and pollutes bodies and relational networks, enslaving its viewers, destroying their families, and dehumanizing those who offer their bodies in it for the consumption of others;
- the enslavement of the sex trade that exists in almost every nook and cranny of North America;
- the racism that, in spite of the good intentions many of us who are white believe we have, still exists in the US and is on display daily in a criminal justice system that is systemically—even if unintentionally—biased against minorities;
- the continuing lack of basic health care available for many of the working poor and their children, even after the passage of the Affordable Care Act;
- the pernicious health effects of having large numbers of liquor stores, tobacco outlets, and fast-food restaurants in lower income neighborhoods, whereas grocery stores with fresh produce are nowhere to be found.

These are only a few of the problems in our culture that rob individuals, families, and whole communities of the *shalom* that God intends for his creatures and his creation. When local churches, out of faithfulness to God and cruciform love for others, begin to educate themselves about these sorts of issues—particularly in conversation with scriptural patterns regarding justice, holiness, and the *missio Dei*—and engage in addressing them, they may indeed become weapons of God's "saving justice" in the body of Christ, the means by which God displays his own holiness. This is part and parcel of what it means for persons and whole communities to be the sanctified

Conclusion

people of God who are continuing to be sanctified. As those who have been liberated by God's saving, life-giving mission, we have been graciously taken up into that mission. We have been set apart for witness to, and active participation in, the saving, reconciling, life-giving purposes of the missional God. This happens only as we become and remain part of a local body of Christ, a people who are corporately and personally being shaped by the Holy Spirit into the image of the cruciform Son, and thereby being restored into the image of the holy, life-giving, Triune God—the *imago Dei*.

To be shaped by the Spirit into the image of the cruciform Son, the image of God, is to become holy; it is to reflect the character of God. That divine character is displayed most fully in a particular (cruciform) pattern of activity that participates in the Triune God's saving, reconciling mission, whose ultimate aim is to draw all into the abundant, Spirit-saturated life of the new creation. Hence, God's means of (re)shaping us into the *imago Dei*, of making us holy, is inseparable from—indeed, primarily constituted by—our participation in, and witness to, the *missio Dei*, the goal of which is to bring creation to its intended destiny.[12]

As we participate in God's mission in our local communities and beyond, may our individual lives and our life together as the body of Christ become a glimpse of creation's intended destiny: when it becomes God's cosmic sanctuary, totally permeated with his life-giving holiness, issuing in abundant life for all.

---

12. I want to be clear once more that, as I said in the very beginning (pp. xvi–xvii), being engaged in God's mission whereby God is making us holy must itself be framed, shaped, and sustained by ecclesial practices internal to the life of the church.

Bibliography

Adewuya, J. Ayodeji. "The People of God in a Pluralistic Society: Holiness in 2 Corinthians." In *Holiness and Ecclesiology in the New Testament*, edited by Kent E. Brower and Andy Johnson, 201–18. Grand Rapids: Eerdmans, 2007.
Barbarick, Clifford A. "'You Shall Be Holy, For I Am Holy': Theosis in I Peter." *JTI* 9 (2015) 287–97.
Barrett, C. K. *A Critical and Exegetical Commentary on the Acts of the Apostles*, Vol. 2. ICC. Edinburgh: T. & T. Clark, 1998.
Barton, Stephen C. "Dislocating and Relocating Holiness: A New Testament Study." In *Holiness Past and Present*, edited by Stephen C. Barton, 193–213. London: T. & T. Clark, 2003.
Bauckham, Richard. *Gospel of Glory: Major Themes in Johannine Theology*. Grand Rapids: Baker Academic, 2015.
———. "The Holiness of Jesus and His Disciples in the Gospel of John." In *Holiness and Ecclesiology in the New Testament*, edited by Kent E. Brower and Andy Johnson, 95–113. Grand Rapids: Eerdmans, 2007.
———. *The Theology of the Book of Revelation*. Cambridge: University Press, 1993.
Bauckham, Richard, and Trevor Hart, *Hope Against Hope: Christian Eschatology at the Turn of the Millennium*. Grand Rapids: Eerdmans, 1999.
Beale, G. K. *The Temple and the Church's Mission: A Biblical Theology of the Dwelling Place of God*. NSBT 17. Downers Grove, IL: InterVarsity Academic, 2004.
Beale, G. K., and Mitchell Kim. *God Dwells Among Us: Expanding Eden to the Ends of the Earth*. Downers Grove, IL: InterVarsity, 2014.
Beavis, M. A. *Mark's Audience: The Literary and Social Setting of Mark 4.11–12*. JSNTSup 33. Sheffield: Academic Press, 1989.
Beck, Richard. *Unclean: Meditations on Purity, Hospitality, and Mortality*. Eugene, OR: Cascade, 2011.
Biddle, Mark E. "The Biblical Prohibition Against Usury." *Int* 65 (2011) 117–27.
Boone, Dan. *Answers for Chicken Little: A No-Nonsense Look at the Book of Revelation*. Kansas City: Beacon Hill, 2005.
Brower, Kent. *Holiness in the Gospels*. Kansas City: Beacon Hill, 2005.

Bibliography

———. "'Let the Reader Understand': Temple and Eschatology in Mark." In *Eschatology in Bible & Theology: Evangelical Essays at the Dawn of a New Millennium*, edited by Kent E. Brower & Mark W. Elliott, 119–43. Downers Grove, IL: InterVarsity, 1999.

———. *Living as God's Holy People: Holiness and Community in Paul*. Milton Keynes: Paternoster, 2010.

———. *Mark: A Commentary in the Wesleyan Tradition*. NBBC. Kansas City: Beacon Hill, 2012.

Brown, Warren and Brad Strawn. *The Physical Nature of Christian Life: Neuroscience, Psychology, and the Church*. Cambridge: University Press, 2012.

Bumstead, Elaine. "Pure Grace: A Simple Well Helps a Bangladeshi Congregation Break Down Barriers and Pour Out Hope." *NCM Magazine* (2011) 14–16.

Campbell, Douglas A. *The Deliverance of God: An Apocalyptic Rereading of Justification in Paul*. Grand Rapids: Eerdmans, 2009.

Carroll, John. *Luke*. NTL. Louisville: Westminster John Knox, 2012.

Childs, Brevard. *Isaiah*. OTL. Louisville: Westminster John Knox, 2000.

Christensen, Michael J., and Jeffery A. Wittung, eds. *Partakers of the Divine Nature: The History and Development of Deification in the Christian Tradition*. Grand Rapids: Baker Academic, 2007.

Crutcher, Rhonda. *That He Might Be Revealed: Water Imagery and the Identity of Jesus in the Gospel of John*. Eugene, OR: Pickwick, 2015.

deSilva, David A. "Clean and Unclean." In *DJG* 142–49.

———. *Honor, Patronage, Kinship, & Purity: Unlocking New Testament Culture*. Downers Grove, IL: InterVarsity Academic, 2000.

Douglas, Mary. *In the Wilderness: The Doctrine of Defilement in the Book of Numbers*. JSOTSup 158. Oxford: University Press, 2001.

Dowd, Sharon. *Reading Mark: A Literary and Theological Commentary on the Second Gospel*. Macon, GA: Smyth & Helwys, 2000.

Evans, C. A., and J. A. Sanders, *Luke and Scripture: The Function of Sacred Tradition in Luke–Acts*. Minneapolis: Fortress, 1993.

Finlan, Stephen, and Vladmir Kharlamov, eds., *Theōsis: Deification in Christian Theology*. Eugene, OR: Pickwick, 2006.

Flemming, Dean. *Recovering the Full Mission of God: A Biblical Perspective on Being, Doing and Telling*. Downers Grove, IL: InterVarsity Academic, 2013.

———. "Revelation and the *Missio Dei*: Toward a Missional Reading of the Apocalypse." *JTI* 6 (2012) 161–78.

———. *Why Mission?* Nashville: Abingdon, 2015.

Fletcher-Louis, C. H. T. "The Destruction of the Temple and the Relativization of the Old Covenant: Mark 13:31 and Matthew 5:18." In *Eschatology in Bible & Theology: Evangelical Essays at the Dawn of a New Millennium*, edited by Kent E. Brower & Mark W. Elliott, 145–70. Downers Grove, IL: InterVarsity, 1999.

Fowl, Stephen E. *Philippians*. THNTC. Grand Rapids: Eerdmans, 2005.

France, R. T. *The Gospel of Mark*. NIGTC. Grand Rapids: Eerdmans, 2002.

Fretheim, Terence E. *Creation Untamed: The Bible, God, and Natural Disasters*. Grand Rapids: Baker Academic, 2010.

———. *Exodus*. IBC. Louisville: John Knox, 1991.

Gaiser, Frederick J. *Healing in the Bible*. Grand Rapids: Baker Academic, 2010.

Bibliography

Garrison, Greg. "Deep in Debt? Church Pays off Payday Loans." *AL*. March 7, 2016. Online: http://www.al.com/living/index.ssf/2016/03/deep_in_debt_church_pays_off_4.html.

Geddert, T. J. *Watchwords: Mark 13 in Marcan Eschatology*. JSNTSup 26. Sheffield: JSOT, 1989.

Ginsburskaya, Mila. "Purity and Impurity in the Hebrew Bible." In *Purity: Essays in Bible and Theology*, edited by Andrew Brower Latz and Arseny Ermakov, 3–29. Eugene, OR: Pickwick, 2014.

Gorman, Michael J. *Abide and Go: Missional Theosis in the Gospel of John*. Eugene, OR: Cascade, forthcoming.

———. *Becoming the Gospel: Paul, Participation, and Mission*. Grand Rapids: Eerdmans, 2015.

———. *Cruciformity: Paul's Narrative Spirituality of the Cross*. Grand Rapids: Eerdmans, 2001.

———. *The Death of the Messiah and the Birth of the New Covenant: A (Not So) New Model of the Atonement*. Eugene, OR: Cascade, 2014.

———. *Inhabiting the Cruciform God: Kenosis, Justification and Theosis in Paul's Narrative Soteriology*. Grand Rapids: Eerdmans, 2009.

———. *Reading Revelation Responsibly: Uncivil Worship and Witness: Following the Lamb into the New Creation*. Eugene, OR: Cascade, 2011.

———. "Romans: The First Christian Treatise on Theosis." *JTI* 5 (2011) 13–34.

———. "'You Shall Be Cruciform for I Am Cruciform:' Paul's Trinitarian Reconstruction of Holiness." In *Holiness and Ecclesiology in the New Testament*, edited by Kent E. Brower and Andy Johnson, 148–66. Grand Rapids: Eerdmans, 2007.

Green, Joel. *Body, Soul, and Human Life: The Nature of Humanity in the Bible*. Grand Rapids: Baker Academic, 2008.

———. "The Demise of the Temple as 'Culture Center' in Luke–Acts: An Exploration of the Rending of the Temple Veil (Luke 23:44–49)." *RB* 101 (1994) 495–515.

———. *The Theology of the Gospel of Luke*. Cambridge: University Press, 1995.

Gunton, Colin E. *Act and Being: Towards a Theology of the Divine Attributes*. Grand Rapids: Eerdmans, 2003.

Hamner, Phil, and Andy Johnson. "Holy Mission: The 'Entire Sanctification' of the Triune God's Creation." *Didache* 5 (2005). Online: http://media.premierstudios.com/nazarene/docs/didache_5_1_holy_mission.pdf.

Harrington, Hannah K. *Holiness: Rabbinic Judaism and the Graeco-Roman World*. New York: Routledge, 2001.

Hastings, Ross. *Missional God, Missional Church: Hope for Re-Evangelizing the West*. Downers Grove, IL: InterVarsity Academic, 2012.

Hays, Richard. "The Conversion of the Imagination: Scripture and Eschatology in Corinth." *NTS* 45 (1999) 391–412.

Hooker, Morna D. *The Gospel According to Saint Mark*. BNTC. London: A. & C. Black, 1991.

Hooker, Morna, and Frances Young. *Holiness & Mission: Learning from the Early Church about Mission in the City*. London: SCM, 2010.

Hurtado, Larry W. *Mark*. NIBC. Peabody, MA: Hendrickson, 1989.

Jenson, Robert W. *Ezekiel*. BTCB. Grand Rapids: Brazos, 2009.

Jewett, Robert. *Romans*. Hermeneia. Minneapolis: Fortress, 2007.

Johnson, Andy. *1 & 2 Thessalonians*. THNTC. Grand Rapids: Eerdmans, 2016.

———. "Ecclesiology, Election, and the Life of God: A Missional Reading of the Thessalonian Correspondence." *JTI* 9 (2015) 247–65.
———. "Holy, Holiness, NT." In *NIDB* 2:846–50.
———. "Lord." In *NIDB* 3:687.
———. "Missional from First to Last: Paul's Letters and the *Missio Dei*." In *Missio Dei: A Wesleyan Understanding*, edited by Keith Schwanz and Joseph Coleson, 67–74. Kansas City: Beacon Hill, 2011.
———. "The 'New Creation,' the Crucified and Risen Christ, and the Temple: A Pauline Audience for Mark." *JTI* 1 (2007) 171–91.
———. "Paul's 'Anti-Christology' in 2 Thessalonians 2:3–12 in Canonical Context." *JTI* 8 (2014) 125–43.
———. "Resurrection, Ascension, and the Developing Portrait of the God of Israel in Acts." *SJT* 57 (2004) 146–62.
———. "Ripples of the Resurrection in the Triune Life of God: Reading Luke 24 with Eschatological and Trinitarian Eyes." *HBT* 24 (2002) 87–110.
———. "The Sanctification of the Imagination in 1 Thessalonians." In *Holiness and Ecclesiology in the New Testament*, edited by Kent E. Brower and Andy Johnson, 275–92. Grand Rapids: Eerdmans, 2007.
———. "Sanctify, Sanctification." In *NIDB* 5:96–101.
———. "Turning the World Upside Down in 1 Corinthians 15: Apocalyptic Epistemology, the Resurrected Body, and the New Creation." *EvQ* 75 (2003) 291–309.
Johnson, Luke Timothy. *The Acts of the Apostles*. SP. Collegeville, MN: Liturgical, 1992.
Juel, Donald, H. *The Gospel of Mark*. IBT. Nashville: Abingdon, 1999.
———. *A Master of Surprise: Mark Interpreted*. Minneapolis: Fortress, 1994.
Kaminsky, Joel, S. *Yet I Loved Jacob: Reclaiming the Biblical Concept of Election*. Nashville: Abingdon, 2007.
Kerr, Alan R. *The Temple of Jesus' Body: The Temple Theme in the Gospel of John*. JSNTSup 220. Sheffield: Sheffield Academic, 2002.
Klawans, Jonathan. *Impurity and Sin in Ancient Judaism*. Oxford: University Press, 2000.
Klutz, Todd. *The Exorcism Stories in Luke-Acts: A Sociostylistic Reading*. SNTSMS. Cambridge: University Press, 2004.
Koester, Craig R. *Revelation*. AB. New Haven: Yale University Press, 2014.
———. *Revelation and the End of All Things*. Grand Rapids: Eerdmans, 2001.
———. *The Word of Life: A Theology of John's Gospel*. Grand Rapids: Eerdmans, 2008.
Levenson, Jon. *Creation and the Persistence of Evil: The Jewish Drama of Divine Omnipotence*. Princeton: University Press, 1994.
———. *Sinai and Zion: An Entry into the Jewish Bible*. Minneapolis: Winston, 1985.
Levison, John R. *Filled With the Spirit*. Grand Rapids: Eerdmans, 2009.
Lincoln, Andrew T. *The Gospel According to Saint John*. BNTC. Peabody, MA: Hendrickson, 2005.
———. "The Johannine Vision of the Church." In *The Oxford Handbook of Ecclesiology*, edited by Paul Avis. Oxford: University Press, forthcoming.
Marcus, Joel. "Idolatry in the New Testament." *Int* 60 (2006) 152–64.
———. *Mark 1–8*. AB. New York: Doubleday, 2000
Markham, Paul N. *Rewired: Exploring Religious Conversion*. Eugene, OR: Pickwick, 2007.
McBride, Jr., S. Dean. "The Essence of Orthodoxy: Deuteronomy 5:6–10 and Exodus 20:2–6." *Int* 60 (2006) 133–50.

McDonald, Nathan. "Did God Choose the Patriarchs: Reading for Election in Genesis." In *Genesis and Christian Theology*, edited by Nathan McDonald, Mark W. Elliott, Grant Macaskill, 245–66. Grand Rapids: Eerdmans, 2012.

———. "Listening to Abraham—Listening to Yhwh: Divine Justice and Mercy in Genesis 18:16–13." *CBQ* 66 (2004) 25–43.

McKnight, Scot. *A Community Called Atonement*. Nashville: Abingdon, 2007.

Middleton, J. Richard. *A New Heaven and a New Earth*. Grand Rapids: Baker Academic, 2014.

Milgrom, Jacob. "Holy, Holiness, OT." In *NIDB* 2:850–58.

Moberly, R. W. L. "The Earliest Commentary on the Akedah." *VT* 38 (1988) 302–23.

———. *Old Testament Theology: Reading the Hebrew Bible as Christian Scripture*. Grand Rapids: Baker Academic, 2013.

———. *The Theology of the Book of Genesis*. Cambridge: University Press, 2009.

———. "Whose Justice? Which Righteousness? The Interpretation of Isaiah V 16." *VT* 51 (2001) 55–68.

Neyrey, Jerome H. "The Idea of Purity in Mark's Gospel." *Semeia* 35 (1986) 91–128.

Pannenberg, Wolfhart. *Systematic Theology*. Vol. 2. Translated by Geoffrey W. Bromiley. Grand Rapids: Eerdmans, 1994.

Parsons, Mikeal C., and Richard I. Pervo. *Rethinking the Unity of Luke and Acts*. Minneapolis: Fortress, 1993.

Perrin, Nicholas. *Jesus The Temple*. Grand Rapids: Baker Academic, 2010.

Peterson, David G. *The Acts of the Apostles*. PillarNTC. Grand Rapids: Eerdmans, 2009.

Rehwald, Jackie. "Springfield Church, Credit Union Create Payday Loan Alternatives for Area Poor." *Springfield News-Leader*, December 2, 2015. Online: http://www.news-leader.com/story/news/local/ozarks/2015/12/01/springfield-church-credit-union-create-payday-loan-alternatives-area-poor/76560376/.

Reynolds, B. E. "Logos." In *DJG*, 2nd ed. 523–26.

Ringe, Sharon. *Jesus, Liberation, and the Biblical Jubilee: Images for Ethics and Christology*. OBT. Philadelphia: Fortress, 1985.

Robbins, Rebecca. "Churches Step in with Alternative to High-Interest, Small Dollar Lending Industry." *The Washington Post*, January 9, 2015. Online: https://www.washingtonpost.com/news/get-there/wp/2015/01/09/churches-step-in-with-alternative-to-high-interest-small-dollar-lending-industry/?Post+generic=%3Ftid%3Dsm_twitter_washingtonpost.

Roberts, J. J. M. "Temple, Jerusalem." In *NIDB* 5:494–509.

Rowe, C. Kavin. "Acts 2:36 and the Continuity of Lukan Christology." *NTS* 53 (2007) 37–56.

———. *Early Narrative Christology: The Lord in the Gospel of Luke*. Grand Rapids: Baker Academic, 2009.

———. *World Upside Down: Reading Acts in the Graeco-Roman Age*. Oxford: University Press, 2009.

Sampley, J. Paul. "1 Corinthians." In *NIB* 10, edited by Leander E. Keck, et al., 773–1003. Nashville: Abingdon, 2002.

Shepherd, C. E. "Purity in the Prophets." In *Purity: Essays in Bible and Theology*, edited by Andrew Brower Latz and Arseny Ermakov, 49–67. Eugene, OR: Pickwick, 2014.

Shiner, Whitney. *Proclaiming the Gospel: First Century Performance of Mark*. Harrisburg, PA: Trinity, 2003.

Bibliography

Swanson, Dwight D. "Leviticus and Purity." In *Purity: Essays in Bible and Theology*, edited by Andrew Brower Latz and Arseny Ermakov, 30–48. Eugene, OR: Pickwick, 2014.

Swartley, Willard M. *Covenant of Peace: The Missing Peace in New Testament Theology and Ethics*. Grand Rapids: Eerdmans, 2006.

Thomas, Gordon J. "A Holy God Among a Holy People in a Holy Place: The Enduring Eschatological Hope." In *Eschatology in Bible & Theology: Evangelical Essays at the Dawn of a New Millennium*, edited by Kent E. Brower & Mark W. Elliott, 53–69. Downers Grove, IL: InterVarsity, 1997.

———. "The Perfection of Christ and the Perfecting of Believers in Hebrews." In *Holiness and Ecclesiology in the New Testament*, edited by Kent E. Brower and Andy Johnson, 293–310. Grand Rapids: Eerdmans, 2007.

Thompson, Marianne Meye. *John: A Commentary*. NTL. Louisville: Westminster John Knox, 2015.

Thompson, Richard P. "Gathered at the Table: Holiness and Ecclesiology in the Gospel of Luke." In *Holiness and Ecclesiology in the New Testament*, edited by Kent E. Brower and Andy Johnson, 76–94. Grand Rapids: Eerdmans, 2007.

Trevaskis, Leigh M. *Holiness, Ethics and Ritual in Leviticus*. HBM 29. Sheffield: Sheffield Phoenix, 2011.

Van Duzer, Jeff. *Why Business Matters to God: (And What Still Needs to Be Fixed)*. Downers Grove, IL: InterVarsity Academic, 2010.

Wagner, J. Ross. "Working Out Salvation: Holiness and Community in Philippians." In *Holiness and Ecclesiology in the New Testament*, ed. Kent Brower and Andy Johnson, 257–74. Grand Rapids: Eerdmans, 2007.

Wall, Robert. "The Acts of the Apostles." In *NIB* 10, edited by Leander E. Keck, et al., 3–368. Nashville: Abingdon, 2002.

———. "Reading Paul with Acts: The Canonical Shaping of a Holy Church." In *Holiness and Ecclesiology in the New Testament*, edited by Kent E. Brower and Andy Johnson, 129–47. Grand Rapids: Eerdmans, 2007.

Wells, Jo Bailey. *God's Holy People: A Theme in Biblical Theology*. JSOTSup 305. Sheffield: Sheffield Academic, 2000.

Winter, Bruce. *After Paul Left Corinth: The Influence of Secular Ethics and Social Change*. Grand Rapids: Eerdmans, 2001.

Wright, Christopher. *The Mission of God's People: A Biblical Theology of the Church's Mission*. Grand Rapids: Zondervan, 2010.

Wright, N. T. *Paul and the Faithfulness of God*. Minneapolis: Fortress, 2013.

Author Index

Adewuya, J. Ayodeji, 135

Barbarick, Clifford A., 91
Barrett, C. K., 122
Barton, Stephen C., 48
Bauckham, Richard, 5, 81, 83–85, 87–88, 90, 95, 99, 104, 153, 155, 157–59, 165–66, 171, 173
Beale, G. K., 3, 48–49, 55, 73, 81
Beavis, M. A., 73
Beck, Richard, 27, 54
Biddle, Mark E., 188
Boone, Dan, 153
Brower, Kent, xi, 50, 53–54, 58, 67, 71, 91, 127, 129
Brown, Warren, 147–48, 186, 189
Bumstead, Elaine, xvi

Campbell, Douglas A., 137
Carroll, John, 69, 107
Childs, Brevard, 36
Christensen, Michael J., 91
Crutcher, Rhonda, 81

deSilva, David A., 27, 50, 60, 72, 118
Douglas, Mary, 27, 29
Dowd, Sharon, 61, 63

Evans, C.A., 114

Finlan, Stephen, 91

Flemming, Dean, x, 80, 92–93, 107–9, 115, 154, 159
Fletcher-Louis, C. H. T., 49
Fowl, Stephen E., 143
France, R. T., 54, 67
Fretheim, Terence E., 4, 9, 19, 20

Gaiser, Frederick J., 57
Garrison, Greg, 189
Geddert, T. J., 73
Ginsburskaya, Mila, 24, 28–29
Gorman, Michael J., x, 51, 75, 80, 88, 91, 93, 94, 100, 127–28, 130, 132, 134, 137, 139, 141–42, 144–46, 153–54, 157–58, 167
Green, Joel, 55, 57, 147, 186
Gunton, Colin E., 132

Hamner, Phil, 176
Harrington, Hannah K., 29, 71, 103, 183
Hastings, Ross, 86, 100–1
Hays, Richard, 148
Hooker, Morna D., 51, 55
Hurtado, Larry W., 67

Jenson, Robert W., 5, 39
Jewett, Robert, 138
Johnson, Andy, 127, 140, 142, 176
Johnson, Luke Timothy, 118, 120–22
Juel, Donald H., 56, 62, 74

Author Index

Kaminsky, Joel S., 12
Kerr, Alan R., 81
Kharlamov, Vladmir, 91
Klawans, Jonathan, 69
Klutz, Todd, 58
Koester, Craig R., 81, 85–86, 89–90, 94, 96, 101, 153, 169

Levenson, Jon, 49, 156, 160, 162, 175
Levison, John R., 136
Lincoln, Andrew T., 96, 102

Marcus, Joel, 23, 56, 58, 124
Markham, Paul N., 148, 186
McBride, Jr., S. Dean, 23
McDonald, Nathan, 11, 15–17
McKnight, Scot, 15
Middleton, J. Richard, ix, 3–5, 9, 12, 15, 19, 14, 16, 82, 171, 177–78
Milgrom, Jacob, 27, 29, 50
Moberly, R. W. L., 12, 18, 35

Neyrey, Jerome H., 51, 67, 69

Pannenberg, Wolfhart, 112
Parsons, Mikeal, 107
Perrin, Nicholas, 55, 71, 81
Pervo, Richard I., 107
Peterson, David G., 109

Rehwald, Jackie, 187, 189
Reynolds, B. E., 80
Ringe, Sharon, 114
Robbins, Rebecca, 189
Roberts, J. J. M., 48–49
Rowe, C. Kavin, 102, 104, 108, 111, 123, 127

Sampley, J. Paul, 135
Sanders, J. A., 114
Shepherd, C. E., 31
Shiner, Whitney, 73
Strawn, Brad, 147–48, 186, 189
Swanson, Dwight D., 58
Swartley, Willard M., 142, 144

Trevaskis, Leigh M., 29

Van Duzer, Jeff, 4

Wagner, J. Ross, 149
Wall, Robert, 107, 122
Wells, Jo Bailey, 19–20,
Winter, Bruce, 124
Wittung, Jeffrey A., 91
Wright, Christopher, 3, 13–15, 22,
Wright, N. T., 134–35

Young, Frances, 51

Subject Index

Note: Every major topic in the index below is referred to in the first section of the last chapter in which I summarize the scriptural patterns regarding holiness and God's mission explored in the book (pp. 181–86).

Abraham (and Sarah), 11–18, 162
Ark of the Covenant, 97
ascension of Jesus, 75, 98

Babel, 9–10, 130, 175
baptism of Jesus, 55–56
beast, beastly, 5, 14, 155, 158–60, 164, 166–67, 169
birth of Jesus, 53–54
body of Christ, 78, 102, 127, 131–32, 134, 139, 145

call, calling. *See* elect, election.
Church as Temple of God/Holy Spirit, 134–37
circumcision, 120–21, 139
crucifixion, 75, 85–88, 99, 164
cruciform, cruciformity, xvi, 17, 75–76, 79, 85, 88, 92–94, 96, 99, 107–8, 125, 127–28, 131, 134, 143, 148–50, 157–58

death as antonym of holiness/ultimate impurity, 29, 59, 62–64, 71–72, 84, 94–97
death of Jesus, 71–74, 76, 85–88, 90, 94–97, 139, 157–59
demonic forces, 57–62, 115

dispensationalism, 153
divine action and human/ecclesial response, 18–20, 150

ecclesial practices internal to the church, xvi–xvii, 193
elect, election, 11–12, 18–20, 22–23, 132–34, 137
exaltation of Jesus, 75, 85–86

faith/faithfulness: of Christ, 76, 79, 104, 129–30, 133–34, 139, 158
of God/the Lord, 36, 43, 99, 125, 129, 131
of God's people, 20, 35–37, 40–41, 63, 86, 90, 101, 104, 121–22, 125, 126, 129, 132–34, 137, 140–41, 148–49, 155, 164, 168–70, 192
inseparable from love, 125, 129, 133, 139–41, 158, 192

glory/honor (*doxa*), 81, 84–88, 96–99, 134–35, 157, 176–77
gospel, 129, 139–40, 168
grace, xviii, 24–25, 35, 120, 131, 150, 151, 171

203

Subject Index

holiness/sanctification: as corporate, 51, 91–92
   as cruciform, 75–76, 79, 88, 92, 99, 158, 172
   cruciform practices as God's means of, 92–94, 148–51
   and divine glory/honor as visible form of holiness, 8–9, 34, 37, 81, 84–88, 92, 99, 156–57, 160, 177
   and election, 19–20, 132–34, 137
   entire/complete, 145, 170, 176, 178
   Holy Spirit as agent of, 102
   of the imagination, 147–51
   Jesus' self-sanctification, 89–94, 98
   and life, 7–8, 29–30, 41–42, 58, 72, 109, 156, 174–75
   and the *missio Dei*, xvi, xvii, 38, 42–43, 47, 57, 59, 70, 80, 82, 84, 87, 92, 98, 102, 110–11, 120, 127, 132, 151, 153, 172, 188, 192–93
   of the name of the Lord/God, 108–15, 122–25, 155–56, 162
   as a process, 148, 193
   and purity/impurity, 21, 24, 28–30, 48, 50–51, 54, 56, 58, 60–65, 71–72, 145–47
   and the pursuit of peace/shalom, 141–45
   requiring ecclesial framework, 147–51
   and righteousness/justice, 26, 35, 42, 129–30, 137–41, 191, 192–93
   and theosis, 91–94
   as transformative, 93–94, 147–51, 189–90
Holy of Holies, 48, 51, 72–74, 82, 163, 177
Holy Spirit, 41–42, 55–56, 73–76, 94–102, 109–12, 116, 117, 119, 121, 131–32, 140–41, 145, 164, 176, 191, 193

idols, idolatry, 7, 23, 29, 33, 38–40, 122–25, 133, 146, 155, 161, 165
image of God/God's son, 4–5, 23, 43, 48, 79, 102, 134, 139, 151, 160, 167–68, 170, 172, 177–78, 190–91, 193

Jerusalem Temple, 48–51, 54–56, 70–76, 81–82, 136, 163
Jesus as true humanity, 86, 99–100, 128–30, 178
Jubilee, 26, 113–14, 188
judgment of God, 13–17, 141, 160–62, 165, 168
justice/righteousness: of God, 14–18, 34–38, 129–30, 141, 144, 160–62, 170, 190–92
   of God's people, 14–18, 32–40, 69–70, 130, 137–41, 190–92
   and holiness, 34–38, 137–41, 191–92
justification, 137–38, 141

Kingdom of God, 19, 56–57, 76, 112–14, 115, 155–56, 158, 165–66, 173

leprosy (skin disease), 29, 59
life/eternal life, 80, 82–84
love: of Christ/God, 86–88, 99, 128–29, 132, 144
   of God's people, 125, 129, 133, 139–41, 158, 192

millennium, 168–71
Missio Dei (Mission of God), xvi–xviii, 4, 6, 8, 11–13, 18, 19, 21–22, 25, 30, 31, 42–43, 47, 70, 76, 79, 83, 85, 89–90, 92, 94, 98, 99–100, 102, 104, 107–10, 116–17, 120, 124–26, 127, 129, 130, 131–34, 137–38, 141–42, 145–46, 150–51, 153, 155, 160, 165, 172–73, 179, 186, 190–93
missional interpretation, xvii

name of God/the Lord, 38–39, 41–42, 108–15, 119–25, 130, 155–56, 167, 177
New Creation, 76–78, 83, 99, 130, 135, 137, 139, 144, 145, 150, 171, 173–79
New Jerusalem, 171, 173–79

Passover Lamb, 95–96, 159

Subject Index

payday lending and the Church's response, 186–91
Pentecost, 109–12
Pharisees, 50–51, 64–66, 68–70, 120
prayer, 112–14
purity/impurity, 21, 27–30, 38–42, 48–51, 54, 58–64, 67–72, 76, 94–97, 116–25, 135–36, 139, 145–47

rapture, 153–54, 165
reconciliation, 98, 100–102, 117–20, 122, 125, 130, 136–37, 143–44
resurrection: in general, 40–41, 116
of Jesus, 74–76, 95, 97, 108, 114, 115
Roman imperial power/cult, 50, 58, 61, 154–56

Sabbath, Sabbath Year, 25–26, 37, 66–67
salvation, 19, 36, 40–41, 63, 82, 111, 119–21, 131, 172
Samaritans, 117–18
Satan, 57–59, 166, 169, 171
sexual immorality, 122, 124–25, 135–36, 145–46
Sin(s) and Sinfulness: as enslaving power, 95–96, 129, 138
forgiveness of, 100–102, 110, 113–14, 119, 191
Sodom (and Gomorrah), 13–18, 31–32, 37, 160

table fellowship, 64–66, 118–20, 122, 125
theological interpretation, xvii
Theosis, 91–94, 131–32
transformation, 39–42, 93–94, 110, 147–51, 189–91
Tree of Life, 7–8, 171, 174–75
Torah/Commands, 22–30, 120–21, 150

wrath of God, 144, 161, 168

Scripture Index

Old Testament

Genesis

1–11	xvii, 3	8:21	8, 9
1–2	4, 6	9:6	9
1:3	80	10	11
1:22	7, 18, 175	10:1–32	9
1:28	4, 6, 7, 10, 156, 175	11	9
		11:1–9	8
1:29–30	7, 175	11:4	9
1:31	4	11:10–26	11
2:3	7, 25, 66	11:30	11
2:7	4, 7, 41, 99, 175	12	11
2:10–14	81	12:1–3	12
2:10	174	12:3	12
2:15	4, 6, 10, 156	17:7	19
3	3, 6, 7	17:14	121
3:5	6	17:16	12
3:8–10	7	18	12, 38, 150, 162
3:8	7, 177	18:2	8
3:12	7	18:15	19
3:16	7	18:19	26, 32, 37
3:15	7	18:20–21	15
3:17–19	7	18:21	32
3:17	173	18:22–23	15
3:22–23	7	18:23	15
5:1–2	9	18:25	15
6:5–6	7	19	17
6:5	8, 13	19:13	13
6:11–13	7, 13	19:17	14

Genesis *(continued)*

19:18	14
19:19	14
19:29	17
22:15–18	18
32:22–32	8
32:30	8

Exodus

1:7	18
3:6–7	19
3:9	13, 32
3:14	157
3:15–17	19
4:22	19
12:10	81
12:46–49	121
13:15	30
15:18	19, 62
16:3	21
16:10	81
19:3	20
19:4–6	19
19:5–6	12
19:6	22, 159
19:10–25	21
19:10–11	30
20:3–4	23
20:8–11	25
20:8	66
20:11	25, 66
21:1–11	26
22:22–23	13
22:25–27	24
22:25	188
24:9–11	8
24:15–18	81
25–26	21
25:8	21
28:4	159
28:36–38	167, 177
30:19–21	65
30:26–30	30
31:13	66
32	23
33:11	8
33:18–23	81, 177
33:18	8
33:19	9
33:20	9
33:21–23	9
34:5–7	81
34:6	99
35–36	21
40:12–13	65
40:34–38	134
40:34–35	21, 81

Leviticus

1–16	24
7:19–21	50
10:1–3	21
10:3	84
11	24, 68
11:44–45	19, 24
12:1–8	54
15:25–30	63
16:16–19	30
17–26	24
17–18	122
18:2–4	21
19	22, 24–25
19:1–2	22
19:2	70
19:3	22, 23
19:4	23
19:9–10	22
19:13	23
19:14	23
19:19	23, 28
19:20–23	23
19:23–25	23
19:27–28	23
19:32	23
19:33–34	23
19:34	24
19:35–36	23
19:36–37	22
20	24

Scripture Index

20:24–26	24
20:26	21
21:16–24	29, 67
25	26
25:1–7	26
25:35–37	188

Numbers

12:12	29
19:13–20	40
19:13	71
19:12	95
21	86
21:9	86
36:25	40
36:26–27	40
36:28	41
36:29	41

Deuteronomy

7:6	132
14:2	132
15	26
15:2	114
15:4	114
23:2	118
32:4	139
32:35	141

Joshua

5:1–7	121

Judges

6:16	8
6:22	8
13:22	8

2 Samuel

8:15	15

1 Kings

6:19–20	175
8:41–43	20
10:9	15
19:14–18	165

Nehemiah

5:3–11	188
9:9	13

Psalms

15:5	188
22:19	95
34:19–20	95
69:22	95
74:12–15	60
77:16–20	60
89:9–10	60
99:4	15
105:6	132
115:4–8	4

Isaiah

1–39	36
1:4	31
1:10	31
1:11–15	32
1:15	33
1:16–17	33
1:17	32–33
1:23	32–33
1:26	34–35, 37
1:27	34, 35
1:29	33
2:2–4	172
2:7	33
2:8	33
2:20	33
3:14–15	33
5:7	32
5:8	33

Isaiah (continued)

5:11–12	33, 34
5:16	26, 34–35, 37, 129
5:18–21	33
5:22	33–34
5:23	33
6:2	156
6:3	34–35, 157
6:5	35
6:9–13	35
6:13	165
11:4–5	15
25:6–8	84
32:15–17	109
36:20–21	38
40–55	35–36
41:8–10	132
42:1	132
44:3	109
46:12–13	36
49:1–7	132
49:6	12
51:5–6	36
51:9–11	60
52:13—53:12	95
53	96
53:7	159
56–66	36
56:1	36
56:2–8	37
58	114
59:17–18	141
59:17	140
59:21	109
60:1–3	37
61	114
64:1	55
65:17–25	43

Jeremiah

5:1	16
9:24	15
22:3	15
34:8–17	26

Ezekiel

18:5	188
18:8	188
18:13	188
23	124
33–39	39
33:10–11	39
33:10	39–41, 110
33:11–20	40
36–37	40
36	55
36:16–32	109
36:16–21	38–39
36:17–18	122
36:17	39
36:18	39
36:20–21	38
36:22–23	41–42, 110–11
36:23	141
36:24–29	40, 43
36:24	110
36:25	39–40, 122
36:26–27	40
36:28	41
36:29	41
36:33	39
37	39
37:1–14	41, 109
37:3	39
37:5	164
37:6	41, 55, 131, 140
37:9	99
37:10	164
37:11	110
37:14	41, 55, 131, 140
37:23	39
37:27–28	81
39:23	39
39:24	39
39:26	39
40–48	43
43	134
47:1–12	6, 81, 174

Scripture Index

Hosea

1:2	124

Joel

2:28—3:1	109
3:1–5	110–11
3:18	81

Amos

5:3	165
5:20–23	31
5:24	32

Zechariah

4:14	163
12:10	96
13:1	96
14:8	81

New Testament

Matthew

1:18–25	54
4:24	57
5:18	196
6:9–10	156
8:2–4	59
8:16–17	57
8:28—9:1	60
9:1–8	57
9:9–13	64
10:1	58
12:6	55
12:9–14	66
12:22–23	57
18:20	55
21:42	55
22:35–40	70
23:21	55
26:6	60, 118
28:18–20	55

Mark

1:1	55
1:5	54
1:8	56
1:10	55, 74
1:15	56
1:23	58
1:24	53, 59, 132
1:34	57
1:39—4:4	59
2:1–12	55, 57
2:15–17	64
2:27	67
3:1–6	66
3:11	54, 58
3:27	62
5	64
5:1–13	58, 60
5:11–13	62
5:2	61
5:3–5	61
5:5	61
5:6	75
5:7	54
5:8–9	61
5:21–43	62
5:21	62
6:7	58
6:13	57
7	68
7:1–3	64
7:15	68
7:13	68
7:17	68
7:18–23	68

Mark *(continued)*

9:14–29	57
10:45	64, 70, 75
11:15–18	71
12:28–31	70
14:3	60, 118
14:36	70
15:37–39	72
15:37	74
15:38	56, 72–4
15:45	72
16:6	75, 158

Luke

1:8–20	55
2:1–7	54
2:21–38	55
2:22	54
2:43	115
4:16	115
4:22	115
4:33	115
4:35	59
4:36	58, 115
4:39	59
4:40–41	57
5:12–16	59
5:12	115
5:17–26	57, 115–16, 64
5:27–32	64
6:6–11	66
6:18–19	57
6:18	58
6:30	115
6:34–36	115, 144
6:36	70
6:40	149
7:11–16	116
7:22	115
7:36–37	65
8:26–39	60
8:29	58
8:40–42	116
8:49–55	116
9	107
9:35	132
9:46–48	69
9:51–56	117
10:27	70
10:30–37	117
11:37–42	69
11:37	65, 69
11:39–40	69
12:33–34	115
14:1	65
15:1–2	64
15:20	70
17:11–19	60, 117
17:18	117
19:1–10	64
22:30	110
23:35	132
24:39	75
24:52	55

John

1:1–4	80
1:4	83, 89
1:3	54
1:14	72, 81, 84
1:18	82
1:29	90, 95
1:32–34	94
2:11	83
2:19–21	82
2:19	95
3:3	82
3:5	82
3:14–17	90
3:14–16	82
3:14–15	85, 86
3:16	86–88, 90, 92
4:10	96
4:14	96
4:46–54	83
5:2–9	83
5:24	83, 90
5:25–29	83
5:26	83, 89
6:1–15	83
6:27	83
6:33	83
6:35	83

Scripture Index

6:38–69	84	13:34–35	88, 92
6:39–40	83	14:6	83, 93
6:44	83, 86, 90	14:12	94
6:47–51	90	14:26	94
6:48	83	15:1–2	83
6:54	83	15:4–5	91
6:63	95	15:5	102
6:68–69	132	15:12–17	88, 92
6:68	53	15:12–13	88
6:69	82	15:13	87
7:18	85	15:16	91
7:37–39	96	15:26	94
7:38	96	16:8–11	101
7:39	94	17	89
8:24	86, 90, 96	17:1	86
8:44	93	17:2	83
9:1–12	83	17:3	83
10:3–4	97	17:4–5	86
10:10	79	17:11	93
10:11–18	87	17:13	93
10:11–15	95, 97	17:14	90
10:17–18	90, 95	17:15–19	89
10:20–23	90–91	17:17–19	89
10:27–28	90	17:17	79, 93
10:30	82	17:19	90
10:36–38	82, 89	17:22	88
10:36	82, 89	19	97
10:37	84	19:5	93
10:38	82	19:24	95
11:1–14	83	19:28	88
11:4	87	19:30	88, 94
11:7–16	87	19:31–32	95
11:25	83	19:31	95
11:36	87	19:34	95
11:40	84, 87	19:36–37	95
11:45–53	87	19:36	95
11:46–53	84	19:39–42	97
12:23–24	85	20	80
12:32–33	85	20:1	97
13–17	87	20:2	97
13	89	20:3–10	97
13:1	87, 96	20:11–13	97
13:2–20	87	20:16	97
13:10	93	20:17	93
13:15	88	20:22	99
13:27	88	20:25–27	75
13:31–32	86	20:28	47, 93

Acts

1:1–2	108
1:8	108, 117, 126
1:9	164
1:14	113
1:24–25	113
2	110, 115
2:5–11	110
2:17–21	110
2:21	111
2:22–36	129
2:22	115
2:23–24	75
2:27	109
2:32–36	108
2:32	112
2:33	109
2:36	110–11
2:37	110
2:41	119
2:42	113
2:44	114
2:46	55, 114
2:47	120
3:1—4:22	115
3:1–26	55
3:14–15	109
3:15	75
3:35	12
4:10–12	111
4:23–30	113
4:27	109
4:30	109, 120
4:32	114
4:33	120
4:34	114
5:15–16	115
5:16	115
6	190
6:1	114
6:3	117
6:4	113
6:8	115
7	xvii
8:4–25	117
8:4	115
8:6–8	117
8:6	115
8:7	115
8:12	115, 117
8:13	115
8:14	117
8:15–17	117
8:17	117
8:26–40	118
9:4–5	127
9:13	109
9:31	118
9:32	109
9:41	109
9:43	118
9:51–56	117
10:2	118
10:3–6	118
10:10–16	119
10:14	68
10:22	118
10:28	119
10:30–37	117
10:34–43	119, 129
10:36	111, 121
10:43	108
10:44–46	119
10:48	121
11:2–4	112
11:2	113
11:14	119
11:18	119
11:19–30	120
11:21	120
11:23	120
11:24	120
11:27	114
11:29–30	120, 125
13	115
13:32	115
13:35	109
14:3	115
14:8–10	123
15:1	120–21
15:3–4	121

Scripture Index

15:5	120
15:8–9	110, 121
15:9	122
15:12	115, 121
15:14	121, 124
15:16	121
15:17	121
15:20	122, 124
15:29	122
16:16–24	123
17:1–9	123
17:11–19	117
17:18	117
17:24	111
19:11	115
19:23–41	123
20:32	109, 117
21:25	122
22:20	108
26:10	109
26:18	109, 117

Romans

1:16–17	129, 138
1:18–32	138, 161
1:21–23	156
3–5	137
3:21–22	129
5	144
5:1–10	144
5:1	138, 142
5:10–11	138
5:18–19	130
6	137, 140
6:4	95
6:7–8	137
6:7	138
6:13	138, 141
6:18–22	138
6:22	137
8:22	61
12:2	149
12:4–5	134
12:17–21	143
12:18	144
12:19	141
14:1–23	143
14:15–21	143
14:19	143

1 Corinthians

1:23	75, 157–58
1:30	130, 134
2:2	157–58
3:16–17	134–35, 145
3:16	163
3:17	135
5	135, 147
6:1–9	136
6:7	143
6:12–20	135, 147
6:14	95
6:16	134
6:18	124
6:19–20	136
8:9–13	143
9:1–27	143
10:14	124
10:16–17	134
12:12–31	134
14:18–19	143
15:28	5, 174
15:44–46	176
15:45	86, 99–100

2 Corinthians

3:17–18	100
4:4	134
4:6	134, 149
4:12	64
5:17	51, 103, 135
5:21	138, 140
6:14—7:1	135, 145
6:16	163
7:1	136

Galatians

2:2	129
2:16	91
3:8	12
5:6	139
5:16	135
5:22	143
6:15	51, 103, 139

Ephesians

1:4–6	136
1:4–5	136
2:11–22	136
2:14–16	142
2:20	163
2:21–22	137
2:21	134
4:24	139
6:14	140

Philippians

1:9–10	149
2:4	143
2:5	143
2:6–11	127–28, 139
2:6–8	87, 133
2:6	69
2:8	130
2:10–11	130, 161
4:2–3	143

Colossians

1:15	48, 79, 104
1:20	142
2:9	48
3:3	131

1 Thessalonians

1:1	131
1:3	133
1:4	132
1:5–8	133
1:5	131–32, 139, 148
1:6–8	133
1:6	133
1:7–8	141
1:8	133
1:9	133, 137–38, 146
2:1–12	133, 148
2:1–9	139
2:10	138–40
2:14	133
3:2	133
3:3	133
3:5	133
3:6	133
3:7–9	143
3:7	133
3:10	133, 140, 148
3:12–13	131, 144
3:12	140, 144
3:13	141
4:3–8	146
4:3	151
4:6	146
4:7	146–47
4:8	140–41, 143
5:8	140
5:12–12	143
5:15	143–44
5:23	142–43, 151
5:24	131

2 Thessalonians

1:3–4	133
1:3	140
2:13	131–32
2:16–17	131
3:6–16	143
3:16	143

Hebrews

12:14	145

Scripture Index

1 Peter

2:5	163

Revelation

1:1	162
1:2	158
1:5	158–59
1:6	163–64, 176
1:13	159
1:20	163
2:2–4	172
2:5	162
2:7	176
2:8–11	155
2:8	169
2:10	155
2:11	176
2:12—3:6	155
2:13	159
2:16	162
2:17	176
2:21	162
3:3	162
3:7–13	155
3:7	158
3:10	155
3:14–22	155
3:18	162
3:21	169
4–5	176
4	157
4:2	156
4:8–11	156
4:8	157
4:14	163
5:1	162
5:5	158
5:6	75, 176
5:7	162
5:9	157, 159, 161, 164–65
5:10	163–64, 169
5:12	157
5:13	157
6	160
6:1	161
6:9	158
7:4–8	166
7:9–17	173
7:9	167, 175
8	160
8:2	161
8:6–7	161
9	xvii–xviii, 158, 160
9:20–21	161–62
10:8	162
11	159, 162–63
11:1–2	163
11:2	171
11:3–13	164–65
11:4	163
11:5	164
11:6	164
11:7	160, 164
11:8	160
11:9	164–65
11:11–12	164
11:11	169, 176
11:12	164
11:13	165, 168, 170
11:15	165, 173
11:17	166
11:19	166
12–22	166, 172
12	166
13:1—14:5	167
13	166
13:1	5, 173
13:7	166
13:16–17	166
14:1	166–67
14:3	167
14:4	167, 170
14:4–5	167
14:6–7	161, 168
14:7	170
14:14–16	168
14:17–20	168
15:2–4	168–69
16–18	168
16:9	168
16:11	168

Scripture Index

Revelation *(continued)*

18:4	155, 166
19:5–9	168
19:6	173
19:7	163
19:11–21	168, 172
19:14	169
19:19	171
19:20	169
19:21	171
20–22	168
20	3
20:1–10	168
20:1–7	172
20:4	169
20:6	169
20:10	169
21–22	4–5, 171, 173–74
21:1	5, 173
21:3	5, 173, 175
21:4	173
21:5	4
21:9–10	163
21:10	171
21:11	21
21:16	175
21:22–23	175
21:24–26	5
21:24	171, 177
21:26	171
22	11
22:1–5	173
22:1–2	174
22:1	81, 174
22:2	171
22:3	173
22:4	9, 83
22:17	176

www.ingramcontent.com/pod-product-compliance
Lightning Source LLC
Chambersburg PA
CBHW020408230426
43664CB00009B/1235